MW00512818

Proportional Representation,

OR

THE REPRESENTATION OF SUCCESSIVE MAJORITIES IN FEDERAL, STATE, MUNICIPAL, CORPORATE AND PRIMARY ELECTIONS.

BY

CHARLES R. BUCKALEW,

LATE U. S. SENATOR FROM PENNSYLVANIA.

With an Appendix.

EDITED BY

JOHN G. FREEZE,

COUNSELLOR AT LAW.

"In all Free States, the evil to be avoided is tyranny; that is to say, the summary of *peril*,' or unlimited power, solely in the hands of one, the few, or the many."—SWIFT.
"Constant experience shows us, that every man invested with power is apt to abuse it. He pushes on till he comes to something that limits him. To prevent the abuse of power, it is necessary that by the very disposition of things, power should be a check to power."—MONTESQUIEU.

PHILADELPHIA:
JOHN CAMPBELL & SON,
LAW BOOKSELLERS, PUBLISHERS AND IMPORTERS,
740 SANSOM STREET.
1872.

TABLE OF CONTENTS.

ANALYSIS OF CONTENTS.

v

EDITOR'S PREFACE.

WITHIN the last few years the public mind has been awakened to many questions relating to government, but to no one more important than that discussed in the volume now presented to the reader. The editor believes it to be a necessity of the times, in view of current discussions of electoral reform, that the papers now collated and arranged should be put into a permanent and accessible form. For not only in Pennsylvania, but in many other states of the Union, the great evils of the present system of voting and of deficient representation, are being earnestly discussed. Therefore, whatever can assist in bringing about just conclusions either as to the necessity of some fundamental changes in electoral action, or, that being conceded, as to the best method of adapting the changes agreed upon to the needs of the people, may be accepted as fit, timely and useful.

Although a number of works, more or less elaborate, have been recently published upon electoral and representative reform, no one of them covers precisely the ground covered by the present one. They have dealt mostly with the theoretical and philosophical aspects of the questions treated, whereas the volume in hand is largely devoted to the practical application of the plan proposed in it for popular acceptance. Herein will be found not only the theory of a reform to extend representation, but sundry acts of legislation for its enforcement, and the returns of elections which illustrate the practical workings of reform and the results to be obtained from it. This information is believed to be more useful and convincing than abstract arguments with the great mass of persons with whom political power is justly lodged by our American Constitution. And as to theory: If the people shall once be satisfied that a system can be applied whereby in popular elections, nearly the whole mass of those who vote shall be represented in government, they will accept it promptly upon the sound theory of equal and exact justice to all.

The matter contained in this volume, it will be observed, is arranged, as nearly as may be, in chronological order, thus exhibiting the growth and modifications of opinion in the author's mind, contemporaneous with movements in other states and publications abroad. And although it consists mainly of legislative arguments, popular addresses and casual papers thrown off or produced as occasion invited during several years, yet the collected volume has nearly the completeness and symmetry of a regular work, with little of surplusage or repetition. There is a regular development of argument, illustration and thought, and each separate, successive part presents the question in hand from a new or enlarged point of view.

The haste with which this volume is put to press precludes careful revision, a correction of former errors of publication and slips unavoidable in oral discourse, but for these the intelligent reader will make due allowance without prolonged apology.

As a citizen of the State, and a resident of the town in which the free vote was first applied at a popular election, the editor has felt the promptings of a laudable, or at least a natural, ambition in presenting this work to the public, convinced as he is that the reform which it presents and vindicates, when accepted generally, will purify elections, establish justice in representation, elevate the tone of public life and give additional credit and lustre to that system of government by the people which is our proudest boast, and our best legacy for those who come after us.

J. G. F.

BLOOMSBURG, Nov. 12, 1872.

PRELIMINARY REMARKS.

MR. DUTCHER, in his recent work on Proportional Representation,* has shown, by elaborate statistics, that of the votes cast at important contested popular elections in the United States, over forty *per centum* are lost or overruled in the computation of results. Of the electors throughout the country who voted for representatives to the Fortieth Congress, no less than forty-two per cent. failed to obtain representation by their votes; and precisely the same percentage of voters failed in elections for representatives to the Forty-first Congress, and again in the elections to the Forty-second. For six continuous years the rate of actual representation in the popular branch of Congress was but sixty per cent. of the votes polled. At the session of the New York Legislature, in 1869, the voters unrepresented in the Senate were forty-one per cent. of the whole, and in the House forty-two; and at the session of 1871, in each House, forty-two.

Mr. Hare is authority for the statement that the percentage of disfranchisement upon votes cast in Parliamentary elections is very nearly as great as in the above examples. He says: "Those who, disagreeing with the majority in their electoral districts, are now in Parliamentary elections outvoted and left without representation,

* "*Minority or Proportional Representation, by Salem Dutcher, N. York,* 1872."

cannot ordinarily be taken at less than two-fifths of the whole electoral body."* It may be assumed that, in contested State and municipal elections in this country, the average proportion of unrepresented voters is as great as in elections for members of Congress and members of Parliament—in other words, that the average rate of virtual disfranchisement of voters in our contested popular elections is fully two-fifths of the total vote. This startling fact is the first one to be considered, and considered attentively, in any intelligent examination of the great subject of electoral reform in the United States; for all schemes for the amendment of popular representation in government must be insufficient and illusory which ignore it or underrate its enormous significance. For it means that our popular elections are unjust; it exposes the principal cause of their corruption, and it may instruct us, if we duly consider it, concerning those measures of change which will most certainly impart health, vigor and endurance to our political institutions.

The plan for securing Proportional Representation presented in this volume, and other plans similar to it in character or object which have been proposed in recent years, strike at this great evil of disfranchisement in popular elections, and are intended to reduce it to its smallest possible dimensions. But the advantages of the plan set forth in the following pages will best appear by comparing it with the old one, which it is intended to supersede.

Under the old plan of majority voting, whenever two

---

* "*Memorandum on the History, Working and Results of Cumulative Voting*," (prepared by Thomas Hare at the request of the English Government,) p. 14.

or more persons are to be elected at one time to the same office and for the same term of service, the law assigns to the voter as many votes as the number of persons to be chosen, and then commands him to distribute them singly among candidates. It restrains and prevents him from exercising his own judgment as to the manner of polling his votes, and, in, fact, undertakes to judge for him and to determine in advance what will be, under all circumstances, a judicious exercise of his right of suffrage. But in this it must blunder extremely and constantly. For as the law maker cannot know the future, cannot from sheer ignorance take into exact account its ever-changing conditions, his injunction or command to the voter must be purely arbitrary, and must be often or commonly unsuited to the circumstances to which it shall come to apply. Hence the virtual disfranchisement and actual non-representation of a large part of the voters is a common fact in all constituencies, large and small, throughout the country, the inevitable consequences of which are deeply injurious and truly deplorable. Misgovernment, injustice, violence, corruption and discontent are created and increased by an unnecessary and absurd restriction upon electoral freedom; by a wholly gratuitous and impertinent interference of law with the free action of the citizen; by an open and palpable violation of the principles of self-government upon which all our political institutions are founded. Only when a constituency shall be unanimous, or nearly so, in opinion and action can the enforced distribution of votes singly among the whole number of candidates operate justly; in all other cases it must result in the non-representation of a part of the electors, and in consequent injustice and evil.

But we turn from this view to the free vote, now proposed to us as an instrument for the improvement of elections and amendment of representation. Its advantages over the majority vote may be roughly stated as follows:

1. It reduces greatly the number of candidates at popular elections, because under it parties will usually nominate only the number they are entitled to and have power to elect. Surplus candidates will not commonly be run, and but few persons will be beaten in struggles for place.

2. It secures nearly complete representation of the whole body of voters in plural elections, by permitting each considerable interest of political society to take to itself its just share of representation by its own votes.

3. It reduces enormously the expense of election contests,—not the legal charges borne by the public, but voluntary outlays by parties and candidates. These will no longer be required to subsidize the floating vote—the balance-of-power vote—the mercenary or impressionable vote—of a district or constituency, as the indispensable condition of success. Whether applied to legal elections or to primary ones; to elections to office or to nominations for office, in this regard its effect will be the same—*to produce, comparatively, cheap elections.*

4. It is a powerful check upon all forms of corruption and undue influence at elections, because it takes away the motive, or most of the motive, to corrupt or pervert them in rendering all ordinary efforts to that end unavailing and useless.

5. It produces satisfaction to voters in gratifying their desire for representation, and thus increases their attachment to the government under which they live.

6. It permits the representation of a greater variety of

opinions and interests in legislative bodies, without impairing the right and power of the majority to rule.

7. It will often continue fit and able men much longer in public service than is now possible, because they will not hold their places subject so much to fluctuation of power *between* parties as to changed preferences in their own party.

8. It will greatly reduce party violence, and give a kindlier tone to social relations among the people, without producing stagnation or indifference to public affairs. In this, as in other cases, justice means peace, but it does not mean stagnation; for it is beyond question that reformed voting "wakes to newness of life," to activity and interest in public affairs, large numbers of persons who, under majority-voting, are inert because disgusted or discouraged by their exclusion from representation. Upon this point Mr. Buxton spoke wisely and soundly in Parliament in the Reform debates of 1867.*

9. It discourages election cheats, whether in the giving, receiving, counting, or returning of votes, because by it the *effect* of cheating is greatly reduced. And, for a like reason, it also discourages the trading of votes, or bartering of the electoral privilege.

10. It is adapted to the bolting of nominations by an aggrieved interest, for such interest, if of respectable size, can represent, by its own votes, without disturbing or changing the whole result of an election.†

11. It renders elections more independent of each other. No one will much influence another; each one will be determined upon its own merits, or upon the issues directly

* Appendix, p. 279.

† See case of Northumberland borough election, *post*, 251.

involved in it, and not with reference to its effect upon other elections.

12. Lastly, it is a certain remedy for the evil of gerrymandering in the formation of Congressional districts, and may be made to remedy, partially or completely, the same evil, in apportionments for members of State Legislatures.

Rightly understood, the free vote is not a plan of minority representation. It is, on the contrary, a plan for the representation of successive majorities in plural elections, by which will be realized, more fully than ever before, our fundamental principle of government by the people.*

It only remains to add, in this place, that in order that this or any other plan of reformed voting shall be thoroughly effectual, it must not stop with the legal elections, but must extend to the primary ones also. In fact, upon plans for the nomination of candidates to office must be fought out the ultimate battle of electoral reform.

* Letter to Secretary Jordan, *post*, p. 182.

PROPORTIONAL REPRESENTATION.

A SPEECH,

DELIVERED IN THE SENATE OF THE UNITED STATES,

JULY 11, 1867.*

THE Senate having under consideration Senate bill No. 131, to give effect to an act entitled "An act to provide for the more efficient government of the rebel States," passed March 2, 1867, Mr. BUCKA-LEW proposed the following amendment as a new section:

SEC. —. *And be it further enacted,* That in the election of Representatives in Congress from the said States mentioned in the act of March 2, 1867, each elector shall be entitled to give as many votes as there are Representatives assigned to his State by apportionment of law, and he may give one vote to each of the requisite number of persons to be chosen, or may cumulate his votes and bestow them at his discretion upon one or more candidates less in number than the whole number of Representatives to be chosen from such State.

After prolonged debate and a vote of the Senate on a question of order, Mr. BUCKALEW delivered the following speech for cumulative voting and in vindication of the amendment which he had proposed:

* *Congressional Globe,* 1st Sess. 40th Cong. 575.

1

Mr. BUCKALEW. The Senate has furnished me a very good argument against the passage of this bill. I think no bill of this kind should be passed and placed upon our statute-book which does not contain the proposition covered by my amendment; and I propose to enter upon an exposition of that amendment and a statement of the arguments by which it is supported.

The plan of cumulative voting has been thoroughly discussed in Great Britain, and is perhaps better understood in that country than in our own. What is it? Where more persons than one are to be elected or chosen by a body of electors, the first idea is that each elector may have votes equal in number to the number of persons to be chosen. Formerly in this country we elected members of Congress in the several States by what was called a general ticket, under which plan each voter in the State voted for as many candidates as there were Representatives in Congress to be chosen from his State, giving to each candidate one vote. That was the system which obtained throughout the United States. In process of time it came to be discovered that this plan of choosing Representatives in Congress by general ticket was a complete and perfect mode of stifling the voice of the minority within a State. A political majority of only five hundred votes in such a State as New York might send twenty-five or thirty members to the lower House of Congress, while the large mass of the minority voters were entirely disfranchised, although nearly as numerous as those who were thus represented in the other House.

This plan of electing by general ticket was therefore abandoned in a number of the States because of its rank and notorious injustice and because of the dissatisfaction which it produced. The habit, however, of so electing Representatives remained in many of the States until Congress interposed by virtue of its power under the Constitution of the United States to regulate this subject, and there is now a law upon our statute-book which provides that Representatives in Congress shall be selected from each State by districts; each State where more than one are to be chosen is to be broken into single districts and a member elected from each. That action by the States and this ultimate legislation by Congress were for the purpose of doing away with the injustice of the former system. It was to enable the minority, or, to speak in other words, to enable the various political interests of society, to have a voice in the councils of the nation, to be heard in these Halls, where laws were to be enacted which would be binding universally upon the citizens. The establishing of the system of single districts for the election of members of Congress was a great reform and a great improvement in American politics; it broke the power of the party majority to this extent, that they could not absorb the whole representation of the State in the popular House of Congress. But when you established the system of single districts you retained still the majority rule for elections in the districts. The majority rule which obtained previously for the States was sent down into these divisions into which the States were broken, and now obtains in the election of Representatives from those several districts. But as society with us has increased in magnitude and in the variety of its interests, inconveniences and evils which formerly were unnoticed or unimportant have grown in magnitude also, and have become exceedingly important, and the majority rule which prevails in the selection of Representatives by districts operates hardly and badly and requires amendment. At least that is my opinion; and in vindication of that opinion, before I conclude I will submit such reasons as have occurred to me in its support.

A majority in a congressional district, although it be a majority of one vote, though it have but a preponderance of one vote over the opposing interest, is entitled to select a Representative, and its voice is heard in the Hall of the people's House. In theory the men who do not vote for the Representative are represented by him; but that theory is simply a falsehood; it is opposed to the fact; it is not true. Instead of representing the men who do not vote for him in his district, the ordinary fact is that the Representative opposes their opinions and contributes all the power which he possesses to render those opinions unpopular and fruitless in the administration of government.

INJUSTICE TO THE MINORITY.

Now, sir, it is a hardship that large masses of the American people should have no voice in the people's House, that they should be shut out from representation in the Hall where popular representation is supposed to prevail with completeness and perfection. Everybody admits that the fact is so, that there is such disfranchisement; and at some times when the cases are very glaring, that disfranchisement arrests public attention and elicits indignant debate.

But we are told that although a minority may be under our present system disfranchised in one district, the opposite party may be disfranchised in another; and so taking the whole State and the whole country together a sort of equilibrium is produced; the party which fails in one district is successful in another, and *vice versâ;* so that when you carry this thing throughout the whole country there is some approach toward justice and a correct result. My answer to that, which is really the main plea for the existing system, is this: in the first place I do not see that the perpetration of injustice in one locality is any compensation for the perpetration of injustice in another; that because a certain minority of voters in Pennsylvania are without a voice in this Government, therefore the non-representation of a different class of voters in Kentucky is justified and made equitable and honorable and of good repute under a republican system. In short, sir, my idea is that when you show me a multiplication of cases of injustice, you have simply swollen your evil in statement and made it more odious, more deserving of blows instead of favor, of opposition instead of support: that the variety of the interests which may be disfranchised under your majority rule as applied to congressional districts is the very fact which pronounces the most weighty condemnation of that rule instead of furnishing it a justification or an apology. Then I have another reply to this suggestion; and that is that it is not true in point of fact that the disfranchisements throughout the country taken together, or the disfranchisements in districts in a particular State taken together, do result in an equilibrium. The fact has never been so; it is not likely to occur; the chances are a thousand to one against it. Therefore, even if there were some soundness in this doctrine of set-off, of setting off one wrong against another, the result would not be the production of an equilibrium of political forces or their just distribution. How was it in the last Congress? Sixteen hundred thousand voters in a particular section of country represented in Congress—the North and West—had but thirty votes; while two million voters in the same section were represented in that same House by one hundred and twenty-eight! Therefore, sir, it is manifestly absurd to talk about the equalization of disfranchisement. There is no such result; there is no equalization.

Mr. President, we have all heard a great deal said in our time about the "sacred principle" that the majority shall bear absolute rule. Well, sir, I deny that there is any such principle in our system of government; and if it could be established, I should deny that it possessed any sacred character. What is our principle, the principle upon which our republican system is founded? It is that the people shall rule; that they shall rule themselves; that we shall have a system of self-government. Does that mean that a part of the people shall rule over another part? Does that mean that they shall be divided numerically, and that twenty shall absolutely control nineteen ; or does it mean volition and action of the whole mass in the business of self-government? We have, however, from what we have supposed to be the necessity of the case, a majority rule at elections. It is a simple rule, nothing sacred in it or about it; an arrangement, a thing of detail, by which we have attempted in a rude manner to apply practically our principle of government by the people ; and this majority rule formerly obtaining in the States and applied to a system of voting by general ticket, yet applies in the districts into which the States are divided. It is the same in its nature and to a great extent it is the same in its effects as before, and the very mischief and evil which led to the abolition of the general ticket plan yet obtains and prevails in elections in single districts. Though mitigated somewhat, it requires, as I think, the vigorous hand of reform.

I have made these introductory remarks in order to approach the subject in an intelligible manner. What is meant by cumulative voting is this: that an elector in any State, whether he belongs to the majority or to the minority, can give his votes for some candidate or candidates who will be elected and who will actually represent him in the Congress of the United States. That is all there is of it. That is the Alpha and the Omega of this whole plan. It is a device by which there shall be actual instead of sham representation in Congress ; by which men who come here into the people's Hall shall represent the men who vote for them and nobody else, and by which it shall not happen that nearly half the people of the United States shall have no efficient or fair representation where the laws are made.

HOW TO CORRECT IT.

How is this object accomplished? The manner of accomplishing it is as simple as the thing is itself. Take the State of Kentucky, about which there is some discussion now, I believe, in the House of Representatives as to membership. She is entitled to nine members in that House. What is proposed is, that an elector in Kentucky may go to the election and vote for nine members, if he choose, to repsent his State in that House, giving each candidate one vote; or bestow his nine votes upon four, if he choose, or upon one, or upon any other number less than the whole. All the provision of law that is necessary is that the elector may vote for a less number of candidates than the whole number to be chosen, and that he may distribute his votes among that less number according to his judgment and discretion, enlightened or directed by his convictions of public duty. That is simple. It does not require a long explanation here; nor to the commonest-minded man in the country is it necessary to go into a protracted argument in order that he may comprehend it. The Senator from Kentucky remarked a short time ago that he was in favor of this reform if it were practicable; he was in favor of some improvement of this kind.

Mr. DAVIS. I did not mean to say that it was impracticable. I am very ready to receive information as to the practicability of it from the honorable Senator.

Mr. BUCKALEW. The Constitution of the United
States says you may regulate the manner of electing
members of Congress; you have interposed already
by law to abolish the evils of the general ticket plan
by which a majority could elect all the members from
a State. Now what I ask you to do is in the same
line of reform with that former legislation; that
you shall go on, and instead of allowing any portion
of the people of a State to be disfranchised, you
shall permit them so to vote that they shall get
actual representation.

Mr. DAVIS. If the honorable Senator will permit me, I will mention as an evidence of my friend-
liness to his principle, that I was a member of the
House at the time that bill was passed, and voted
for it; and I was then upon the Committee of Elections, and I made a report in favor of the bill.
Some of the States then voted by general ticket,
and some did not. Some voted by the district
system, with districts entitled to send two or three
or four Representatives, as was the case in the honorable Senator's State. That measure was deemed
entirely a Whig measure; it was opposed by the
Democracy; and there were four States, according
to my best recollection, two of which I remember,
Mississippi and New Hampshire, who refused obedience to the law, and continued to elect their Representatives upon the exploded general ticket system,
defying the law of Congress. But their representation, elected on the general ticket system, was
accepted in the next House by a majority. I merely
make this statement of my being a friend to that
measure to give some assurance to the honorable

Senator that I am not hostile to the principle of his proposition.

Mr. BUCKALEW. Well, sir, whatever may be said of this measure, it is certainly practicable. It requires nothing but an act of Congress of half a dozen lines permitting an elector in any State choosing members of Congress to bestow his votes on any number of candidates less than the whole. Nothing further is necessary than that the votes so taken shall be reported, counted by the Secretary of the Commonwealth in a State, and the returns signed by the Governor in the usual way, and sent to the Speaker of the House of Representatives. The scheme requires no machinery; it requires no involved legislation; it involves no difficulty in putting it into execution.

ILLUSTRATIONS OF THE NEW PLAN.

Now, let me show how this scheme would work by a particular example. Take the case of Vermont, a State with sixty thousand voters, forty thousand of whom are members of the majority party, and twenty thousand of the minority. By act of Congress—the existing apportionment law—that State is entitled to three members. The numbers I have stated are very nearly the exact numbers of voters in that State. Every one at a glance can see what ought to take place. The majority having forty thousand votes should choose two members of Congress from that State, and the minority having twenty thousand votes should choose one member. Then there would be just representation. Then there could be no complaint in any quarter. Then our principle of the representation of the people would be applied in the particular case, and no human being can conceive of any argument or objection against the result.

This plan of cumulative voting renders just that result certain—renders it morally impossible that any other should take place; and why? Because the minority cumulating their votes upon a single candidate can give him sixty thousand votes; each elector giving his candidate three votes, it would count him sixty thousand. The forty thousand constituting the political majority in the State, if they attempt to vote for three candidates, can give them only forty thousand each. If they cumulate their votes upon two candidates, (which is what they are entitled to,) they can give them sixty thousand votes each; so that two men will be elected to Congress representing the majority and one man representing the minority, and it is impossible for either one of those political interests to prevent the other from obtaining its due share of representation.

Take the case of Pennsylvania, with twenty-four members. In that State at the last congressional election there were polled five hundred and ninety-six thousand one hundred and forty-one votes. The majority party polled three hundred and three thousand seven hundred and ninety and the minority two hundred and ninety-two thousand three hundred and fifty-one. It thus appears that there was a majority in favor of one political interest in that State at that congressional election, amounting to eleven thousand four hundred and thirty-nine votes. Multiplying that by five—one-fifth of the population ordinarily being the voters of the State—and you see that that surplus which one party possessed of votes over the other represents a population a little exceeding fifty-five thousand—less than one-half the number of inhabitants in the State entitled to a representative in Congress—so that this surplus of votes of one party over the other represents a minority fraction upon a ratio of apportionment of members of Congress to the State. The returns of that election (held in October last) were as follows:

PENNSYLVANIA CONGRESSIONAL DISTRICTS.

	Republican.	Democratic.
I	7,728	12,192
II	12,612	9,475
III	12,520	11,516
IV	14,551	12,126
V	12,259	11,800
VI	11,447	14,009
VII	12,011	8,531
VIII	6,999	13,188
IX	14,298	8,675
X	13,186	12,971
XI	9,121	15,907
XII	13,274	15,280
XIII	11,940	10,653
XIV	14,190	12,675
XV	12,489	15,830
XVI	13,589	12,964
XVII	11,298	9,979
XVIII	14,734	12,688
XIX	15,107	12,481
XX	17,106	15,222
XXI	13,023	12,669
XXII	12,720	9,655
XXIII	14,197	10,012
XXIV	13,391	11,853
	303,790	292,351
	292,351	

Majority.................................. 11,439

Ratio of votes for a Representative, according to votes polled...24,839

Now, sir, what is the result? Judging by the actual votes polled at that congressional election, there should have been an equal division of Representatives in the House, standing 12 to 12 ; or, if a Representative should be assigned to the majority interest on account of the excess of its vote, the numbers would stand 13 to 11. But in point of fact, under your single district system, the result in that State is that the delegation stands 18 to 6. instead of being equally divided between parties according to the actual votes which were polled at the election. But under this plan of cumulative voting, what would take place? As each political interest in the State knows that its vote is .about the same as that of the opposing one, and that if it attempt to obtain more than its fair share of representation, it may actually lose instead of gaining, it will be forced to concentrate its votes upon twelve candidates, or upon thirteen at the most, and it is impossible that by any ingenuity or device whatever it can increase its representation in Congress above about what its actual numbers entitle it to. If it should make the attempt, the opposite party would gain an advantage as the result of the sharp practice attempted upon them.

I have taken Vermont and Pennsylvania. Now take the case of Kentucky. There are nine members of the House elected from Kentucky, all of one political complexion. They are now demanding membership in the House, and they are met by a refusal for reasons which I need not discuss, and which it would be, perhaps, improper to discuss here. Suppose a just system of election had pre-

vailed in Kentucky, would the whole nine have
been Democratic—a clean delegation of one political
opinion? No such thing would have been possible.
At that election the majority was about forty thousand for the party that prevailed.

Mr. DAVIS. Larger than that.

Mr. BUCKALEW. I thought it was about forty
thousand. As I make the number of voters required for the election of a member of Congress,
that would represent nearly two members. Therefore the preponderance of one political interest in
Kentucky over the other would represent two members. That would leave seven members of Congress
to be equally divided between the two political interests; one party having four and the other three,
and the result would be that the representation in
the House would have been divided, more unequally, to be sure, than in most cases, but still not
with gross inequality between the two parties that
contend for mastery in this country.

Take the case of Maryland at the last election.
You find that representation in the House of Representatives is not just, considering the men who
gave the votes by which those Representatives were
elected; that instead of there being but one Republican Representative from Maryland there should
be two on account of the actual votes polled in that
State. Then, sir, take the case of Connecticut, an
election recently held, and a most notable trial of
political strength in the North. There, where the
vote was a tie substantially, where the preponderance
of one side over the other was very slight, not more
than about a thousand or twelve hundred, perhaps,

the delegation stands three to one, whereas it should be equally divided according to the actual votes polled and returned according to law.

I cite these cases of recent State elections, and elections which on the whole have been favorable to that interest in the country which when the votes are taken in the aggregate is in the minority, and I cite the other two cases of Vermont and Pennsylvania as other illustrations. But nearly every State might be mentioned in illustration of the argument.

Thus, sir, whether you go to the North or to the West, or confine your researches to the central portions of the country, you find gross misrepresentation of the people of the United States in that House which was peculiarly intended to represent them, and to represent them completely, year by year. The Senate was intended to be a more permanent body, and to possess somewhat of a different character. What I propose, then, is the correction of this injustice, whether it exist in the States I have mentioned or in any other States represented in Congress, and to guard against its extension to the States which you are about to restore under your legislation to their former places in the Union, and with regard to which a reform of this kind is more important than it is to the States of the North, the centre, or the West.

ITS ADVANTAGES.

Mr. President, I will now proceed briefly to state in succession, not to elaborate, several distinct arguments by which cumulative voting can be sustained, vindicated, and made good as I think against all

objection. In the first place, this plan is one of
justice; it is recognized as just by every one who
hears me upon its mere statement; it will be recognized as just by any man in the country to whom
you carry the proposition and submit it for his judgment. It will deal equal, even-handed justice
among political interests in the country, whether
they exist now or are created by the exigencies of
our affairs hereafter.

In the next place, this plan would bring into
public life and keep in public life many able men
who are now excluded under your single district
system. A man of ability in a State can never
reach the Hall of the House of Representatives as
a Representative of the people unless there be a
majority in his district to send him; and if he commence a career in public life, with high ambition
before him, and devote himself zealously to the
service of the people, and so qualify himself for
high statesmanship, and to take rank in Congress as
men take rank in the Parliament of Great Britain,
he knows that a little shifting of the political scale
in his district will leave him out. Those who agree
with him in opinion cannot continue him in the
public service. The result is that you have no
twenty, thirty, or forty-year men in Congress.
They are mostly men of the moment; they are two
and four-year men in the House, and the example
extends even here. If a member of this body gets
re-elected his friends think it is a subject for warm
congratulation, regard it as a wonderful result to be
wrung from a caucus and from managers at home.
But, sir, I insist that in this country, as abroad, the

House of Representatives ought to be the great House of our Legislature; its Hall should be resorted to for words of eloquence, for profound logic, and for the exhibition of the highest traits of American statesmanship. How is it and how must it be as long as you keep members there two, four, and six years only? They have no opportunity to grow up into distinction; they have no opportunity to mature their abilities and become able statesmen.

The result is that the weight of that House in the Government is far below what it should be. This may increase the relative importance of the Senate; but upon the whole it is not a desirable condition of things, and the continuance of this system of rapid rotation in the membership of the House of Representatives bids fair to be one of those injurious influences which will bring republican institutions into contempt.

I say then, sir, that this plan of election by cumulative voting will allow electors of a particular party in a State to continue their favorites in Congress, and will result in improved statesmanship in the House of Representatives, elevating that branch of the national Legislature, and, of consequence promoting the public interests.

Again, sir, one great advantage of this plan is that it abolishes gerrymandering in the States, cuts it up by the roots, ends it forever. That is one of the most crying evils of the time. Now, sir, I venture to say that from Maine westward to the Pacific Ocean, in the last ten years, in no State whatever, has there been an honest and fair district apportionment bill passed for the selection of members of

2

Congress. Nowhere, in no State, has there been a fair apportionment, unless, indeed, it was in a particular and exceptional case where the two branches of a Legislature were divided in political opinion and one checked the other; but ordinarily, as we know, in the course of northern politics, legislative bodies have been of the same political complexion in the upper and lower houses; and I venture to say that whenever this was the fact, unfair and dishonest apportionment bills have been passed.

Under the present system the temptation to party is too great to be resisted; party interest appeals to members of a Legislature, and they yield to. its demands and enact injustice into law. The party that does this knows perfectly well that when a future apportionment shall be made, the opposite party, if it be in power, will retort this injustice, perhaps with increased force. Thus you have a competition between political interests with reference to the apportionment of the States continually increasing in injustice, leading to degradation of the Legislatures and the corruption of the people. The plan of cumulative voting, however, dispensing with single districts in a State, avoids altogether this capital evil and mischief of gerrymandering and brings it to an end so far as the selection of members of Congress is concerned.

Well, Mr. President, in the southern country, as already hinted by me, I consider this plan of cumulative voting to be indispensable to the harmony, to the welfare of that section of the Union. You have vast masses of voters belonging to two different races there who are to be brought into antagonism

to each other at the polls, and that in and through
every State of the whole ten now unrepresented.
How will you have them vote? Against each other,
voting each other down under the majority rule,
producing bad blood and riot and turbulence upon
thousands of occasions, with wide-spread discontent
and dissatisfaction through the whole social body?
Will you permit the majority rule of elections to
have uninterrupted effect there, causing results like
these? Will you make no provision for amendment, for counteracting and countervailing these
manifest evils and dangers?

Take the case of Georgia, with seven members.
You can see what the result would be under cumulative voting following a regular registration of
voters. It could be known beforehand about what
number of representatives the colored voters and their
white allies were entitled to, and how many representatives under that registration the other elements
of population would be entitled to. The election would
take place quietly, without collision; neither side
could deprive the other of its fair share in the result.

I should like to enlarge on that point, but I shall
not do so; for the reason that the decision of the
Senate ruling the amendment proposed by me out
of order upon this bill does not render a discussion
of the effects of this plan in those States, in connection with the coming elections, as important as it
would otherwise be.

I go over, as briefly as I can, the different heads
of the argument, in order that they may be considered here and elsewhere, because this is not the
end of this subject. A proposition which is just in

itself, which is capable of being vindicated by debate, which is important and vital to the working of our representative system, cannot be kept down or suppressed. If it be pushed aside at one time it will recur upon us, it will return again and again, until it be determined upon its merits and according to an enlightened public sentiment developed or produced by discussion.

In the last place, Mr. President, this plan of cumulative voting will be a most valuable check upon fraud at elections. No measure ever proposed in this Union would have so extensive and salutary an effect in checking election frauds and corruption as this plan of fair and honest voting which I defend. Do you not discover at a glance in looking over the States of the Union the main source from which electoral corruption issues, the main cause that brings it into existence? What is that? Why, sir, the motive put before every candidate in every district of the country that is anything like close, the strong incentive and the strong temptation is to corrupt a few votes in order to turn them into his scale and carry his election over an opposing candidate. And when one candidate resorts to this mode of promoting his interests, the opposing candidate feels justified in acting in the same way; and thus it is that an iniquity perpetrated on one side begets similar iniquity upon the other. There is a pitting of corruption against corruption, in the closely contested districts at all events, or most noticeably at commercial points, and our system of government is thereby poisoned at its very fountain. The evil is growing yearly.

As the country becomes denser in population, as wealth accumulates, as the various interests of society become more diverse, its affairs more complicated and dependent upon legislation, this evil of electoral corruption must increase and swell in volume. You must correct your arrangements for elections in order to check it. Cumulative voting will check it. There will be no longer a struggle for district majorities, a struggle for a few votes for one man over another, because one party in a State casting its votes for the number of men or about the number of men it can elect according to its numbers in that State will elect them against the whole world, and there will be no motive to corrupt anybody, no turning of the scale by any species of illegitimate influence which may be brought to bear. Then, no little local interest can come to a political party and command terms from it, command its action. Then no man with his pocket full of accumulated gain can go to election agents and through them corrupt a part of the electoral body to turn the scale in his own favor, provoking thereby similar corruption on the other side. Then illegitimate, pernicious, and selfish interests in a State will not use the machinery of your electoral system for the purpose of poisoning the sources of political power, because there will not be a sufficient motive. It is these contests for majorities between candidates that cause the major part of the evil of which we complain.

CORRUPTION OF THE PRESENT SYSTEM.

Sir, we have not in this regard attained to the full height and depth and breadth of possible evil.

But we have declined far below the purity of former times. The Senator from Massachusetts [Mr. WIL-SON] thinks our elections in this country are models of purity, that nobody is corrupted, that there is little departure from honest principles in their management. Notwithstanding his opinion, I think that this evil is already extensive enough with us to alarm every patriot and every honest man. I could if it were necessary and time permitted put my finger upon cases in my own State which would establish a very different opinion (at least as to that section of the Union) from that which the Senator from Massachusetts announces.

Let me illustrate the extent to which, under a system of elections by the majority rule, corruption may be carried for the purpose of obtaining these local majorities. I take cases from England—some parliamentary boroughs. In the debate in the House of Commons on the 30th of May last a provision of the reform bill was pending which had been proposed by the ministry for the disfranchisement of certain boroughs, on the ground of the corruption of the electors therein. Four boroughs were to be struck from the list of those to be represented hereafter in Parliament, (whether the inhabitants were to be counted as electors of the counties in which they were located or not was not determined at the last accounts.) There had been an examination by a board of commission of the subject of corruption in those boroughs at the previous parliamentary election. Witnesses were examined under oath; the case of each borough was thoroughly investigated, and the facts were laid before

Parliament. What did the report of the commission show? The statement is a startling one, and here it is:

CORRUPTION IN ENGLISH BOROUGHS.

	Registered Voters.	Impure Voters
Totness	421	158
Reigate	912	346
Great Yarmouth	1647	528
Lancaster	1498	916

In Totness and Reigate the corrupt voters were thirty-eight per cent. of the whole; in Yarmouth thirty-two per cent., and in Lancaster sixty-four!

The reason why Yarmouth shows the lowest in this scale of infamy, is that by act of Parliament some years since the freemen were disfranchised, and suffrage was confined to householders; so that the percentage of corrupt voters is only thirty-two per cent., whereas in Lancaster, a borough of somewhat similar character, the percentage amounts to sixty-four per cent. This is shown by a detail of the voters in Lancaster. There, of freemen, there were 980 registered, of whom 708 were proved to be impure; whereas of the householders, 439 registered, the number of corrupt was only 208. Here three-fourths of the freemen were bribers or bribed, whereas less than one-half of the householders were corrupt.

These are the facts as proved, and they of course do not include the corruption in those boroughs which was not detected by the commission, of which there may have been a considerable amount. You see here to what length electoral corruption may be carried under the district system—because in England their boroughs are districts—where the ma-

jority or the plurality rule obtains, and where there
is a motive for a corrupt man to struggle for the
balance of power in order to turn the scale. One
great objection I have always had to colored suffrage, and which I have stated upon this floor, has
been this: that thereby you cast into the hands of
corrupt and ambitious and evil men in this country,
a vast opportunity for mischief, for using this mass
of votes for their own improper purposes. Looking
from the practical point of view upon this question,
I supposed that it connected itself with the subject
of corruption; but if you had a system of cumulative voting in the South, each political party there
would have the power to secure to itself due representation in Congress in spite of another; the
causes of corruption would be cut off or limited,
and you could have a system comparatively pure.
Sir, I show you these English examples as a warn-
ing, as pointing out to you the great danger to
which our representative system is liable, particularly in that section with which your measures of
reconstruction are concerned.

Mr. President, I had prepared some time since a
complete analysis of the recent elections in the
States represented in Congress, from the best means
of information within my power, for the purpose of
showing the operation of our existing system under
the majority rule; but, sir, it is not necessary for
me to go over that. All I shall say upon that
point is that you cannot examine the facts as to any
State, taking your figures from any authentic publication, without perceiving that your representative
system requires reform; that you must advance

from the position you have heretofore maintained as to the manner in which the right of suffrage shall be exercised by our people; and the farther this investigation shall be carried the more thorough will this conviction be.

Mr. President, I have done what I supposed to be a duty in calling attention to this question, presenting it to the consideration of the Senate, knowing perfectly well that it will be again before us, and feeling assured that the proposition will eventually triumph here on this floor and throughout the country, that you will make your plan of taking the sense of the people in the election of members of Congress just, equitable, reasonable, fair; that you will make and shape it according to the information which you now possess, instead of continuing your present imperfect arrangement; that as you extend the basis of suffrage, as you make changes in the foundations of political power, you will improve the plans upon which your system shall be worked and made to accomplish its proper objects.

MILL AND GREY ON REFORMED VOTING.

I have in conclusion only to cite authority, which will be brief upon this question. In the first place I will read from an author of the first rank—from John Stuart Mill's work on parliamentary reform, page 28. He is speaking of districts which shall elect each three members of the Parliament, and is proposing the application of improved modes of voting to them:

"Assuming, then, that each constituency elects three representatives, two modes have been proposed, in either of which a minority, amounting to a third of the constituency, may, by acting in concert, and determining to aim at no more, return one of the members. One plan is, that each elector should only be allowed to vote for two, or even for one, although three are to be elected. The other leaves to the elector his three votes, but allows him to give all of them to one candidate. The first of these plans was adopted in the reform bill of Lord Aberdeen's government; but I do not hesitate most decidedly to prefer the second, which has been advocated in an able and conclusive pamphlet by Mr. James Garth Marshall.

" The former plan must be always and inevitably unpopular, because it cuts down the privileges of the voter, while the latter on the contrary, extends them. And I am prepared to maintain that the permission of cumulative votes, that is, of giving either one, two, or three votes to a single candidate, is in itself, even independently of its effect in giving a representation to minorities, the mode of voting which gives the most faithful expression of the wishes of the elector. On the existing plan, an elector who votes for three can give his vote for the three candidates whom he prefers to their competitors; but among those three he may desire the success of one immeasurably more than that of the other two, and may be willing to relinquish them entirely for an increased chance of attaining the greater object.

" This portion of his wishes he has now no means of expressing by his vote. He may sacrifice two of his votes altogether, but in no case can he give more than a single vote to the object of his preference. Why should the mere fact of preference be alone considered, and no account whatever be taken of the degree of it? The power to give several votes to a single candidate would be eminently favorable to those whose claims to be chosen are derived from personal qualities, and not from their being the mere symbols of an opinion. · For if the voter gives his suffrage to a candidate in consideration of pledges or because the candidate is of the same party with himself, he will not desire the success of that individual more than that of any other who will take the same pledges or belongs to the same party.

" When he is especially concerned for the election of some one candidate, it is on account of something which personally distinguishes that candidate from others on the same side. Where there is no overruling local influence in favor of an individual, those who would be benefited as candidates by the cumulative vote would generally be the persons of greatest real or reputed virtue or talents."

In his subsequent work on representative government he has gone elaborately into an investigation of the existing evils of the representative system as shown in Great Britain, and has laid elaborately the foundations of an argument upon grounds distinct from those which I have stated, although in some cases approaching them, for the adoption of this or some other adequate plan of reform; and in that subsequent work he repeats his recommendation of cumulative voting as one of sensible and material reform. He proceeds, however, to state that his own opinion inclines to a still further reform, the introduction of a system of personal representation, which I shall not discuss here because the occasion does not invite it, because I do not suppose it is a system which can be within a twelvemonth or within several years debated and understood and adopted by the American people. It is one much more complicated, requiring perhaps a higher state of political experience, or a more advanced stage of discussion for its comprehension and adoption by our people.

I have quoted the authority of Mr. Mill in favor of cumulative voting as a convenient, practicable, just, and useful measure of reform, confident that his authority will be accepted both by the Senate and by the people of this country as the highest perhaps which can be produced upon a question of

this character. Next I quote from Earl Grey's
work on Parliamentary Government and Reform,
seventh chapter. This is a new edition, published
in 1864. He says:

"The first of the reforms of a conservative tendency which I
should suggest, and one which I should consider a great improvement under any circumstances, but quite indispensable if
any changes favorable to democratic power are to be admitted,
would be the adoption of what Mr. James Marshall has called
the 'cumulative vote;' that is to say, the principle of giving
to every elector as many votes as there are members to be elected
by the constituency to which he belongs, with the right of either
giving all these votes to a single candidate or of dividing them,
as he may prefer.

"The object of adopting this rule would be to secure to minorities a fair opportunity of making their opinions and wishes
heard in the House of Commons. In order that it might fully
answer this purpose, the right of returning members to Parliament ought to be so distributed that each constituency should
not have less than three representatives to choose. Supposing
that three members were to be elected together, and that each
elector were entitled to three votes, which he might unite in
favor of a single candidate, it is obvious that a minority exceeding a fourth of the whole constituency would have the
power of securing the election of one member. It is probable
that in general three members would be thus returned, each
representing a different shade of opinion among the voters.

"The advantages this mode of voting would be calculated to
produce, and the justice of making some such provision for
the representation of minorities, or rather, the flagrant injustice of omitting to do so, have been so well shown by Mr. Marshall in the pamphlet I have already referred to, and by Mr.
Mill in his highly philosophical treatise on Representative
Government, that it is quite needless for me to argue the question as one of principle. But I may observe that, in addition
to its being right in principle, this measure would be in strict
accordance with the lessons of experience if read in their true
spirit. One of the most remarkable peculiarities of the British

House of Commons, as compared to other representative bodies, is that it has always had within its walls members representing most of the different classes of society, and of the various and conflicting opinions and interests to be found in the nation. Much of the acknowledged success with which the House of Commons has played its part in the government of the country has been attributed (I believe most justly) to this peculiarity.

"The changes made by the reform act, and especially the abolition of the various rights of voting formerly to be found in different towns, and the establishment of one uniform franchise in all the English boroughs, (with only a small exception in favor of certain classes of freemen,) tended somewhat to impair the character of the House in this respect. The greatly increased intercourse between different parts of the country, and the rapidity with which opinions are propagated from one extremity of the kingdom to another, have had a similar tendency; and there is no longer the same probability as formerly that different opinions will be found to prevail in different places, so as to enable all parties to find somewhere the means of gaining an entrance to Parliament for at least enough of their adherents to give expression to their feelings."

And then he goes on with an elaborate investigation and application of this scheme to the House of Commons. There has been, therefore, not only an inquiry abroad, but an assent from minds very differently or variantly constituted, in favor of cumulative voting; from Mr. Mill, a representative of radical opinion, than whom there is no one more eminent in political literature; and then, again, from Earl Grey, representing a more conservative shade of political sentiment in that country. Why has not this plan been adopted in Great Britain and applied in practice, and why has it not been incorporated in the existing reform bill? Because in that country they have not the same advantages that we have for its introduction. Here our existing States offer the facilities for introducing this plan without inconvenience, whereas in Great Britain, where they have their districts formed, districts which have existed for centuries, where the habits and relations of the people have been formed for long periods of time, until they have become inveterate, it is almost impossible to make up political constituencies upon whom to apply this plan of voting. In our States, however, in nearly all of which more members than one are to be elected by the same body of electors, the introduction of this plan is both possible and convenient.

I conclude, Mr. President, by saying that I shall attach, probably, to my remarks a tabular statement, summing up the results of representation as they are exhibited by the existing system in the composition of the Fortieth Congress, excluding, possibly, some of the returns which I do not possess. Now, I submit to the Senate, and to whoever in the country may pay attention to our proceedings and see my remarks on this occasion, that upon grounds of both reason and authority this proposition has been sustained; and that if it be introduced into this country, whether in one State or in many States, or universally throughout the country, in any event it will bear the character of a material, useful, and necessary reform of our political system.

SPEECH

ASSEMBLY BUILDINGS, PHILADELPHIA,

TUESDAY EVENING, NOV. 19, 1867.

Fellow-Citizens of the City of Philadelphia:—

You have had stated to you the circumstances under which I appear in your presence to speak upon the subject of representative reform. Without any introductory remarks, without pausing over preliminary topics, I shall proceed to the subject-matter of my discourse.

Ours is said to be a Government of the people, meaning by that term the whole electoral body with whom the right of suffrage is lodged by our constitution. The people, considered in this sense, are said to rule themselves, and our system is therefore described as one of self-government. Those who are bound by the laws are to enact them. Power is in the first instance exerted by them and obedience yielded afterward. All rests upon their voluntary assent and upon their free action. But, as it is impossible that the whole mass of the political community should assemble together for the purpose of enacting or agreeing upon those rules of conduct which are to bind the citizens, and as it would be impossible for such an enormous body, even if it were convened, to act with convenience or to act at all, we, like the people of other countries in former times have resorted to what is known as the representative system.

From the impossibility of convening ourselves together to determine those great questions which pertain to the political and social bodies, and about which government is employed, we have determined to select from among ourselves a certain number of persons with whom shall be lodged all our powers connected with legislation and with government, and whatsoever they shall determine shall be to us and to all men within our borders the law of individual conduct.

Well, now, gentlemen, in carrying on this system of representative government the manner in which the agents of the people shall be selected becomes in the highest degree important. Although by our theory, although by our fundamental principle of self-government by the people, all the people are to be represented in the making of laws and in the administration of government, in point of fact we have not attained to this result. We have fallen short of it in our arrangements, and hence it is that men of intelligence and of sagacity, driven to their conclusions by thorough examination and by full inquiry, have been compelled to declare that our system is imperfect, and imperfect to such an extent that the quality of our government is deeply affected, and many pernicious things have place in its administration.

Instead of there being under the representative system, as it is known among us, a representation of the entire electoral body, of all the individuals who compose it, there is in fact a representation of only a part. In other words, representation instead of being complete and coextensive with all those who are to be represented and who are to be bound by the action of government, is partial and restricted to a part only of the political body.

Well, gentlemen, in the infancy or in the early stages of a Government an imperfection of this kind may be permitted or overlooked. The affairs of society when they are not complicated, before the community has become rich, before its affairs, social and political, become involved and intricate, may admit of very rude and imperfect arrangements, and yet the people may be well governed, the laws may be just and wholesome and administered in a proper spirit and with complete success. But, as wealth accumulates, as population becomes dense and great cities grow up, as vices are spread through the social body, and as widely extended and complicated political action becomes necessary, those earlier and simpler arrangements—imperfect always—become positively pernicious and hurtful; and the necessity arises for their correction, and that the system of government shall be purified and invigorated by amendment.

In your popular elections which are held or taken under the majority or rather under the plurality rule, (which ordinarily amounts to the same thing,) at your popular elections the smaller number of voices which are spoken in the election of represent-

3

atives who are to enact your laws are stricken from
the count. When the officers charged with the
duty of collecting the voices of the people come to
make up the count and declare the result, they
strike from the poll or the return all those who
when numbered are the smaller quantity or the
smaller political force. Then after your representatives selected in this manner by a majority merely,
by a part of the community, are convened together,
when they come to act in the business of government, to enact laws, they again act by a similar rule.
The majority in the representative body pronounce
the opinion and decree of that body, and what they
pronounce becomes law, binding upon all the people. Now, what is observable in this statement of
facts? Why, that in the first place, in selecting
representatives you strike off a part of the political
body; then, again, in representative action you
strike off the minority of the representative body,
who represent another portion or mass of the popular electors. The result is that your laws may be
made by men who represent a minority of the people who are to be bound by the laws so made. A
representative majority may not be, in point of fact
—and often is not—a representative of the majority
of the people.

When we come to consider in addition to this that
the representative majority, whether in a State
Legislature or in Congress, in modern times or comparatively corrupt times, when pernicious and selfish
interests invade the halls of legislation, ordinarily
acts under what is known as the caucus system; you
perceive how far we have departed from those popu-

lar principles upon which we professed to found our
system originally, and which we supposed would
give vitality and energy to its action. A caucus, a
private consultation of majority members, rules the
action of the representative majority. That majority rules the entire representative body, and that
representative body is composed of representatives
of only a part of the political community. Is it
not then established by this inquiry that instead of
our representative system being what we originally
intended it to be, and what we had supposed it
would be, it is in its practical action characterized
by imperfections which must arrest universal attention when the facts are examined and provoke a cry
for some measure of amendment and reform? And
if a project of reform and amendment can be
brought forward which is practicable, reasonable
and wise, it will be our business to embrace it with
promptness and with gladness of heart.

PLANS OF REFORM.

Now, what do we desire? We may desire that
the whole people, instead of a part of them, shall
be represented in the Government, and that is precisely what I propose. In accomplishing this object, differences of opinion, as in all cases of new
investigations, may be expected. One may have
one project and another another. In a time of inquiry, of movement in the public mind, it is not
well and it is not to be expected that all minds
should run in the same channel, and that out of
the inquiries which individuals enter upon the
same ultimate proposition should be evolved by

each. How will we then obtain representation in government of the entire mass of the people? Let us come to that question, and in coming to it inquire into the several plans or projects which have been suggested to secure this object. They may be classed under three heads. In the first place, it has been proposed in various forms that by law there should be a restricted or limited mode of voting. Again, it has been proposed that the elector in all elections of representatives and of other officers where more than one are to be chosen, may bestow his votes upon a smaller number than the whole; in other words, may exercise what is known as the cumulative vote. Again, there has been proposed in Great Britain and elaborately defended in that country what is called the system of personal representation, by which an elector shall be emancipated from the ordinary bonds and trammels of party organization, and shall be as an individual and not as a member of a party represented in Parliament or other body of a similar constitution.

THE LIMITED VOTE.

Now, as to the first of these, that is, the limited or restricted vote—I use these words because I have none more expressive or convenient at hand—as to this limited vote: When you pass to your places of election and proceed to choose for yourselves the election officers who shall hold elections during the year in your several election districts, what do you do?

Each elector votes for one inspector, and yet two are chosen. Here is a limitation upon the voter.

Instead of voting for both, the law says that he shall vote for but one. What is the practical result throughout the State under this law? Why, that one inspector belongs to the majority party in each election district, and the other belongs to an opposing one. In other words, both the parties into which our political society is ordinarily divided are represented in the election boards. Thus you secure representation of the entire mass of the electors, and yet you secure it by a limitation upon the votes of individual electors.

What has been the practical result of this arrangement, which is found in your State election law of 1839? Has the result been good or bad? Why, there is not a man who hears me, or an intelligent, honorable citizen in this Commonwealth, who would not cry "shame" if that law were repealed. It is a law by which elections are kept comparatively pure, by which fraud is prevented and fairness is secured to the citizen in polling his vote.

I believe in this city, when you come to choose assessors in your several wards, those interesting persons who have control over your pockets [laughter], who take valuations of your property, whose action as public officers is most interesting to you, each elector votes for one, and yet two are selected. In this case you are secured, I presume, against partiality and injustice in the administration of the tax laws by dividing those officers between political parties.

I am told, also, that in selecting your school directors each school division or ward has twelve directors who have charge of your school system—one-third, that is four, elected in each year. In voting, each elector votes for but three, so that it ordinarily happens that the fourth man chosen each year will be of a different opinion politically from the majority of his fellow-directors; will represent in the government of the school district one kind of opinion, while the greater number of his colleagues will represent another.

At the last session of your State Legislature a law was passed which took from the commissioners of counties and sheriffs the selection of jurors for the several courts throughout the Commonwealth. Great complaints were made in this matter, especially in the interior of the State. You had a particular arrangement in the city which has not been disturbed, to wit: the selection of jurors by the judges of the several courts, in order to insure impartiality and fairness and prevent the intrusion of political interests or passions in the selection of your jurors. But in the interior the duty of selecting jurors, which was formerly charged upon the commissioners and the sheriffs of the several counties, was taken away at the last session of the Legislature and confided to two officers in each county, who are to be called jury commissioners. The president-judge in each county has some function or duty in connection with these officers—it is somewhat doubtful what it is; the law was badly drawn—but substantially the power of selection heretofore exercised by the ordinary officers of counties to whom I have referred is now to be confided to these jury commissioners.

How are they to be chosen? As in the case of

inspectors of election, where one candidate alone is
voted for, but two are to be chosen. By this means
it is to be supposed that there will be fairness in the
selection of jurors throughout the State, and the
abuse which has heretofore prevailed will be removed from our system—the abuse that in Republican counties Democratic citizens were excluded to
an unreasonable extent from the jury-box, and that
on the other hand in Democratic counties Republican jurymen were unreasonably excluded. Here
again is a limitation upon the elector. He shall
vote for but one of these officers, who are to select
the men who may sit upon questions which relate to
his life, to his property, or to his reputation, and yet
by this limitation fuller representation of the people
and fairness in trials are secured. I think that a
much wiser arrangement might have been made
than that. If I had possessed power to mold the
law upon this subject I would have simply changed
the mode in which county commissioners are chosen.
I would have had them selected upon the plan of
the cumulative vote (which I will presently explain)
or upon the plan of the limited vote. We would
have obtained substantially in that way the same
result without two additional officers and without
certain inconveniences which attend upon the existing law. But the object was laudable and the effect
which will be produced by that law will be salutary.
Public opinion will take hold of it and uphold it
hereafter as a just and wise arrangement, compared
with the one it superseded.

Let me illustrate this idea of limited voting which
has obtained in our State by a case taken from the

State of New York. Under the constitution of that State every twenty years the question of reforming the State constitution is to be submitted to a vote of the people, and in case they vote in favor of a convention to amend the constitution one is to be called. It happened last year that a convention was to be called, and Governor Fenton proposed to the Legislature that in addition to the selection of delegates from the representative districts of the State (one from each) there should be thirty-two delegates selected at large, and in selecting these thirty-two delegates each elector in the State to vote for but sixteen. His recommendation was adopted by the Legislature, so that the existing constitutional convention of New York (it has not concluded the performance of its duties) is constituted of representatives elected from the representative districts, and of thirty-two delegates from the State at large. Of the latter, sixteen belong to each political party, for such was the inevitable effect of the plan adopted. Many men went into the convention and are now sitting in it who could not have been elected in their several local districts, because the party with which they were associated was in the minority therein. In selecting delegates from the State at large this was possible, and able men were selected on both sides—men of great weight and great wisdom. These cases of limited voting in our own State which I have mentioned and this case in New York will suffice so far as our own country is concerned.

Now, let me carry you to England for a short time to see what has been done there in this same direction. In 1854, under the administration of

Lord Aberdeen, Lord John Russell introduced a reform bill which underwent protracted discussion in the House of Commons. One feature of that bill was that in all constituencies electing three members of Parliament no elector should vote for more than two, the result of which would have been to give to the minority class of electors ordinarily the third member. That bill, however, did not become a law; it fell, and other reform bills introduced since into Parliament have failed. But during the present year a bill was passed through Parliament to amend and reform the representation of the people of England in the House of Commons. That bill having passed the House of Commons and being under consideration in the House of Lords on the 30th of July last, Lord Cairnes moved to amend clause 8 of the bill by adding, "at a contested election for any county or borough represented by three members, no person shall vote for more than two candidates." This was substantially, if not in exact terms, the same as the clause in the Russell reform bill of 1854. After undergoing debate this amendment was adopted in the House of Lords by the following vote: contents, 142; non-contents, 51, or by the large majority of 91 in its favor. The bill being returned with this and other amendments to the House of Commons was again considered in that House. Finally, upon the 8th of August, after prolonged and exhaustive debate, in which men whose names are known throughout the earth participated, upon motion to strike out this amendment made by the House of Lords the vote stood—ayes 204, noes 253, being a majority of 49 in favor of retaining the provision, and it was retained by that vote; and the bill subsequently passing and receiving the approval of the Crown it became and is now the law of Great Britain, (from which country we derive our political descent and many of our principles of free government, including that of representation.)   Henceforth, in the election of members of the lower house of Parliament, where a constituency select three members, two shall be given to the majority and one to the minority of the electors, assuming that the latter constitute so large a mass as one third of the whole number.   This is the most notable instance of the application of the limited vote to secure the representation of the whole political mass of the community or of a particular constituency charged with the duty and power of selecting representatives for the enactment of laws.

By these instances, selected in our own country and abroad, it is manifest that attention has been largely drawn to this question of amendment in representation—of mitigating the evils and inconveniences which must always arise under an unchecked, unmitigated, unamended majority rule.

THE CUMULATIVE VOTE.

But, gentlemen, I pass from the consideration of this mode of amending representation to the second form which propositions for that purpose have assumed; in other words, I pass to the discussion of the topic which is most interesting at this time for our consideration.   I mean the plan of *cumulative voting*, as it has been named.   This was in the first instance proposed, explained, and advocated

by James Garth Marshall, a subject of the Crown
of Great Britain; and, by his proposition and his
advocacy of it, he has given his name to the political history of his country and to the political history of representative institutions everywhere in
future times: for no one previously had mastered
this subject with such grasp; no one had looked
into it with such intuitive perception of all its
characteristics and was able to strike precisely the
point where reform could be most safely and effectually introduced. It is preferable, infinitely preferable, to all propositions for securing the representation of all interests in society by any limitation
upon the elector's vote in the manner of the various
propositions which I have already described.

This system or plan of cumulative voting has
been indorsed by John Stuart Mill in his work on
Parliamentary Reform and in his work on Representative Government, and since supported by him
ably in the House of Commons. It has been
recommended, also, by Earl Grey in his work on
Parliamentary Reform, edition of 1864. It was
proposed during the consideration of the recent
Reform bill in the House of Commons by Mr.
Lowe, on the fifth of July last, and after debate
received the very respectable support of 173 votes.
It is beginning to attract in this country that degree
of attention which it merits, and which is naturally
provoked by the inquiry which has taken place
abroad. I shall describe it in a moment. For the
present I will simply say that the third proposition
of reform, known as *personal representation*, which
looks to other objects and to other consequences, I

shall not attempt to discuss to-night. It invites us
over too wide a field of investigation for the time at
our disposal; and I may add that it involves so
many considerations and so much of prolonged
debate that, within the ordinary duration of a meeting, it would be impossible to exhaust the subject
or to come to any intelligent conclusion upon it. I
presume, also, speaking generally concerning it, that
it will be a considerable time before we shall be in
possession of that amount of experience and of discussion which are requisite to its adoption in this
country.

Now, what is cumulative voting? I propose that
what is known by this term shall be applied to the
election of representatives in Congress and to the
choice of electors of President and Vice President
of the United States. It admits, also, of application
to the selection of senators and representatives in the
several State Legislatures, and to the selection of
county commissioners, and many other officers.
In what I shall say at this time, however, I shall
confine myself, in the discussion of this plan, mainly
to the election of Representatives in Congress. This
reform can be introduced by act of Congress without
any constitutional change; and the plan can be applied to the election of presidential electors by the
Legislatures of the several States, who, under the
Constitution, have committed to them the power of
providing the manner in which those electors shall
be chosen. What, then, is cumulative voting? It
is that where more than one officer is to be chosen
the elector in the first place shall possess as many
votes as there are persons to be chosen, and next, he

may bestow those votes at his discretion upon the whole number of persons to be chosen, giving one vote to each, or upon any less number, cumulating his votes upon one, two, three, or any other number less than the whole. That is simple in its statement, although its effect, the practical character of the proposition, requires some reflection and prolonged experience to its entire comprehension. What is its effect? It is that any political interest in a community, whether in a State or in a division of a State, if it can ascertain about the relative proportion which its strength bears to the whole mass of the vote, or to the vote of an opposing interest, may cast the suffrages of its members in such manner that they will tell upon the result; and it will happen that every man, or about every man who votes, will vote for a candidate who will be chosen, and there will be no such thing as unrepresented minorities left. They will be wiped out of the system; they will no longer exist. To speak of this as a plan for the representation of minorities is an abuse of terms, because it conveys no idea which attaches to the plan. Far be it from us to arm a minority with power which we know even majorities abuse! The proposition now submitted to us is not that there shall be majorities and minorities known in election returns, but that the men who vote shall vote for those who will be chosen, and who will in point of fact represent them.

I cannot better illustrate the scheme than by the case of Vermont, which I have used on another occasion. There are 60,000 voters in Vermont, of whom 40,000 are members of the Republican party

and 20,000 of the Democratic party. I speak in
round numbers. By law that State is entitled to
three Representatives in Congress, because her
population, under the Constitution of the United
States, authorizes the allotment of that number to
her. Now, what ought to take place there? The
majority should elect two Representatives, having
40,000 voters, and the minority should elect one,
having 20,000 voters; but can that be so in point of
fact at present? If the electors of that State vote
for three Representatives by general ticket the majority would elect the whole three. If the State be divided up into single districts, it is a matter of chance
how the result will be, whether all three districts
will have majorities of the same political complexion
or not. I say it is a matter of chance; nay, more
than that, it is a matter of honesty in the Legislature of the State, and any political majority that
has control of the Legislature will very likely form
the districts to suit its own interests. We know
that these things occur everywhere. By cumulative voting, by authorizing the 20,000 minority
electors of that State to give each three votes to one
candidate, that candidate would receive 60,000 votes,
and the majority cannot defeat him. The majority
voting for two Representatives can elect them, but
they cannot elect the third. Suppose they attempt
to vote for three candidates, they can only give each
of them 40,000 votes, and the minority candidate
has 60,000. If they attempt to vote for two, as they
ought to do, that being the number they are entitled
to, they can give them 60,000 votes each, the same
number that the minority candidate has. If they

attempted to vote for one they would give that one candidate 120,000; but of course they would not throw away their votes in that foolish manner. The practical result would be that the 40,000 majority electors in that State would vote for two candidates and elect them, and the 20,000 minority electors would vote for one and elect him, and results analogous to this would occur all over the United States if this system were applied. In every State the freemen, each possessing an equal right with his neighbor, would each vote for a Representative or Representatives in Congress who would speak his voice and obey his will, and thus you would obtain throughout the country, in each State, an actual representation of the whole mass of people on both sides; honest representation instead of a sham; a government by the majority in point of fact in Congress instead of an accidental result, which may be one way or the other, and is just as likely to be minority rule as anything else, and always and under all circumstances unjust rule.

Oh! gentlemen, what would happen then? Some little men in the State Legislature, destitute of honor but greedy of gain and of personal objects, would no longer gerrymander your States [applause], would no longer sit in quiet chambers concocting injustice by law, studying how they can prevent their neighbors from being represented in the government and get an undue share of public power for themselves and for their friends. That iniquity would be ended, and would be no more heard of among us. Why, gentlemen, at this moment, from the British possessions upon the northeast to the

Golden Gate of the Pacific, there is probably not
one honest apportionment law for members of Congress, and you will scarcely ever have one, unless in
an exceptional case where one political interest shall
have control of the upper branch of a Legislature
and another of the lower, holding each other in
check, and compelling some degree of fairness in
the formation of the law.

I do not desire to speak on any topic which may
bear a partisan complexion. I am almost afraid to
cite cases lest I shall be thought to have an object
or purpose not openly avowed. Let me tell you the
difficulty in this case is in human nature, and you
must frame your system so that mischief will not
result. "It is necessary," said a great and wise
man, "that by the very constitution of things power
should be a check to power." What said Dr.
Priestly? "There is no earthly power that has
not grown exorbitant when it has met with no control." Take these words of men who thought
wisely and profoundly, and then look at your existing political action and see whether it is not a
struggle for power instead of a struggle for justice;
whether it is not a struggle by each interest to obtain all it can and to retain all it can, and to keep
away from an opposing interest anything like a fair
distribution of power or fair treatment.

It is necessary, then, gentlemen, that by your
fixed arrangements in your constitutions and laws
you shall curb the injustice of human nature; that
you shall so arrange your system that evil and selfish
men cannot pervert it to their own purposes and
to the injury of others. A system of cumulative

voting secures the government of the real majority
of the people. Instead of striking off a part of
them in the popular elections, they are all represented in the representative body, whether Congress
or the State Legislature, and there by a single
operation the vote is taken, the majority pronounced,
and a proposed law is enacted or defeated. Instead
of unjust representation and an eventual decision by
a representative majority moved and governed by a
caucus, you will have fair, equal, extended, complete
representation of the whole mass of the people and
the proper voice of the majority pronounced in the
representative body.

I repeat, this is no plan for minority representation
merely; it is a plan for the representation of the
whole people, a device by which the majority shall
rule and shall pronounce its voice in a fair and
honest manner. Again, a system of cumulative
voting would secure to you in your legislative bodies
men of high ability, and secure them for long
periods of time, because elections would not be subject to the uncertainties which attend ordinary elections under the majority rule. A political party in
Pennsylvania, constituting about or near one-half
its electors, assuming that the State would be permanently entitled say to twenty-four members (the
present number), can keep about a dozen men con-
tinuously in Congress for a long period of time
Just as long as they retain the confidence of their
constituents they will be elected, because the merit
of this plan is that one part of the community cannot vote down another. Each will get its due share
of Representatives, and can keep it always simply

4

by giving votes only to the number which they are entitled to have and which they can elect. This system would secure contentment to men constituting minorities, as they are now known, because such minorities would be abolished at popular elections, and, although their representatives should be voted down in representative bodies, they would be heard there, and it is a great satisfaction for a man to be heard even when judgment is pronounced against him. That is what we suppose to be one great advantage of courts of justice; a man has his day in court and he is heard; judgment is not pronounced in his absence or without a hearing. Just so minorities in our country, as they are now constituted, are dissatisfied and they always will be dissatisfied under the present system. Let them be heard, and if the decision is against them in the legislative body they will acquiesce, because they have had fair treatment. This is human nature. Every one can see that that would be so. Would we not, therefore, be less liable to revolt, to convulsion, to war? Content your people, improve your system so that it will work happily and properly, and you crush out the seeds of political convulsion. [Applause.]

A CHECK ON CORRUPTION.

I shall not go over the other heads of the argument at length, because time will not permit me. I insist as a principal argument, however, for this mode of taking the sense of the electoral body, that it would be a great check upon corruption. Now, what causes corruption at our elections? What brings it into being? I submit that question to

you, gentlemen, as men of ordinary experience.
What is it? One candidate wants to get a majority
over another candidate. The district may be close,
or at least each side may have hopes of carrying
it; passion is aroused; to use a common expression
the blood is up; ambition calls, private interest
prompts. Here and there we know, for so the fact
stands revealed to us, a candidate, or the friends of
a candidate, will resort to corrupt means. For what
purpose? To get the balance of power, to turn the
scale; not to corrupt the great body of the electors,
but to gain the tenth, the twentieth, or the fiftieth
man who holds in his hands the balance of power
between political interests. In this manner these
contests for local majorities and for State majorities
between parties call into existence all the evil and
corrupt influences which attend our elections. A
man at Harrisburg or at Washington is expected to
distribute patronage around his district, so that he
can get votes to beat somebody else when he comes
before the people again. A man with his pocket
full of accumulated gain, the result of his own thrift
and cunning or the accumulation of his ancestors,
wants a few votes to make a majority against an
opposing candidate, and he gives money to election-
eering agents and does not inquire how it is applied.
After a while great complaints are made in your
community of a corrupt election. You hear such
expressions as "shocking," "horrible," "what is
the country coming to; what is the social body and
what is the political body coming to?" Corruption
raises its head in America; it is the danger in our
path; it is the giant we have to fear, whose blows

will lay low our republican system if it shall ever
be prostrated. Does not your majority rule invite
all these evil influences? Go out and make
inquiry about your last congressional election in
certain districts, and you will hear, "Oh, money
carried it; here was a boss who was bought up;
he had control of fifty or one hundred men;" in
another district another had control of fifty or one
hundred electors, and the election was turned. It
required only a few votes to win, and away goes the
victor to his post of duty, to make laws for the
American people. I am not talking of things
abroad. This cry comes to you in this city. Yes,
corruption is increasing in America. And what
invites it? I will answer in a word—it is the
majority rule at popular elections which invites it;
it is because you have an unjust or imperfect system
by which nearly one-half of the community have
their voices stifled; the corrupt man buys a few
votes, and thousands of his fellow-citizens have no
voice in the Government; they are outvoted; five
votes will do it, if they create a majority, as well as
five thousand. Adopt a plan by which every political party and every political interest, if it choose,
can elect its men and can elect as many men as its
numbers entitle it to, and you are done with this
abuse of corrupting votes to turn the scale, you are
done with this purchase of majorities, you are done
with this scandal of your system, and you have
taken the most effectual guarantee which, with our
present information, it is possible for us to secure
for its integrity and perpetuity hereafter. [Great
applause.] Under a system of cumulative voting,

in the present Congress the delegation from this State would stand twelve Republicans and twelve Democrats. Why? Because each party has three hundred thousand votes in this State, and each one knowing that its strength was about equal to the other, would have cumulated its votes upon twelve men and elected them, and there would have been a fair representation of the State. Vermont would have had two majority and one minority members as I have shown. Kentucky, which sends nine Democratic members, would have sent at least three Republicans in her delegation, under a sound mode of voting; and Maryland, instead of one Republican member out of five, would have sent two; in Connecticut, instead of three Democratic Representatives out of four, there would have been two, because the vote of the State was about a tie; and so throughout the Union. You cannot take a State and examine the facts relating to it in any authentic publication without seeing this element of injustice entering into your system and poisoning it at its very fountain.

I need hardly say—and this is, perhaps, a delicate branch of my speech—that if in any part of this Union we are to have two classes of voters, distinguishable by race or color, a very considerable part of the mischief and evil which the opponents of the extension of suffrage apprehend would be prevented or removed by the adoption of the cumulative vote. Instead of the cry being raised, "one race votes down another and has its heel upon it"—we have heard that all over the North, and we know how powerfully it has influenced the elections—instead of that cry it would be announced that each race obtained representation in proportion to its numbers, without direct antagonism or collision. This, however, is an argument for gentlemen in a different position from myself. As to them it ought to be decisive in favor of their rendering support to the plan of cumulative voting which I advocate.

CHOICE OF PRESIDENTIAL ELECTORS.

Now, gentlemen, a few words as to the application of this system to the selection of presidential electors. General Jackson proposed that the people of the United States should vote directly for President and Vice President, instead of voting for electors in their several States, and this proposition, at several times, has been brought forward in Congress. At the last session it was again introduced by Mr. WADE, now President of the Senate, and was defended by him in an argument. Great complaint is made that the people are not heard directly in the choice of President; that the electoral colleges are useless or inexpedient; that they should be removed from our system, and each voter be permitted to vote directly for the President of his choice.

Gentlemen, a system of cumulative voting by the citizens of Pennsylvania, which can be provided by an act of their Legislature as I understand the constitution, would secure to our citizens, if not the precise objects sought by the friends of that reform, at least greater advantages than it would confer. The result would be that each of the political interests existing in this State would select as many electors as they were entitled to by their numbers, and each

would be felt proportionably in the presidential
election. How is it now? Do you not know what
is coming on next year in our State? Six hundred
thousand votes are to be polled for presidential electors. Each party has about three hundred thousand. What is going to take place? From Lake
Erie to the Delaware this State is to be convulsed;
a thousand disagreeable circumstances are to attend
the election; men's minds are to be taxed and wor-
ried for months; men of property are to have their
attention turned to the security of their investments.
All the unpleasant and illegitimate influences which
attend elections, and to which I have referred, will
be called into existence in that great approaching
struggle. And why? Because whichever interest
obtains a majority in this State, though it be a majority of but one vote, secures twenty-six electoral
votes for President of the United States, and the
struggle will be for the little majority which turns
the scale. Now, do we not all see at a glance what
the fact is? Each party is entitled to thirteen of
these electors, or about that number, because they
are composed of American freemen who are entitled
to an equal voice in our common government. But
both cannot secure electors; the whole twenty-six
must be given to one side, and perhaps that result
will determine the government of this country not
only for four years to come but for four centuries.
We enter upon the canvass as a game of chances,
fearful that the most adroit and unscrupulous interest of the two in the State can command the result;
that there will not be a fair struggle between the
men who are honest and those who are not. Let

us have honest voting; let each party have the
presidential electors that its numbers entitle it to,
and let them be felt upon the general result; let
the people in each of the other States vote as we
vote, and let the majority of Americans decide the
contest.

CONVENIENCE AND JUSTICE OF NEW PLAN.

Finally, this plan of representative reform is
convenient in a high degree; it is both practicable
and convenient.   It requires in this State nothing
of legislation except simply to permit a citizen who
has, say, twenty-four votes for members of Congress
and twenty-six for presidential electors, to cast those
votes as a freeman, according to his own choice and
pleasure; let him bestow them upon any smaller
number, for instance, giving two to each of twelve
candidates, or four to each of six.   Trust the people,
and their common sense will regulate their action.
You do not need intricate laws, constitutions tink-
ered, or a great scheme of reconstruction. [Laughter.]
You are simply asked to trust the people, and permit them, when they possess votes, to cast them
as they think best; as their judgment may be
directed by views of public interest or public duty.
If we should have that system for electing members
of Congress and presidential electors next fall, we
could each go to the polls and vote for twelve Representatives in Congress to sit for Pennsylvania, and
for thirteen electors of President and Vice-President; or, if any one should think that the political
interest with which he is associated is flourishing

and growing in strength, so that it is entitled to
one additional member, he could vote for thirteen
Representatives. If he should be mistaken in his
calculation, he would fail as to one of his votes;
numbers would be counted exactly, and there would
be no injustice.

Now, I must point out one additional special
injustice of the ordinary majority rule at elections,
unmitigated by any such plan as that proposed.
Observe that the party which prevails at the election does not merely carry the day, does not merely
get its votes counted and get the result appropriate
to the counting of them; but it gets all the power
which belongs to the other side in addition to its
own.   Suppose that the two parties in Pennsylvania
are so divided that one has 300,000 votes and the
other 301,000.   In choosing electors of President
and Vice-President the 301,000 who prevail, who
have 1000 majority, do not merely get their votes
counted in the presidential election, do not merely
influence the result in selecting our Chief Magistrate by their own votes, but they have in effect
counted into their vote the votes of their opponents,
the other 300,000.   Your 301,000, constituting the
majority in the State, wield the political power of
the whole 601,000—wield not only their own appropriate power but a power which does not belong to
them but belongs to the political interest opposed to
them.

That is what sharpens this injustice of disfranchisement, and that is the reason why, in legislative
bodies, a little turning of the popular scale gives
one party or another, when in point of fact parties

are nearly equal, such a mass of preponderating power.

Take the elections which occurred in 1866 in the States north and west, the States formerly called the free States. In those elections 2,000,000 voters (in round numbers) voted Republican tickets for members of Congress in the respective States. The other party, the Democracy, polled in those States at those elections a little over 1,600,000 votes. What was the result? To Congress 1,600,000 voters chose twenty-eight Representatives only, and the 2,000,000 voters one hundred and forty-three! The proportion between the two great masses of our electoral population, known by the respective party names, was twenty to sixteen in votes actually polled in the States to which I have referred. The Representatives to Congress selected at those elections from those States, instead of standing as twenty to sixteen, stood one hundred and forty-three to twenty-eight. And why? Because under the majority rule at elections in those States the majority not only obtained representation in Congress for its own votes, but obtained the greater part of the representation that belonged to the other side. Under a system of cumulative voting representation in Congress would have stood about in the proportion of twenty to sixteen, just as the actual votes ran in those States. Do you not see how the whole policy of your Government can be changed; how the voice of the people may be stifled; how republican institutions may be made a farce and a sham, and that under a system which you are falsely

told secures the fair rule of a majority as a principle
that is sacred?

AN OBJECTION ANSWERED.

Gentlemen, I have already occupied so much time
that I must omit any detailed examination of the
arguments against cumulative voting. I can notice
only one or two of them briefly. It is said that a
system of elections such as I have described would
deprive particular localities of representation; that
there would be a combination of great and powerful
communities within a State against some particular
districts, and those districts which now have Representatives would be disfranchised. This argument
has been made in Great Britain; it is likely to be
repeated here, and it is perhaps the only one deserving any considerable attention. Of course my
political reading and political thought have been
against the undue concentration of power at any
particular point, whether Washington, Harrisburg,
Philadelphia, or elsewhere, and I have been in favor
of its distribution, as far as possible, into all the
local communities into which the State or the country is divided. And this objection, from my point
of view, deserves respectful treatment and respectful
answer. I have to observe, then, that, in my opinion, particular localities within a State would have
a due voice and due influence in the selection of
candidates; that if they were selected by a common
body, by a State convention, any attempt to disfranchise any particular section of the State would be
met by a counter combination in the interest of fair
play, and that the practical result would be that

there would be on the whole a fair distribution of political power in the different parts of the State by the selection of candidates. If, however, any difficulty were apprehended on this ground, there might be a rule adopted by which nominations should be made by districts, a thing very often done in counties and also in States. It would be a rule to a party in making its selections that there should be a distribution of its candidates according to district divisions, either those established for other purposes by some general State law or established by the particular party organization for its own purposes of selection or distribution.

But the conclusive answer to the objection is this, that any important locality would have the power to defend itself against such injustice; and that is one of the merits of this system of cumulative voting. If there was an attempt to disfranchise the city of Philadelphia, to prevent her returning her four members to Congress, and the thing was gross and glaring, what could she do under a system of cumulative voting? Just combine her vote on her four men and elect them in spite of all the other electors in the State, and thus any attempt at injustice in any section of the Commonwealth might be resented by the people aggrieved by cumulating their votes upon one or more local candidates of their own. They could defeat any such attempt at injustice and defend themselves against it, and the fact that they had such power of defense would always secure a just distribution of nominations.

Again, candidates being thus voted for by the whole State, there would be opportunities for making better selections than are made by the district system. Let me take an illustration on this point. What a misfortune it would have been if the narrow intellectualities of our modern political reasoners had controlled in England when Edmund Burke was a candidate before the electors of Bristol in 1780; a distinguished member of Parliament, whose name is given to the literature of the world for all future ages. He stood up in the British Parliament defending the just rights of the American colonies. Words in our behalf which yet echo through the world were heard with admiration and pride even by those opposed to him in the House of Commons. But they were heard with other feelings in Bristol, which he represented in Parliament; and when he went down to his constituents, instead of re-electing they rejected him; he was voted down; his own district had a local majority against him of men who hated America, who were with the king in the war he waged against our fathers. Their passions and prejudices were roused against their eloquent representative who had defended America in the Parliament of the empire; he was defeated under the majority rule and a single district system. Fortunately, he was returned to Parliament by another constituency, who thought it an honor to be represented by him, and he continued in the House of Commons as long as he lived, adorning it by his eloquence and his genius, and giving his name to his country and to the world as a cherished recollection for all time. In our country, under similar circumstances, such a man would remain out of Congress or out of other legislative body upon a

defeat in his district. He would be ostracised from
the councils of his country, his voice silenced, his
career would be closed. What does cumulative
voting do? It enables the freemen of a State to
select their Burkes and their Websters, their Clays
and Calhouns, wherever they may be in a State, and
to use their abilities so long as they please in shap-
ing the legislation and administration of the government of the country. [Applause.] No ability, no
merit, no eminence, no greatness, could be stifled in
any of our States under this system. The majority
rule, which would seem to have been invented to
submerge merit and to lift mediocrity, would no
longer operate its course unchecked in American
politics; the freemen of our country would have a
breadth of choice which they would exercise, I
doubt not wisely, to the advantage of themselves
and of future generations.

Our experience in this State and in other States
is not in favor of carrying the idea of single districts very far. I drew the amendment to the Constitution of our State by which your city is broken
into single districts. [Applause.] What was the
idea of that amendment? It was that one political
interest should not absorb the whole sixteen or
eighteen representatives you send to the Legislature;
that a little shifting majority one way or the other
should not cast that large number of votes on one
side or the other at Harrisburg. The idea was to
break up the political community, and allow the
different political interests which compose it, by
choosing in single districts, to be represented in the
Legislature of the State. Unfortunately, when that

arrangement was made for your city (and for Pitts-
burg also, to which it will soon apply), this just,
equal, almost perfect system of voting, which I have
spoken of to-night, was unknown; it had not then
been announced abroad or considered here, and we
did what best we could.   Now, however, if a change
were to be made, I suppose the same current of
opinion and of sentiment would have course in this
State which has prevailed in New York, where the
system of single districts throughout the State for
the election of members of the Assembly or lower
legislative branch of that State has lost credit.   The
idea is very generally abandoned by thinking and
reflecting men in that State.   It is a failure; it has
not produced the results which it was supposed
would flow from it.   Cumulative voting, however,
comes in, and it is a principle which is capable of
extended application to popular elections, where
more than a single officer is to be chosen.   It can
be applied to the election of Senators and Representatives in the Legislature from your city and
from each of the counties of the State, or from districts into which the State might be divided, and
you may thus get in the government of your State
that fair and equal representation which you ought
to claim and which is your due as citizens of a free
State.

After some further remarks, Mr. BUCKALEW concluded as follows:

Gentlemen, I have said most of what I proposed
to say this evening, so far as points of argument are
concerned.   I omit some minor points, and I omit
filling up the outline of the argument.   I have said

what I supposed was most essential. And now, in conclusion, let me say that I appear here to discuss this subject before you for no purpose of idle display or of amusement, but with a proper object; with an idea to its examination and discussion by others; and what I shall desire, and what will repay me a thousandfold for any inconvenience in attending here and any effort in speaking, will be the support of the press and people of Philadelphia to a new, improved, and honorable system of electoral action by which our representative system in this country will be vastly improved, and by which the future of our country will receive an additional guarantee and security which will not fail it hereafter in peace or in war.   [Great applause.]

[The foregoing address was delivered before a large and intelligent audience at the request of some gentlemen of Philadelphia, who desired the subject of reformed voting to be presented to the people of that city.   Hon. Alexander Cummings presided over the meeting and introduced the speaker with appropriate remarks.   The address was reported by D. F. Murphy, the accomplished United States Senate Reporter, and was published in the daily newspapers the following morning.]

SENATE COMMITTEE REPORT.

IN THE SENATE OF THE UNITED STATES.

MARCH 2, 1869.

Mr. BUCKALEW, from the Select Committee on Representative Reform, submitted the following

REPORT.*

[To accompany bill S. No. 772.]

THE bill referred to the committee, and now reported by them, presents a question which deserves deliberate examination both because it is important and because it is new. It proposes to secure fair and complete representation to every important political interest in the country; to strike an effectual blow at corruption in popular elections; to secure more of harmony and contentment than now exist among the people, and to improve the composition of the popular branch of Congress by facilitating the introduction and continuance of men of ability and merit in that body. That these results may to a great extent be secured by it is, by the friends of the measure, most positively affirmed. If the claim made by them on its behalf be substantially true,

* *Congressional Globe*, 3d Sess. 40th Cong., Appendix, p. 268. Sen. Com. Report, same sess., No. 271.

or true to any considerable extent, and the plan be capable of convenient application, it will merit strong commendation and prompt adoption.

THE PLAN.

Representatives being assigned to a State under the constitutional rule of distribution, each elector in the State shall possess as many votes as there are representatives to be chosen. He shall possess his due and equal share of electoral power as a member of the political body or State. Thus far we deal with familiar ideas which have heretofore obtained. It is next proposed that the elector shall exercise his right of suffrage according to his own judgment and discretion, and without compulsion of law. He shall bestow or distribute his votes upon or among candidates with entire freedom, and shall be relieved from that legal constraint to which he has been heretofore subjected. He may select his candidate or candidates anywhere within the limit of his State from among all its qualified citizens, and he may exert his political power upon the general representation of his State instead of the representation of a particular district within it. Here is unquestionably a large and valuable extension of privilege to the citizen, a withdrawal from him of inconvenient and odious restraint, and a more complete application of that principle of self-government upon which our political institutions are founded. And what is material for consideration is, that while all the advantages of a plan of election by general ticket are secured, all its inconveniences and evils are avoided.

FORMER PLANS—THEIR IMPERFECTIONS.

Formerly when elections of representatives in Congress were had by general ticket, a great inconvenience resulted which became at last offensive and intolerable. For a political majority in a State, organized as a party, and casting its votes under a majority or plurality rule, secured in ordinary cases the entire representation from the State and the minority were wholly excluded from representation. ·To avoid this inconvenience and evil which had become general throughout the country, Congress interposed, and by statute required the States to select their representatives by single districts, that is to divide their territory into districts, each of which should elect one member. This contrivance, dictated by Congressional power, ameliorated our electoral system, mitigated the evil of which general complaint had been made, and was an unquestionable advance in the art of government amongst us. But retaining the majority or plurality rule for elections and restricting the power and free action of the elector, it was imperfect in its design and has been unsatisfactory in practice. It has not secured fair representation of political interests, and it has continued in existence in a somewhat mitigated form the evils of the plan of election by general ticket which it superseded. Still, one body of organized electors in a district vote down another; electoral corruption is not effectually checked, and the general result is unfair representation of political interests in the popular house of Congress. Besides, the single district plan has called into existence inconveniences peculiar to itself and which did not attach to the former plan.

It excludes from Congress men of ability and merit whose election was possible before, and thus exerts a baneful influence upon the constitution of the House. Two causes operate to this end. In the first place no man who adheres to a minority party in any particular district can be returned, and next, great rapidity of change is produced by fluctuation of party power in the districts.

Again, the single district system gives rise to gerrymandering in the States in the formation of districts. Single districts will almost always be unfairly made. They will be formed in the interest of party and to secure an unjust measure of power to their authors, and it may be expected that each successive district apportionment will be more unjust than its predecessor. Parties will retaliate upon each other whenever possible. The disfranchisement suffered through one decade by a political party may be repeated upon it in the next with increased severity, but if it shall happen to have power in the legislature when the new apportionment for the State is to be made, it will take signal vengeance for its wrongs and in its turn indulge in the luxury of persecution.

MODES OF VOTING DESCRIBED.

The manner in which the right of suffrage shall be exercised, always a question of high importance, is one of difficulty also. It has been regulated in various ways in our States and in foreign countries, but must be considered in many respects as still open to debate. We have pretty generally adopted the vote by secret ballot for popular elections, but whether votes be given by secret or open ballot, or by voice, a question will remain as to the manner in which they shall be bestowed upon or distributed among candidates. Where but one representative or other official is to be chosen by a constituency, it is readily understood that a single vote is to be given by each elector to the candidate of his choice, and such is the uniform regulation. But where more than one person is to be chosen by a constituency, the manner of bestowing votes upon candidates is a question of more difficulty, and various regulations have been made or proposed concerning it. Several of these it is necessary to mention and describe before proceeding to the main matters to be examined in this report.

The vote by general ticket.—By the general ticket plan of distributive voting the elector has assigned to him a number of votes equal to the whole number of persons to be chosen, and is authorized to bestow them singly upon a like number of candidates. Upon this plan presidential electors are chosen in all the States except Florida.

The vote by single districts.—By the single district plan the general constituency is divided into parts by territorial lines and each part constituted a sub-constituency to vote separately and choose one person. The voter casts a single vote for his candidate and has no participation in the action of the general constituency beyond the giving of his district vote. Upon this plan, prescribed by statute, representatives in Congress are now chosen.

The limited vote.—The limited vote obtains

where the voter is forbidden to vote for the whole
number of persons to be chosen by the constituency,
but is authorized to give single votes to each of a
less number or a single vote to one.

The cumulative vote.—The cumulative vote is the
concentration of two or more votes upon one candidate or upon each of a greater number. It may obtain whenever the voter has assigned to him more
votes than one and is permitted to cast them otherwise than singly among candidates.

The unrestricted or free vote.—The unrestricted
or free vote obtains where the voter has assigned to
him a number of votes equal to the whole number
of persons to be chosen by the constituency, and is
permitted to cast them according to his own discretion and choice without legal restraint.   In such
case he may bestow them all upon one candidate,
or distribute them singly among candidates, or
cumulate them upon more candidates than one, or
cast a part of them singly and a part of them
upon the principle of cumulation, precisely as his
judgment may direct him and the possibilities of
the case may permit.

SUPERIORITY OF THE FREE VOTE.

The unrestricted or free vote is more comprehensive and flexible than the others, and it includes many of their features and may be used to
accomplish their objects.   It involves or includes
the vote by general ticket without the restriction
that but one vote shall in any case be given to a
candidate.   It may be used to accomplish the purposes of the limited vote and of single district
voting in a just, effectual, and popular manner, and

it includes completely the cumulative vote, with which it is in character closely allied. In brief, it combines the advantages of other plans without their imperfections, while it is not open to any strong objection peculiar to itself. The ingredient, however, of greatest value and importance contained in it, and the one particularly fitted to regenerate and give credit to elections is the principle of the concentration of votes. In fact for practical purposes in dissertation or argument upon the question of electoral reform, the terms "cumulative vote" and "free vote" may be interchangeably used, though the latter is most appropriate and accurate to indicate a plan which commonly involves distribution as well as concentration of votes, and sometimes even the giving of single votes to particular candidates.

HOW FAR IT CAN BE APPLIED.

The bill now reported by the committee applies the unrestricted or free vote to the selection of representatives in Congress from the several States, and the proposed amendment to the Constitution of the United States reported by the committee on the 29th of January will, if adopted, empower Congress to apply that vote (or some other proper reform) to the selection of electors of President and Vice-President of the United States.

By the fourth section of the first article of the Constitution power is clearly conferred upon Congress to pass a bill regulating the manner of holding elections for the choice of representatives. The times, places, and manner of holding such elections are to be prescribed in each State by the legislature thereof, but the Congress may at any time make or alter such regulations. This power was exercised by the passage of the act of Congress which provides that representatives shall be chosen in the several States by single districts instead of by general ticket, which had been the general practice before, and it is equally competent for Congress to prescribe a still different manner for choosing them, subject only to such other provisions of the Constitution as may relate to the same subject. The free or cumulative vote or other like reform may, therefore, be introduced simply by the enactment of a statute. No constitutional amendment will be necessary for the purpose. But as to the choice of presidential electors the case is different, as before stated. The first section of the second article of the Constitution provides that each State shall appoint electors "in such manner as the legislature thereof may direct." Congress may determine the time of choosing the electors and fix a uniform day on which they shall give their votes, but cannot prescribe the manner in which they shall be chosen. To accomplish any reform in the manner of choosing them through the instrumentality of an act of Congress, an amendment to the Constitution will be necessary. That such amendment is desirable, and that it is necessary also to the introduction of any reform whatever in the manner of choosing electors, will be hereafter shown.

ARGUMENTS FOR ITS ADOPTION.

Recurring now to the question of representative reform raised by the bill reported by the committee,

we will proceed to state those grounds of argument
which recommend the adoption of the unrestricted
or free vote.

ITS SIMPLICITY AND CONVENIENCE OF APPLICATION.

The first consideration to be taken into account is
the simplicity and convenience of this plan of reform.
It is easily understood, convenient of application,
and will readily adapt itself to all new or changed
conditions of political society. It is self-adjusting,
and requires no law whatever to enforce it or afford
it a sanction beyond the act which shall simply call
it into existence. The number of representatives to
which a State shall be entitled being first ascertained
under the rule of distribution contained in the Constitution, the law will simply declare that each voter
of the State shall have as many votes as there are
representatives to be chosen from his State, and at
that point will stop, leaving the voter perfectly free
to cast his votes according to his own judgment and
discretion.

The voter may then exercise his right according
to any of the plans relating to the distribution or
concentration of votes which have heretofore been
the subject of discussion, including those which
have and those which have not been prescribed by
legal enactment. But inasmuch as our political
communities will always be divided into political
parties, (or so long as our free institutions remain
to us,) it must happen that the voter will exercise
his right with direct reference to his party associations—to the interests of the party to which he shall
belong. He will vote (as he votes now) as a party

man, and for candidates who have been selected
by some form of nomination—by some agreement
or concert of action among men of common views
and common interests. The inevitable result will
be that political parties and the voters who compose
them will obtain fair and complete representation
by distributing or concentrating their votes in such
manner as to secure it, and nothing can be more
certain than that they will be better judges of
their own interests than the lawmaker possibly
can be. For they will act with a full knowledge
of all the facts which pertain to an election—of the
relative strength of parties at the time—the probable amount of the aggregate vote to be polled, and
generally of the effect of their voting in any particular manner. Of all these matters the lawmaker
must be profoundly ignorant, or must conjecture or
assume them at random. He cannot foreknow the
future, nor adapt his arrangements to the ever-
changing conditions of political society.

It is for this reason that imperfection will always
attach to the limited vote as a general plan to be
applied to popular elections. The lawmaker cannot
know that his arbitrary limitation will operate justly
and secure his object at some future time. If he
could know the exact relative strength of parties
in future years, he might apply his limitation to a
constituency with confidence. Adjusting it to the
facts, he could obtain a proper result. As this
cannot be, the limited vote can be but partially
applied to elections and must in most cases be un-
satisfactory. It has rarely been applied to constituencies selecting more than three representatives,

and can never be accepted as a plan for extensive use and application.

The unrestricted or free vote, however, is not open to these observations. It will adjust itself to all cases, and it will have the most important and effectual sanction; for it will be put under the guardianship of party interest, always active and energetic, which will give it direction and complete effect to the full and just representation of the people.

ITS CONFORMITY TO REPUBLICAN PRINCIPLES.

The unrestricted or free vote is in strict conformity with democratic principles, and realizes more perfectly our ideas of popular government. For by it the whole mass of electors are brought into direct relations with government, and particularly with that department or branch of government (the principal one in power, if not in dignity) which makes the laws. All will participate really in choosing representatives, and all will be represented in fact. Now, the beaten body of electors choose nothing, unless it be mortification, and are not represented at all. For the theory that they are represented by the successful candidates against whom they have voted—that those candidates when installed in office represent them—is plainly false. An elected official represents the opinions and the will of those who choose him, and not of those who oppose his selection. As to the latter he is an antagonist and not a representative; for his opinions are opposed to theirs, and their will he will not execute. And this must always be the case where political parties act upon elections and a majority or plurality rule assigns to one party the whole representation of the constituency. Our present system of representation is therefore essentially partial and imperfect, and our great object in reforming it must be to make it full and complete. If we cannot secure this object perfectly, it will be our duty, as it should be our pleasure, to approach it as nearly as possible.

Now, inasmuch as by extending to the elector that freedom of choice and of selection which the law has heretofore forbidden, we can strike from our system of representative elections almost entirely the element of disfranchisement and bring the whole electoral body into direct and useful relations with the representative body, we may congratulate ourselves that our reform, while it will be rich and fruitful of results in the purification of elections, in imparting energy and wisdom to government and contentment to the people, will also be strictly republican in character and democratic in principle, and will apply more perfectly than ever before those ideas of self-government which inspired our ancestors when they established our political institutions.

THE FOUR GREAT REASONS FOR IT.

But we proceed to state the main reasons for the unrestricted vote, without dwelling upon introductory points or upon those secondary reasons which, while they may commend this plan of reform to us, will not alone command its adoption. Those great reasons (which speak with imperative voice to statesmen and to free constituencies everywhere) are four in number, and they will be mentioned in their proper order.

1. *It is just.*

The unrestricted or free vote should be permitted because it is just. That this quality pertains to it in a high degree and constitutes one of its main characteristics is beyond all question. It gives an equal voice to every elector of a State, secures the elector from the peril of utter disfranchisement, and affords to him also that freedom of choice which is indispensable to his complete and useful exercise of his right. A vote at any point or place in the State is precisely as valuable and as important as at any other point or place; location of the voter is immaterial as affecting his right or his consequence in the electoral body, and no preference in privilege or power is given or advantage allowed to one elector over another. Besides, (and this is the great consideration,) any material disfranchisement of electors is rendered almost impossible; for every political interest, of any considerable magnitude, in a State, will have the complete opportunity afforded it of concentrating its vote upon a proper number of candidates and those candidates will be chosen, not merely because they have more votes than other candidates, (as under our present system,) but because they are the recipients of an adequate support. One mass of voters will not vote down, defeat, or disfranchise another. One candidate will not beat another in the ordinary sense of that expression. The full comprehension of this point may require reflection by those to whom it is new, but no reflection is necessary to perceive the justice of a plan

which will substantially strike disfranchisement from
our electoral system.   Lastly, it is but just that the
elector should have a greater freedom of choice than
is now allowed him, that his judgment should have
freer action, that he should enjoy all possible facilities for performing his duty to his country in exercising his right of suffrage.   At present he is hedged
about and constrained by legal regulations which,
while wholly unnecessary to the public order and
peace, cripple and impede him in the performance
of his duty.   He is held responsible for the character and action of the government, for in theory he
controls it by his vote, and yet he does not possess
all those facilities and rights the possession of which
will justify that responsibility and enable him to
discharge all its obligations.

In the matter of selecting representatives from
his State to Congress—perhaps the most important
of all electoral operations known in our country—
he is allowed to participate in the selection of but
one out of the whole number.   The State may be
entitled by 6 to 12 or to 20 representatives, but the
judgment of the elector can be exercised upon the
choice of one only.   As to all the rest, he is excluded from taking part in their selection.   Besides,
his choice of a single representative must be exercised within and for a particular district, arbitrarily
established by law, with such boundaries, population, interests, and political complexion as may happen to be convenient or agreeable to a majority in
the legislature of the State.   And practically he
must select his candidate from among the men of the
district and is excluded from all choice beyond it.

And when to all this we add that the elections held in single districts are necessarily subjected to a majority or plurality rule, which very commonly renders a large part of the votes cast unavailing for the purpose for which they are given, we have the case fully presented as one of inconvenience and hardship upon the elector. The law has been busy where it should have been inactive, and the voter is bound by inconvenient and injurious restrictions, which he can neither evade nor defy. It is time that the hand of power be lifted from the citizen and he be permitted to perform his electoral duties with all possible freedom.

The justice of the proposed reform is therefore evident. It extends popular power upon a principle of equality, limits disfranchisement, and provides the voter with necessary facilities for the exercise of his right.

With good reason therefore did the London *Times* in speaking of clause 9 of the reform bill of 1867, (triumphantly carried in both houses of Parliament upon full debate, and similar in principle to the proposition before us,) declare—" that the idea of modifying our electoral machinery so as to secure in three-membered constituencies the proportionate representation of both the great divisions of party, *has made its way by its inherent justice.*"

2. *It will check corruption.*

The unrestricted or free vote will greatly check corruption at elections. It will take away the motive to corrupt, and thus strike an effectual blow at the source of a great evil.

Now, money and patronage are usually expended upon elections to secure a majority or plurality vote to one or more candidates over one or more other candidates, and are directed or applied to the comparatively small number of electors in the constituency who hold the balance of power between parties. Those persons being bought or seduced, victory is secured. The importation of voters into a State or district, or their fraudulent creation within it, is with a like object. And such corrupt influence or practice when resorted to by one party, provokes like conduct in an opposing one, until both become tainted with guilt and unfitted for vindicating the purity of elections. This evil grows in magnitude yearly, and it will continue to increase until those motives of interest which produce it shall be weakened or destroyed.

A new right to the elector, whether in the form of the free or cumulative vote, or of personal representation, or a new protection to him in the form of the limited vote, will check corruption; but of these remedies the first is most practicable and effectual. The limited vote (as will be hereafter shown) cannot have extensive application, and it is but a rude contrivance. Personal representation is a scheme of great theoretical merit; it has been tried partially in Denmark, and it has received elaborate vindication from authors of distinction in England, in Switzerland, and in France. But it may be put aside from the present discussion, because it is comparatively intricate in plan and cumbrous in detail, because it assails party organization, and because some of its most important effects cannot be distinctly foreseen. It is so radical in character, so revolutionary in its probable effects, that prudence will dictate that it should be very deliberately considered, and be subjected to local experiment and trial before it shall be proposed for adoption upon a grand scale by the government of the United States.

But why will the cumulative or unrestricted vote check corruption? It will have this certain effect, it will operate efficiently to this end, because it will render any ordinary effort of corruption useless and unavailing. *The corruption of voters will not change the result of an election: It will elect no candidate and defeat no candidate* in contested States or districts, unless indeed it be carried on and carried out upon a gigantic scale, beyond any ordinary example of the past or probable occurrence of the future.

An average or common ratio of votes for a representation in Congress, taking the whole country together, is now 25,000, and it will be much greater in future times. Assume then that 600,000 votes are to be cast in Pennsylvania at an election, of which each political party has one-half, and that 24 representatives are to be chosen. This is a supposition very nearly conformed to actual numbers in that State. Now it is evident that either political party, by resorting to the cumulative vote, can elect 12 representatives, and thus secure to itself exact and just representation, and no art or effort of the opposite party can prevent it. But suppose, further, that corruption shall assail the election, and that some thousands of votes shall be changed thereby, or that in the interest of one of the parties so many

6

as 10,000 or 20,000 voters shall be imported into
the State, or be fraudulently created or personated
within it, in either case there will be no effect produced; the result will be unchanged; in short, in
the case supposed, a fraudulent *increase* of its vote
(and of the total vote) by a party, to the extent of
20,000, will not give to it any advantage, nor will
its corrupt acquisition of 5000 or 10,000 votes from
the opposite party. It follows that corruption will
in no ordinary case be resorted to; it will be effectually discouraged and prevented. And even in the
extreme case of the corruption of a large number
of voters in a State, the resulting evil will be reduced to its minimum.

What has been said concerning the choice of representatives will apply with equal, if not greater,
force to the choice of presidential electors. If the
representative presidential electors were chosen in
the several States (save those which have but one)
upon the plan of the cumulative vote, there would
be as to them due representation of the people in the
electoral colleges, and the elections for choosing them
would receive a much needed purification. Millions
now expended upon those elections would be kept
out of the hands of political agents and be applied
to better and nobler uses.

That freedom of the vote will have the effect
claimed for it will more clearly appear from considering the manner in which the present plan of
elections operates to invite and produce corruption.
By considering the evil which exists we will be
better able to judge the merits of the remedy proposed. Popular elections in the States for federal

or national purposes are either by a general ticket for the whole State, or by a single ticket in district divisions. As before stated, the former obtains in the choice of presidential electors; the latter, in the choice of representatives to Congress. But to both is applied the plurality rule and a struggle invited between candidates and parties for preponderance of vote.

Whichever can be made to outnumber an opposition upon the return will win the whole result and will wield the entire power of the constituency in an electoral college or in Congress. Antagonism is thus made an essential element of the proceeding, and the result presents to us the spectacle of victor and vanquished, the former crowned with honor and exultant in his strength, the latter humiliated and powerless. And it is important to observe that the successful party does not obtain merely a power proportioned to its vote, does not merely obtain full representation for itself, but obtains the whole power of the constituency. The whole vote cast against it or withheld from it is virtually counted to it and added to its true vote.

An issue thus made up for popular elections must be one portentous of evil; and, so far as it is unnecessary to secure popular representation, must be denounced as plainly unjust as well as injurious.

3. *It will be a guarantee of peace.*

The free vote will be a guarantee of peace to our country, because it will exclude many causes of discord and complaint, and will always secure to the friends of peace and union a just measure of politi-

cal power. The absence of this vote in the States
of the south when rebellion was plotted, and when
open steps were taken to break the Union, was
unfortunate, for it would have held the Union men
of those States together and have given them voice
in the electoral colleges and in Congress. But they
were fearfully overborne by the plurality rule of
elections and were swept forward by the course of
events into impotency or open hostility to our cause.
By that rule they were largely deprived of representation in Congress. By that rule they were shut
out of the electoral colleges. Dispersed, unorgan-
ized, unrepresented, without due voice and power,
they could interpose no effectual resistance to seces-
sion and to civil war. Their leaders were struck
down at unjust elections and could not speak for
them or act for them in their own States or at the
capital of the nation. By facts well known to us we
are assured that the leaders of revolt, with much
difficulty, carried their States with them. Even in
Georgia, the empire State of the south, the scale
was almost balanced for a time between patriotism
and dishonor; and in most of those States it
required all the machinery and influence of a
vicious electoral system to organize the war against
us and hold those communities compactly as our
foes.

In those same States the free vote will now allay
antagonism of race, and will substitute therefor the
rivalry of parties formed with reference to the policy
of the general government. The tendency of party
is to form upon national issues, and not upon State
ones, and this tendency will operate more strongly

if causes of offence between races shall be removed or lessened. And what can accomplish this more perfectly than the free vote? For under it one race cannot vote down and disfranchise the other; each can obtain its due share of power without injustice to the other, and there will be no strong and constant motive (as now) to struggle for the mastery. This fact (the importance of which cannot be overestimated) will allay animosity and prevent conflict. And because the free vote will have this certain effect it will nationalize parties in the south and will be to the whole country an invaluable guarantee of order and peace.

In extending suffrage largely, in extending it to include many hundreds of thousands of voters of another race than our own, it will become us to look to our electoral machinery and to amend it in those parts which have been found defective, or which do not seem well adapted to the new strain to be put upon it. Unquestionably there is a large mass of honest opinion in the country opposed to colored suffrage, and many of those who support it in Congress and out-of Congress, put their support of it upon the ground of necessity—upon the ground that in order to secure the fruits of emancipation it is necessary that the emancipated be armed with the power of self-defence. A majority of this committee hold that colored suffrage is allowable and expedient, that the objections to it are to a great extent misconceived, and that the fears felt and expressed by many as to its results will not be realized. But all must agree that this great experiment of extended suffrage, being once determined upon, should have a fair trial; that all the conditions proper to its success should, as far as possible, be established by the government. And those who sincerely believe that the experiment will have bad results must approve a plan of voting which will certainly mitigate its possible evils. But the salutary effects of the free vote as a guarantee of peace, though well illustrated by the southern States, will not be confined to them. Everywhere it will decrease the violence of party contests and create more amicable relations than now exist among our people.

4. *It will improve the character and ability of the House.*

The unrestricted or free vote will secure men of ability and experience in the House of Representatives. It is believed that changes are now too frequent in that House, and that the public interests suffer detriment from this cause. The committee give their unqualified approval to that provision of the Constitution which assigns short terms of service to members of the House. But frequency of election does not involve rapidity of change. Popular power may be retained over the House, and yet the great part of its members be continued by reelection for a considerable period of time; in other words, frequent elections and permanent membership are not incompatible.

But, in point of fact, the members of the House are frequently changed so that members of less than four years' service always constitute a large majority, and it is a rare case that a member continues beyond a third term. Under such a system or practice of rapid change, the average character of the House for ability cannot be high. Two and four year men can know but little of the business of government, can be but imperfectly qualified to curb abuses in the executive department, and to expose or comprehend the true character of most questions of domestic and foreign policy.

There are several reasons which account for frequent change in the membership of the House, of which the single-district system is chief. The fluctuations of party power is next in importance, but is intimately connected with the former. The single-district system has carried the idea of local representation to excess, and has produced a class of inconveniences peculiar to itself. The idea of assigning a representative by law to a special district within a State is naturally supplemented by the idea of rotation in the representative privilege among the localities within the district. Hence, very commonly party nominations are made in turn to the several counties, parishes, or other municipal divisions of the district, which necessitates the frequent selection of new men for representative nomination. The claim of locality becomes more importunate, and it is often more regarded than the claims or fitness of candidates in making party nominations, and this although there is no diversity of interest among the people in the different parts of the district. The other cause which we have mentioned co-operates with this, though subordinate to it in effect. Changes of party power in districts, where one party does not largely predominate over another, are at all times likely to occur, and to defeat

the member of the House from the district, although
his own party may desire to continue him in the
public service.   These causes of change would have
but slight operation if delegations from States were
elected by general ticket, and would have still less
if they were selected upon the plan of the cumulative or free vote; and the general ticket system
being quite inadmissible, upon the reasons which
apply to it, we are driven to the cumulative or free
vote as the practical and effectual measure of reform.
It will continue members of merit for long periods
of time in the House, because it will relieve them
and those who support them from the causes of
change above mentioned.   They can be re-elected
with certainty so long as the party whose representatives they are desire their continuance in service,
and it may be reasonably expected that some men
of distinction and intellectual power will always be
found in the House whose period of service counts
by 20 or 30 years.   They will be the great representatives of party, and will give lustre and power
and usefulness to the House, while they will be the
objects of profound attachment and of honest pride
in the States they represent.   Congress will become,
much more than at present, a theatre of statesmanship and a fit representative of a great people, whose
extended territory, diverse populations, and varied
interests demand great ability and wisdom in the
enactment of the laws.   Our present system, admirably calculated to repress merit and lift mediocrity,
will be supplanted by one which will produce precisely the opposite result.

At present a member of the House holding his

seat insecurely cannot devote himself to public business with that zeal and confidence which his position demands. He is involved all the time in a contest for official existence, and his energies are thereby absorbed and wasted. If he has a just ambition to serve the people he must repress rivals at home, must overcome a rule of rotation in his district, and fortify himself against fluctuations of party power. It will be expected of him that he shall distribute the patronage of the government to men who will be efficient in his support for re-election; and thus appointments to office and government contracts are to be his peculiar study, and their distribution a leading object of his labor. And he must be liberal in his expenditure of money upon elections to retain his popularity and place; and the more of political contribution from abroad he can obtain to influence elections in his district the more admired and the more secure he will be.

In brief, his time and his efforts, instead of being expended for the public, must be expended on personal objects if he desires to remain for any considerable time a representative of the people. Undoubtedly many of the best men of the country must be deterred from entering upon a congressional career, continuance in which requires such sacrifices to an evil system, so much of unpleasant effort, attended with uncertainty and probable mortification.

But freedom to the elector has one special advantage, hitherto unnoticed, over single-district voting. Under the district system a large part of the men of a State are absolutely barred from election to Congress. They cannot be chosen in districts where their party has not a preponderance of vote. The difference in strength between parties may be slight, but it will virtually constitute a rule of exclusion, which will always be rigidly enforced. But the cumulative or free vote opens the doors of the people's house to any citizen of a State whenever those who agree with him in opinion in his State will give him a competent support. They can elect him to Congress regardless of State or district majorities. This is an advantage of immense value if republican principles be true, and republican institutions be worthy of being carried to their utmost limit of perfection as fit and proper for the use and enjoyment of mankind.

EXAMPLES OF REFORM.

But let us turn from general argument upon electoral reform to particular cases which will illustrate its application. And first of cases in our own country:

In Pennsylvania and in other States inspectors of elections are chosen upon the plan of the limited vote. Each voter is authorized to vote for but one inspector, and yet two are to be chosen. Thus, whenever the minority party in an election district can poll one-third of the whole vote they can secure one of the inspectors, and obtain representation in the election board of the district. This arrangement protects elections from fraud and injustice, and is everywhere within the States which have adopted it strongly sustained by public opinion. In fact, even in districts where the majority has more than a two-thirds vote the attempt is rarely made by them to choose the second inspector.

In Pennsylvania also jury commissioners in the several counties are chosen upon the same plan. But one is voted for by each elector, and yet two are chosen.

For selecting delegates at large to the New York constitutional convention in 1867 a similar plan was adopted. Upon the recommendation of Governor Fenton the legislature provided that thirty-two delegates at large should be chosen by the people—in addition to the delegates from the representative districts—and that in choosing them each voter should vote for but sixteen. The consequence was that each political party obtained sixteen of the delegates at large, many of whom could not have been chosen upon a district plan, or upon a general ticket devised in the ordinary way.

These instances in our own country illustrate the principle of reform now in question, and many others might be cited. They show distinctly that successful attempts have been made by our people to break away from an unjust system of voting, and to secure to themselves those advantages which full representation is so well calculated to produce.

ENGLISH REFORM.

But English authority and example may be called in to aid the argument in a still more effectual manner. The papers appended to this report from authors and statesmen of high standing who have in recent years examined this subject of popular representation with great fullness and power, may be consulted with profit by any one desirous of understanding the general grounds of argument in favor

of reform. And the debates and proceedings of
Parliament in 1867 upon the reform bill may also
be examined in connection with the returns of parliamentary elections in 1868 for further and most
valuable information.

On the 4th of July, 1867, Mr. Lowe (the present
chancellor of the exchequer in the Gladstone administration) moved the following amendment to
the reform bill in the House of Commons:

POWER TO DISTRIBUTE VOTES.

At any contested election for a county or borough represented by more than two members, and having more than one
seat vacant, every voter shall be entitled to a number of votes
equal to the number of vacant seats, and may give all such
votes to one candidate, or may distribute them among the candidates as he thinks fit.

This amendment (which was for the free vote including the principle of cumulation and applicable
generally to elections where more than one member
was to be chosen) was debated on the day when
offered and on the day following, and received the
very handsome support of 173 votes—a large vote
for a new proposition upon its first trial of strength.
Mr. Lowe's amendment was identical in principle
and almost identical in terms with the bill now
reported by this committee. The English proposition applied to the election of members of Parliament, the American applies to the election of members of Congress, but in both a free vote, including
the right of cumulation, is the essential idea, and the
object in view more complete and just representation
of the people.

On the 30th July, 1867, the reform bill being

under consideration in the House of Lords, Lord Cairns moved to insert the following new clause, to come in after clause 8 of the bill:

At a contested election for a county or borough represented by three members no person shall vote for more than two candidates.

This amendment, after an elaborate debate, was adopted by a strong vote: contents, 142, not contents, 51; and an additional amendment was then also adopted without a division that "at a contested election for the city of London" (which is entitled to four members) "no person shall vote for more than three candidates."

The success of those amendments (which were concurred in by the House of Commons on the 8th of August) constituted an important event in the history of representative institutions, for they recognized and gave application to a principle of justice which will endure the test of trial and of time, a principle which will hereafter receive indefinite extension, and wherever extended will purify elections, insure contentment to constituencies, and elevate the character and improve the action of free government.

Mr. Gladstone, speaking in the House of Commons, and confining his attention to his own country, declared that the proposition or principle contained in those amendments, if adopted at all, must be adopted with the certainty that "it must unfold and expand itself over the whole country and completely reconstruct the system of distribution of seats." And generally those who supported it in both houses of Parliament foretold and rejoiced in the prospect of its future expansion.

Those amendments constitute the ninth and tenth clauses of the reform act of 15th of August, 1867, and their effect is illustrated by the parliamentary elections of 1868.   We give the returns for certain districts:

PARLIAMENTARY ELECTIONS, 1868.

Herefordshire, three members. Average tory vote, 3360; average liberal vote, 2074. Two tories and one liberal elected.

Cambridgeshire, three members. Average tory vote, 3924; average liberal vote, 3310. Two tories and one liberal elected.

The liberals also obtained the third member in each of the tory counties of Oxford, Bucks and Dorset.

Liverpool borough, three members. Average tory vote, 16,404, average liberal vote, 15,198. Tory majority, 1206.

In Liverpool the second seat, previously held by the tories, was attacked by the liberals; the result was a failure, as shown by the above vote. But the third member was most justly secured to the liberals under the certain operation of the limited vote, provided by clause 9 of the reform act.

Under the operation of the same clause the tories obtained the third member for Leeds, and they carried members also in Manchester and London.

Blackwood's Magazine, a tory organ, (it has called itself "the oldest of the tories,") although it admits

that its party has suffered loss to the extent of at
least four seats by the minority clause, says:

That to the principle of that clause, fairly and consistently
worked out, it has no objection whatever.—*Blackwood's Magazine, January,* 1869.

This expression of opinion by a leading organ of
the party which suffered somewhat under the minority clause, is a valuable testimony in favor of
the principle of electoral reform which that clause
was intended to promote.

DIFFICULTIES OF ENGLISH REFORM.

Mr. Disraeli in debate on the 5th of July, 1867,
pointed out one great practical obstacle to the adoption of the cumulative vote in England which does
not exist in this country. It happens that the
Scotch and Welsh districts are nearly all one-member districts with liberal majorities. The proposed
reform is, therefore, inapplicable to those parts of
the kingdom as at present organized for election
purposes, and if it were applied to England alone,
upon an extensive scale, it might give undue influence and power in the House of Commons to Scotch
and Welsh members. They would control the
house upon all party questions. Full representation
in England would tend to equalize the strength of
parties in the house, and then the Scotch vote cast
wholly on one side would always turn the scale.

But putting this consideration aside, and taking
the English districts as they stand, we find that
most of them are not adapted or well adapted to
the cumulative vote. A great part of them are
boroughs, electing one member each. In Schedule

A of the reform act are no less than 38 such boroughs, added to those which existed before, and in Schedule B, nine additional. Other boroughs choose two members each, as do divisions of counties, 35 of which are fixed in the reform act, Schedule D. The triangular districts, those which elect three members each, are not numerous, and we are not aware that any district elects a greater number, save London, which elects four. The limited vote is now, however, applied to London and to all the triangular districts, whether boroughs or counties, and it is to be expected that by the reorganization and consolidation of districts hereafter, reform will be greatly extended.

REFORM IN THE UNITED STATES.

But the difficulties and obstacles which exist in Great Britain do not exist with us. Our States are well suited to the application of the free vote. There are now only six of the whole number to which it will not apply as a plan for representative elections, to wit, Delaware, Florida, Kansas, Nebraska, Nevada, and Oregon. They constitute the one-member States, and would be unaffected by the new plan. But from this class Kansas will pass at the next apportionment, leaving but five States out of 37 to compose this class; and as they would select but five representatives out of about 250 who will constitute the House, their influence upon general results would be unimportant if not inappreciable. It is to be remarked, also, that these States, in common with the other States, might come under the operation of the free vote if that vote should be applied to presidential elections, because each of them will be entitled to choose three electors.

THE TWO-MEMBER STATES.

The two-member States are Rhode Island and Minnesota, and both will probably change their position at the next apportionment of representatives. . Rhode Island will fall off to one member and Minnesota rise to three. Other States, however, two or three in number, may take their place, and hence it will be worth while to consider the position of two-member States with reference to the plan of the free vote. It has been sometimes said, without due reflection, that the cumulative vote is not suited to elections where two persons are to be chosen by a constituency, because if it have practical effect it will give equal representation to the majority and minority. But the frequent application of the limited vote to dual elections—as in the cases of inspectors of elections and jury commissioners in Pennsylvania—may cause us to pause and examine this objection with some care before we accept it as a sound one. Carefully examined, it may turn out to be more specious than solid, and we may further discover that in the case of the representation of our States in the Federal Government there is an important fact which bears upon this objection and deprives it of any appearance even of strength or force. In the first place let us test the objection and illustrate its futility by a supposed case. Take a constituency of 32,000 electors, 20,000 of whom are tories and 12,000 liberals, entitled to elect two members to Parliament. As there

7

are 32,000 voters and two members to be chosen, the full ratio or number of voters for a member is 16,000. Assign now one member to the tories and the just demand of 16,000 tory voters is complied with and exhausted. They can have no further claim to representation. What have we left? Why, on the one hand 4000 tory voters, and on the other 12,000 liberals, and the simple question for us to determine is whether the 4000 or the 12,000 shall have the second member. The cumulative or the free vote will give that second member to the 12,000 liberals; unjust voting will give him to the 4000 tories.

But let us cite cases of actual parliamentary elections in 1868, for two-member districts, in further illustration: Northeast Lancashire, two members, average tory vote, 3615; average liberal vote, 3458.

Two tories elected upon a majority of 157. The ratio for a member was 3536, so that 79 tory voters obtained the second member, while 3458 liberals were disfranchised.

Take next two districts in Kent. Middle Kent, two members; average tory vote, 3245; average liberal vote, 2873. West Kent, two members; average tory vote, 3389; average liberal vote, 3279.

Two tories were chosen from each district. In Middle Kent 186 tory votes carried the second member, and in West Kent 55; while in the two districts 6152 liberals were entirely disfranchised.

East Derbyshire, two members; average liberal vote, 2069; average tory vote, 1974. Yorkshire, West Riding, (South,) two members; average liberal vote, 8032; average tory vote, 7935.

In these districts four liberals were elected; in one the second member was carried by 48, and in the other by 49 votes; while 9909 tories were wholly disfranchised.

Where, then, a minority in a two-member constituency exceeds one-third the whole number of voters therein, it does not seem unreasonable to assign to them the second member, and thus, in fact, an equality of representation with the majority. It is a case where complete or exact justice is impossible; there must be disfranchisement to some extent; but that disfranchisement should be reduced to its minimum, and made to press as lightly as may be upon the constituency. What, then, can be said as to two-member constituencies is this— that any rule of voting for them must (in the very nature of the case) be imperfect in result, but that the cumulative vote, or an equivalent plan applied even to them, will be one of reform and improvement.

But an important consideration remains to be mentioned. Our States are represented in *both* houses of Congress, and not merely in one; a fact which changes entirely the character of this question in the two-member States. In Great Britain there is no representation of the people, or even of districts, in the upper house of Parliament. Compensation to a constituency for loss of political power in the House of Commons cannot be obtained by them in the House of Lords. With us the case is widely different. The political majority in a State will ordinarily have both the senators from the State; in other words, the whole representation of the State in the Senate.   If, then, in two-member States they have but one-half the representation of the State in the House, (as against a minority of one-third or upwards,) the aggregate of their representation in Congress will still be many times over what it should be upon any principle of justice or of numbers.

THE THREE-MEMBER STATES.

It is agreed pretty generally that the cumulative or free vote is admirably suited to three-member constituencies.   The States which now elect three members each are Arkansas, California, New Hampshire, Vermont, and West Virginia.   In such States the majority will always have two members, and the minority, if it exceed one-fourth the whole constituency and one-third of the majority vote, can obtain the third.   Upon constituencies or districts of this class—called indiscriminately "three-handed," "three-cornered," or triangular—much of the debate in Great Britain as to reform in popular voting has been expended.   The question as to them in particular is fully expounded in the papers (drawn from British sources) which are appended to this report.

THE GREAT STATES.

Having exhausted the list of States which elect less than four members, we find that 24 remain. Of these, Connecticut, South Carolina, and Texas each elect four members, and the remainder various numbers, up to New York, which chooses 31.   They may be taken together in this examination as an additional, though by far the most important class of States.   They choose 218 out of the 243 ·members

of the House. In this class all the great States are
before us, and all of secondary rank, challenging
the wisdom of Congress to reform and amend our
political system in some effectual manner. For our
country has in some respects outgrown the system
provided for us by the care of our ancestors; new
necessities press upon us; great evils afflict us, and
it has become the duty of statesmen not merely to
administer or to carry on our plan of government,
but to amend it also; and to this end we are to invite and welcome the best thoughts of men abroad
and at home upon political reform, and give them,
as far as possible, application and practical effect.

Now there can be no question that if parties in
the great States obtain representation according to
the number of their votes, one of the greatest possible reforms in a republican government will be
secured. All the arguments heretofore mentioned
apply to those States with special force, because they
contribute the main body of members to the House
and a defective plan of election operates within them
with extensive effect. As to them, reform will be
most important and useful, and no reasonable effort
should be spared in attempting to apply it.

We have in fact as to the great States no point
left for examination except the single one of practicability. Will the free vote work and work well in
the great States? Those who distrust popular intelligence and judgment may deny, while those who
confide in the people will affirm, the practicability
of the plan. But there is one leading consideration,
which in the judgment of the committee is decisive
upon this question. It is that where free action

shall be permitted each political party will pursue its own interests with activity, intelligence, and zeal, and will inevitably obtain for itself its due share of representative power. Thus where a party shall have one-third of the popular vote of a State it will cumulate its vote upon one-third the number of representatives to be chosen. Where parties are nearly equal in strength in a State the weaker one will cumulate its vote upon one-half the number of persons to be chosen, or within one of that number. Where a party has a small majority in a State, and particularly where it is increasing in numbers, it will cumulate its vote upon one or two more than one-half the number of candidates. And finally, in States with large delegations, a party with so small a vote as one-fourth or one-fifth the whole number will cumulate its vote upon the small number of one, two, three, or more representatives, according to the proportion which its vote shall bear to the total vote of the State. The due working of the plan is secured by the selfish interests with which it deals, and we may congratulate ourselves that under the plan the very efforts of parties to secure power for themselves will result in justice—that is, in the division of power between them according to their respective numbers.

Now, it is idle to say that voting in the great States will be confused and uncertain. On the contrary, it will run according to party organization at all times, and will adjust itself naturally and inevitably to all changes of opinion and organization in the political body. And as political parties constantly divide society into parts, the relative strength of which can at any time be approximately stated, there need not be uncertainty or confusion in the polling of votes. And even in times of transition and change, when popular power is departing from one party and attaching itself to another, or when some third party takes ground upon a particular issue, or faction diverts a fragmentary vote from a great party, the amount of disturbance and consequent uncertainty produced will not be considerable, and can be readily estimated for all practical purposes, in fixing the number of candidates which any party shall support. The merit or practicability of a rule of elections is not to be judged upon a supposition which is unlikely or exceptional; but even in the cases supposed, the elements of error and mistake will be reduced to their smallest possible quantity. Where the relative strength of party is uncertain—that is, cannot be exactly known or estimated, or where the boundary of power between them is near the dividing line between ratios of representation, it will rarely happen that a mistake will be made beyond the extent of one member, and the general result for the State will be but slightly disturbed.

THE CHOICE OF PRESIDENTIAL ELECTORS.

The proposed amendment to the Constitution of the United States, regarding the choice of electors of President and Vice-President of the United States, reported by this committee on the 29th of January, (adopted by the Senate subsequently, but lost upon disagreement between the two houses,) deserves distinct examination, particularly as full debate upon it in the two houses of Congress could not be had when it came up for consideration, for want of time.   That amendment is as follows :

The second clause, first section, article two of the Constitution of the United States shall be amended to read as follows : Each State shall appoint, *by a vote of the people thereof qualified to vote for representative in Congress,* a number of electors equal to the whole number of senators and representatives to which the State may be entitled in the Congress; but no senator or representative, or person holding an office of trust and profit under the United States, shall be appointed an elector; *and the Congress shall have power to prescribe the manner in which such electors shall be chosen by the people.*

The amendment has two objects: first, to secure to the people at all times the right of choosing electors themselves: and second, to authorize Congress to prescribe the manner in which this popular right shall be exercised.   In other respects the amendment follows the language of the existing Constitution and introduces no change.   At present electors are to be appointed as the Legislatures of the several States may direct, and there is no uniform rule for the whole country.   Although in most of the States the practice has been to choose them by a popular vote, this has not been a matter of constitutional right in the people, but of legislative permission, and liable at any time to be taken away.   That the authority to appoint electors should be fixed in the Constitution by a uniform rule, and not be left to legislative discretion is, we believe, a general opinion, and it rests upon good grounds of reason and experience.   South Carolina formerly chose her electors by a vote of her legislature, and the people had no voice in the proceeding; but by her present constitution, formed under the reconstruction laws, their appointment must be directly by the people. It may be questioned whether a State constitution can take away the discretionary power vested in the legislature by the Constitution of the United States, which is "the supreme law of the land," but this action by South Carolina shows that popular right requires a constitutional guaranty against the caprice, ambition, or corruption of legislative bodies. Florida has by law placed the appointment of her electors in her legislature, and a recent attempt in Alabama to fix a similar arrangement in that State was only frustrated by an executive veto. It may be apprehended that in some future election of President and Vice-President closely contested, the legislature of a State or the legislatures of several States may take to themselves the appointment of electors, prevent their choice by the people, and change the result of the election. This is a danger to be carefully guarded against, to be wholly removed from our electoral system, not only because it contains an element of injustice, but because it may provoke convulsion and civil war.

The next provision of the amendment that Congress may prescribe the manner in which electors shall be chosen by the people is most important and valuable. It is true that this clause only permits and does not require congressional action, but its necessity for the introduction of any reform in the manner of choosing presidential electors is perfectly certain, as will be presently shown. The objection that because this clause will take power from the legislatures of the States and vest it in Congress, or

rather will authorize Congress to interpose and control the action of State legislatures, it will increase
federal power and tend to consolidation, ought not
to prevail against the amendment, and that for
several reasons. In the first place, the choice of
presidential electors is a federal question as much
as the choice of members of Congress, and may
properly be subjected to similar regulation as to the
manner in which it shall be performed. In the
next place, the original design of the electoral colleges has wholly failed. They were intended to be
bodies for deliberation and free choice; in other
words, to exercise judgment and discretion in giving
their votes to candidates for President and Vice-
President. It was expected that they would not in
form and theory merely, but in fact and truth *choose*
the two principal executive officials in the government of the United States, and it is to be noticed
that the "*manner*" in which they shall choose is
carefully "prescribed" by the Constitution. They
are to meet on a fixed day in their respective States
and vote by ballot for President and Vice-President,
(one of whom at least shall not be an inhabitant of
the same State with themselves,) and shall make
distinct lists of their votes, signed and certified, and
transmit them under seal to the President of the
Senate. But the manner in which the electors
themselves should be chosen was not prescribed (or
authority conferred upon Congress to prescribe it)
for two reasons: first, because the convention did
not determine what authority should appoint them ;
and second, because the actual choice of President
and Vice-President was intended to be in the col-

leges themselves, whose "manner" of choosing was distinctly fixed.

These considerations are now of no force. On the contrary, when it is expressly provided that the people shall choose the electors, and it is understood that the colleges shall simply represent them and execute their will, the regulation of the manner in which the electors shall be chosen falls, as before stated, within the same reason which applies to the regulation of the manner of choosing representatives in Congress; and it falls, also, within the reasons which originally induced the regulation of the manner in which the electoral colleges were to exercise their powers. The amendment therefore, is in conformity with principles already contained in the Constitution, and does not introduce any "portentous novelty" into our system.

But the most important reason in favor of this branch of the amendment remains to be mentioned. *It is absolutely necessary to secure reform in the manner of choosing electors.* They are now chosen by general ticket in nearly all the States, and the only practical alternative to this plan is legislative choice, which is still worse, and struck at by the prior clause of the amendment. Now, the general ticket plan is very objectionable, as is well known, and yet the States cannot change it. Theoretically, by virtue of an express clause of the Constitution, the State legislatures may direct the manner in which electors shall be appointed at their pleasure, but practically they cannot or will not exercise that power in the direction of reform. Always, whenever they have not taken to themselves the power of appointing electors, they have provided that they should be elected by the people upon the general ticket plan, and that plan, so long as they allow a popular vote at all at Presidential elections, they will not abolish or amend. The explanation of this is not difficult, and it will be easily understood by any one familiar with our political history, and with the character of our political parties.

By the general ticket a political majority in a State can wield the whole power of the State in an electoral college—not merely a power proportioned to their own numbers, but a power proportioned to the joint vote of their own and of an opposing party. They obtain not only the power appropriate to themselves, but also the power appropriate to their opponents or rivals. Now it is not to be expected that a party in a State will voluntarily surrender such an advantage, though tainted with odium and injustice, or that their representatives in the State legislature will surrender it; for it is a law of party to obtain all the power possible, and to yield no advantage except upon compulsion or for adequate compensation.

But if considerations of justice and the general good could have weight with the State legislatures, and overrule with them the suggestions of selfish interest, still reform could not be secured. A change, in order to operate fairly, should be uniform throughout the whole country, and be applied in all the States at the same time. But State action in the way of change must be successive, extending over a period of years, and would not probably be uniform or universal. And so no State could well venture to take the initiative, as its political majority would make a certain sacrifice for an uncertain or imperfect reform. If a political majority in the legislature of Indiana should desire to have electors chosen by single districts, they could not afford to adopt the plan alone. For they would discover at a glance that if other States did not adopt it they would weaken their party without any possible compensation. While they would divide power in their electoral college with an opposing party, that opposing party, by holding on to the general ticket plan in another State, (Kentucky, for instance,) would obtain an advantage which might determine the general result of the Presidential election. Upon the whole, then, we must conclude that without an amendment of the Constitution, any reform whatever in the manner of choosing Presidential electors is impossible.

But it is said by many that the electoral colleges should be abolished and the people be permitted to vote directly for President and Vice-President. An amendment of the Constitution to effect this purpose has been often proposed, but has never been submitted to the States for adoption, and for a very good reason, which is, that they would have rejected it. Nor is it now possible to obtain the ratification of such an amendment by three-fourths of the States. The reason is a plain one. All the small States, and all the States of secondary rank, are interested largely in retaining their representation as States in the electoral colleges. They have now each two electors without regard to population, whereas under the plan proposed they would be confined to the principle of numbers and would influence the result of an election only in proportion to their actual votes polled. No less than 24 States out of 37 would lose from about one-fourth to two-thirds of their present political weight in presidential elections by the change. This fact is decisive. Instead of ratifications by three-fourths of the States there would be prompt rejections by a majority of them if this proposition should be submitted.

But although the electoral colleges cannot be abolished by constitutional amendment, they may be greatly reformed. They may be made to represent more truly the will of the people and the States, or the people alone, by an amendment of the Constitution which shall prescribe, or shall authorize Congress to prescribe, the manner in which their members shall be chosen. It may be provided that the two electors of each State, commonly called senatorial electors, who represent the principle of State equality, shall be chosen in one manner, and the remaining electors of the State, who represent the principle of numbers in another, or that all the electors shall be chosen in the same way. If the former plan should be preferred, the senatorial electors might be chosen by general ticket, and then, as to them, there would be no change from the present practice. But it could be provided that the representative electors in the one case, or all the electors in the other, should be chosen by single districts, or upon the principle of the free vote. The single district plan would be a very great improvement, and it would be free from some of the objec-

tions which lie against it when applied to the choice
of representatives in Congress; but the free vote
would be infinitely preferable to it, because it would
be more convenient, because it would prevent corruption, and because it would secure a more full and just
representation of the people in the electoral colleges.

It is the opinion of the committee that under
their amendment, as reported, Congress would be
authorized only to prescribe uniform rules for choosing electors; rules applicable to the whole country,
and operating equally in every State. But if this
opinion should be questioned, a slight change of
phraseology in the amendment would remove all
doubt.

To the suggestion that Congress might attempt
itself to district the States in order to perpetrate
party injustice, there are several answers. In the
first place, it is not at all certain that Congress would
form districts more unfairly than they would be
formed by State Legislatures. In the next place, it
is not at all likely, and hardly possible, that Congress would undertake this work, which would be to
it both inconvenient and odious. It possesses now
the same power of controlling the manner of choosing representatives which it is proposed to confer
upon it in regard to choosing electors, and yet it
has never undertaken to district the States for representative elections, in which it is more directly interested than in those for electors. But again, if
thought expedient, the amendment might be modified so as to exclude the direct action of Congress
in the formation of districts. It is hardly necessary
to add that the adoption of the free vote for the

choice of electors would avoid this and all similar questions of debate.

CONCLUSION.

The committee must now conclude their examination of a most important subject. They have not been able, on account of the pressure of other duties, to fill up completely the argument in favor of the free vote, or to answer in form the possible objections which may be made to its adoption. But they have endeavored to present fairly the main arguments which should weigh with Congress and with the people in its favor, and by due explanation of its purpose and character to vindicate it against misconception and cavil. As to the objections which may be made that it would delocalize representation, that it would introduce some degree of confusion, that it would decrease political activity, and that it is opposed to the doctrine that the majority shall rule, they must content themselves with declaring that in their opinion none of those objections are well taken or well suited to undergo debate, and that they were thoroughly answered in the two Houses of Parliament in 1867. The last one, in particular, is preposterous, for it is one of the main merits of reformed voting, that it will secure the true rule of the majority, and give to it a sanction it does not now possess. The whole mass of the electoral population being represented by reformed voting in the representative body, the vote will be there taken upon any question in controversy, and the voice of the majority duly pronounced. But at present minority rule may obtain. For in the first

place, all minorities at popular elections are struck
out of the returns, and next the minority vote in
the representative body is overruled when a decision
is there made, so that we have, in fact, the rule of a
majority of a majority, which very likely represents
only a minority among the people, particularly when
a plurality rule is applied to the popular elections.

The argument for reform may be summed up in
a few words.   By it we will obtain cheap elections,
just representation, and contentment among the
people; by it we will also secure able men in the
people's House; by it our political system will be
invigorated and purified; by it our country will
"take a bond of the future" that our government
shall be a blessing and not a curse; that our pros-
perity shall be enduring; that our free institutions
"shall not perish from the face of the earth."

SENATE BILL, No. 772.—(40TH CONGRESS, 3D SESSION.)

IN THE SENATE OF THE UNITED STATES,

JANUARY 13, 1869.

Mr. BUCKALEW asked, and by unanimous consent
obtained, leave to bring in a bill entitled "A bill to
amend the representation of the people in Congress;" which was read twice and referred to a
select committee consisting of Messrs. Buckalew,
Anthony, Ferry, Morton, Warner, Rice, and Wade.

MARCH 2, 1869.

Mr. WADE, from the Select Committee on Representative Reform, reported the bill without amendment, as follows:

8

A BILL to amend the representation of the people in Congress.

Be it enacted by the Senate and House of Representatives of the United States of America in Congress assembled, That in elections for the choice of representatives to the Congress of the United States, whenever more than one representative is to be chosen from a State, each elector of such State, duly qualified, shall be entitled to a number of votes equal to the number of representatives to be chosen from the State, and may give all such votes to one candidate, or may distribute them, equally or unequally, among a greater number of candidates; and the candidates highest in vote upon the return shall be declared elected.

APPENDIX.

It has been thought proper and is found convenient to place in an appendix various citations of authority in favor of representative reform from parliamentary debates and from the writings of English authors. These evidences of the progress of thought abroad upon one of the most important and interesting questions which relate to representative government, it is believed are worthy the attention of both statesman and citizen in this country— of all who desire the progress and improvement of free institutions and a satisfactory issue to our great experiment of democratic government.

A few general observations may fitly precede what follows. In the first place, it is to be remarked that reform in Parliament as secured in 1867, in regard to the mode of popular voting, broke through the lines of party and was obtained independent of party support.

In both houses of Parliament whigs and tories, liberals and conservatives, independent and radical members, ·were found together in support of an amendment which was intended to do justice to the people and improve the representative body. In the upper house of Parliament in fact the opposition became at last narrowed almost to the ministry and their immediate dependents—a fact which induced the chief minister of the Crown in the lower house, to abandon the opposition which he had at first proclaimed. In this country also the question of reform in the manner of popular voting is not one of a party character, and cannot be made such. It appeals to all good citizens and to all thoughtful men, in whatever political organization they may be found, and demands of them an independent and patriotic support. Already men of different opinions upon ordinary questions of party, and others of independent views, have stood forward among us as urgent advocates of reform. Of these, outside of Congress, honorable mention is to be made of Mr. J. Francis Fisher, Mr. Greeley, Mr. D. G. Croly, and Mr. Simon Stern. Mr. Greeley's proposition in the New York constitutional convention of 1867, for the division of his State into 15 senatorial districts, each of which should elect three senators upon the principle of the cumulative vote, was one of much merit, and will deserve, upon some future occasion, to be revived, and will also deserve to be imitated in other States.

ARGUMENTS IN PARLIAMENT.

In the House of Commons, July 4, 1867, Rt. Hon. Robert Lowe, on moving his amendment for

the cumulative vote to the reform bill, addressed the
house at length.   He said:

> That he must not be understood as coming forward to argue
> for any protection to the minority . . . but between the
> members of the constituency there should be absolute equality;
> the majority should have nothing given to it because it was a
> majority; the minority should have nothing taken away from
> it. . . . Let each voter have an equal number of votes not
> dependent upon the use he makes of them; let him be at lib-
> erty to dispose of them as he likes. . . . The tendency of
> the present system was to make that stronger which was al-
> ready strong, and that weaker which was already weak.   By
> an arbitrary and unreasonable rule it strengthened the major-
> ity; by the same arbitrary and unreasonable rule it weakened
> the minority.   On abstract justice, therefore, the present rule
> could not be maintained.   The proper way to alter it was to
> give each elector as many votes as there were vacancies, and
> leave him absolutely free to dispose of them as he pleased—to
> give all to one person, one to each of three, or two to one, and
> one to another.   By that means they would be doing nothing
> unjust or unfair to the majority or to the minority.   They
> would be merely putting them on a level, and leaving them
> on perfectly fair ground.   That was the abstract argument.
> There were different ways by which the end might be accom-
> plished.   Some proposed to give only a single vote to each
> elector; others recommended that when there were three can-
> didates each elector should have two votes.   He preferred to
> give each elector three votes, and allow him to dispose of them
> as he pleased.   The objection to the two first proposals was
> that they would operate in the way of disfranchisement, and
> would take away something people already possessed; because
> on the supposition that there were three candidates they had
> already three votes.   The system he proposed had greater flex-
> ibility and better adapts itself to the general purposes of elec-
> tions. . . . They would find that in this way opinion in con-
> stituencies would ripen.   Opinion in that house would ripen to
> changes, and the house would become a more delicate reflex
> of the opinions of the constituencies.   The existence of such a

system of gradual growth, not only of opinion but in the representation of opinion, would, to a great extent, prevent the necessity of external agitation, and be a great discouragement to it. There was nothing more worthy of the attention of statesmen in the new state of affairs than anything which would have the tendency to prevent that violent oscillation which they now witnessed. What happened in the United States? The minority of thousands might as well not exist at all. It is absolutely ignored. Was their country (England) in like manner to be formed into two hostile camps, debarred from each other in two solid and compact bodies? Or were they to have that shading off of opinion, that modulation of extremes, and mellowing and ripening of right principles, which are among the surest characteristics of a free country, the true secrets of political dynamics, and the true preservatives of a great nation? He said then that what he proposed to the house was in itself just, equal, and fair, founded on no undue or unfair attempt to give a minority an advantage they were not entitled to exercise, and that it was peculiarly applicable to the state of things on which they were entering. . . . He might justly add that the principle of the amendment was large enough to include boroughs returning two members, as well as those which had three, and if it were worth while he was prepared to contend that upon abstract principle it ought to be applied to both classes of boroughs.— Hansard, Parl. Deb., 3d series, clxxxviii. pp. 1037-'41.

In the House of Lords, July 30, 1867, Lord Cairns spoke at length in support of his amendment for representation of minorities in three-membered constituencies. He said he would state the advantages of the system he had proposed:

These must obviously be looked at from three points of view —the advantages to the general legislation of the country, the advantages to the members who would be selected under an arrangement of this kind, and the advantages to the constituencies themselves. Now, with regard to the legislature, the advantages which I think would be gained by this system

would be these: you would obtain in the persons of those who
would be the representatives of the minority in these large constituencies a body of men of great intelligence, and of great
independence; you would have those elements of advantage
which exist in the representation of small boroughs, and, at the
same time, you would be perfectly free from the disadvantages
and defects of the small borough system. . . . Questions are
constantly arising which in one aspect are questions of general
political interest, but which are more or less connected with
local interests, and bear upon local claims; and thus a question
which, in a general point of view, is of political interest to the
whole country is sometimes colored and affected in many ways
by the way in which it is viewed in different localities. No
doubt, in discussing general questions of political interest, it
would be of the greatest possible advantage to hear how those
questions were viewed not merely by different localities but
by different bodies of men in the same locality. That result
you would obtain by the plan which I propose. . . . I will
pass to the consideration of the advantages which would be
gained by the representatives of those large constituencies
themselves. . . . You would have from the same constituency two members representing the majority and one representing the minority, communicating freely with each other,
and without the slightest tinge of jealousy or apprehension that
the interests of one would jar or conflict with the interests of
the other in the constituency. . . . Again, with regard to
the constituency itself—and this is one of the most important
views of the case—observe the advantages which would be
gained: First, I believe you would gain the greatest possible
local satisfaction; there is nothing so irksome to those who
form the minority of one of those large constituencies as finding
that from the mere force of numbers they are virtually excluded from the exercise of any political power; that it is vain
for them to attempt to take any part in public affairs; that the
elections must go in one direction, and that they have no political power whatever. On the one hand the result is great dissatisfaction, and on the other it is disinclination on the part of
those who form the minority to take any part in affairs in
which it is important they should take a prominent and con-
spicuous part. . . . In addition to that, it would do much to

soften the asperities of political feeling which sometimes, though not often, prevail in. large constituencies. . . . Of this I am sure, (and although some treat it as an objection I think it a great advantage of the scheme,) that contests would be very much diminished in large constituencies where contests are most expensive, so expensive that the mind almost recoils at hearing the sums which they cost. Contests practically would come to an end; and as they did, so would danger of bribery and corruption. You would have great constituencies divided into great component parts; you would have each portion well represented; you would have freedom from expense, freedom from the irritation of political feeling, and from the curse of all elections, bribery.—Hansard, 3d series, clxxxix. pp. 433–'41.

The views of Earl Russell in favor of dividing the representation of large constituencies between parties, have been often expressed. In debate in the House of Commons upon the reform bill of 1854, he spoke as follows:

Now it appears to us that many advantages would attend the enabling the minority to have a part in these returns. In the first place there is apt to be a feeling of great soreness when a very considerable number of electors, such as I have mentioned, are completely shut out from a share in the representation of one place. . . . But in the next place I think that the more you have your representation confined to large populations, the more ought you to take care that there should be some kind of balance, and that the large places sending members to this house should send those who represent the community at large. But when there is a very large body excluded it cannot be said that the community at large is fairly represented.--3d Hansard, clvi. 2062.

In his Essay on the English Constitution, (edition of ·1865,) he wrote as follows:

If there were to be any deviation from our customary habits and rooted ideas on the subject of representation, I should like to see such a change as I once proposed in order to obtain representatives of the minority in large and populous counties and towns. If, when three members are to be elected, each elector were allowed to give two votes, we might have a liberal country gentleman sitting for Buckinghamshire, and a conservative manufacturer for Manchester. The local majority would have two to one in the House of Commons, and the minority would not feel itself disfranchised and degraded.

In the House of Lords, in 1867, he gave a vigorous and able support to the Cairns amendment, which now constitutes clause nine of the reform act of that year. He said:

I believe by means of such a plan you would introduce into the House of Commons men of moderate views, whose influence would tend to reconcile parties on those occasions which now and then arise when neither extreme is completely right, and when the influence of moderate men is of much use in allaying the heat of party passion. . . . Suppose a town has 20,000 voters, and that 12,000 are of one side in politics and 8000 of the other, would not that town be better represented if both the 12,000 and the 8000 were represented than if only the 12,000 were represented? The gentleman who first impressed me with those opinions as to three-cornered constituencies, mentioned to me that in a great manufacturing town where there was a very considerable conservative minority, men of the greatest respectability, men of wealth, and men of education were in such a state of political irritation, from the fact of feeling themselves reduced to the position of mere ciphers at elections, that they were sometimes ready to support candidates of even extreme democratic opinions. . . . I can well understand men who are extremely intolerant and exclusive in politics objecting to give any voice to those whose political views are distasteful to them; but I cannot understand such an objection being urged by those who are in favor of having public opinion fairly represented.—Hansard, 3d series, clxxxix. pp. 446–'47.

Upon the consideration of the reform bill of

1831 in the House of Commons, Mr. Praed, distinguished as speaker and poet, expressed himself as follows:

> If we desire that the representatives of a numerous constituency should come hither merely as witnesses of the fact that certain opinions are entertained by the majority of that constituency, our present system of election is certainly rational, and members are right in their reprobation of a compromise, because it would diminish the strength of the evidence to a fact we wish to ascertain. But if we intend, as surely we do intend, that not the majority only, but the aggregate masses of every numerous constituency, should, so far as is possible, be seen in the persons and heard in the voices of their representatives—should be, in short, in the obvious literal sense of the word "represented," in this house—then, sir, our present rule of election is in the theory wrong and absurd, and in practice is but partially corrected by the admission of that compromise on which so much virtuous indignation has been wasted.—3d Hansard, v. 1362.

THE CUMULATIVE VOTE.

BY EARL GREY.

"The first of the reforms of a conservative tendency which I should suggest, and one which I should consider a great improvement under any circumstances, but quite indispensable if any changes favorable to democratic power are to be admitted, would be the adoption of what Mr. James Marshall has called the 'cumulative vote'—that is to say, the principle of giving to every elector as many votes as there are members to be elected by the constituency to which he belongs, with the right of either giving all these votes to a single candidate, or of dividing them, as he may prefer. The object of adopting this rule would be to secure to minorities a fair opportunity of making their opinions and wishes heard in the House of Commons. In order that it might fully answer this purpose, the right of returning members to Parliament ought to be so distributed that each constituency should not have less than three representatives to choose. Supposing that three members were to be elected together, and that each elector were entitled to three votes, which he might unite in favor of a single candidate, it is obvious that a minority *exceeding* a fourth of the whole constituency would have the power of securing the election of one member. It is probable that in general three members would be thus returned, each representing a different shade of opinion among the voters.

"The advantages this mode of voting would be calculated to produce, and the justice of making some such provision for the representation of minorities, or, rather, the flagrant injustice of omitting to do so, have been so well shown by Mr. Marshall in the pamphlet I have already referred to, and by Mr. Mill, in his highly philosophical treatise on representative government, that it is quite needless for me to argue the question as one of principle. But I may observe that, in addition to its being right in principle, this measure would be in strict accordance with the lessons of experience, if read in their true spirit. One of the most remarkable peculiarities of the British House of Commons, as compared with other representative bodies, is, that it has always had within its walls members representing most of the different classes of society, and of the various and conflicting opinions and interests to be found in the nation. Much of the acknowledged success with which the House of Commons has played its part in the government of the country has been attributed (I believe most justly) to this peculiarity. The changes made by the reform act, and especially the abolition of the various rights of voting formerly to be found in different towns, and the establishment of one uniform franchise in all the English boroughs, (with only a small exception in favor of certain classes of freemen,) tended somewhat to impair the character of the house in this respect. The greatly increased intercourse between different parts of the country, and the rapidity with which opinions are propagated from one extremity of the kingdom to another, have had a similar tendency; and there is no longer the same probability as formerly that different opinions will be found to prevail in different places, so as to enable all parties to find somewhere the means of gaining an entrance to Parliament for at least enough of their adherents to give expression to their feelings.

" Hence there is a danger that the House of Commons may cease to enjoy to the same extent as formerly the great advantage of representing the various classes and opinions to be found in the nation. That danger would be greatly aggravated by rendering the constituencies more nearly equal than they are; but the simple change involved in adopting the cumulative vote would do much towards guarding against it, since with this mode of voting it would be impossible that any considerable party in the country should be left unrepresented in Parliament. The tendency of the alteration would be conservative in the best sense of the word, while at the same time, in many cases, it would have the effect of relieving liberal politicians from a disadvantage to which they are unfairly subjected. On the one side it would prevent the representation of the large town constituencies from being monopolized, as at present, by candidates ready to pledge themselves to the support of democratic measures. Even in the metropolitan boroughs we might reasonably expect that some members would be returned really representing the higher and most educated classes of their inhabitants, who are now practically without any representation at all except that which they obtain indirectly by means of members chosen by other constituencies. Thus in the large towns it would put an end to the unjust monopoly on the part of radical politicians; and on the other hand, in those counties where a conservative majority now excludes a strong liberal minority from any share in the representation, it would correct a similar tendency in the opposite direction. In both cases this system of voting would be calculated to give more weight to the independent ·electors, who are not thorough-going partisans on either side, and to favor the return of candidates deserving their confidence." —*Parliamentary Government Considered with reference to Reform, edition of* 1864, p. 203.

LIMITED AND CUMULATIVE VOTING.
BY JOHN STUART MILL.

"Assuming that each constituency elects three representatives, two modes have been proposed, in either of which a minority, amounting to a third of the constituency, may, by acting in concert, and determining to aim at no more, return one of the members. One plan is, that each elector should only be allowed to vote for two, or even for one, although three are to be elected. The other leaves to the elector his three votes, but allows him to give all of them to one candidate. The first of these plans was adopted in the reform bill of Lord Aberdeen's government; but I do not hesitate most decidedly to prefer the second, which has been advocated in an able and conclusive pamphlet by Mr. James Garth Marshall. The former plan must be always and inevitably unpopular, because it cuts down the privileges of the voter, while the latter, on the contrary, extends them; and I am prepared to maintain that the permission of cumulative votes, that is, of giving either one, two, or three votes to a single candidate, is in itself, even independently of its effect in giving a representation to minorities, the mode of voting which gives the most faithful expression of the wishes of the elector. On the existing plan, an elector who votes for three can give his vote for the three candidates whom he prefers to their competitors; but among those three he may desire the success of one immeasurably more than that of the other two, and may be willing to relinquish them entirely for an increased chance of attaining the greater object. This portion of his wishes he has now no means of expressing by his vote. He may sacrifice two of his votes altogether, but in no case can he give more than a single vote to the object of his preference. Why should the mere fact of preference be alone considered, and no account whatever be taken of the degree of it? The power to give several votes to a single candidate would be eminently favorable to those whose claims to be chosen are derived from personal qualities, and not from their being the mere symbols of an opinion; for if the voter gives his suffrage to a candidate in consideration of pledges, or because the candidate is of the same party with himself, he will not desire the success of that individual more than that of any other who will take the same pledges, or belongs to the same party. When he is especially concerned for the election of some one candidate, it is on account of something which personally distinguishes that candidate from others on the same side. Where there is no overruling local influence in favor of an individual, those who would be benefited as candidates by the cumulative vote would generally be the persons of greatest real or reputed virtue or talents."—*Thoughts on Parliamentary Reform*, 2d ed., 1859.

OF TRUE AND FALSE DEMOCRACY—REPRESENTATION OF ALL, AND REPRESENTATION OF THE MAJORITY ONLY.

BY JOHN STUART MILL.

It has been seen that the dangers incident to a representative democracy are of two kinds: danger of a low grade of intelligence in the representative body, and in the popular opinion which controls it; and danger of class legislation on the part of the numerical majority, these being all composed of the same class. We have next to consider how far it is possible so to organize the democracy as, without interfering materially with the characteristic benefits

of democratic government, to do away with these
two great evils, or at least to abate them in the
utmost degree attainable by human contrivance.

The common mode of attempting this is by limit-
ing the democratic character of the representation
through a more or less restricted suffrage. But
there is a previous consideration which, duly kept
in view, considerably modifies the circumstances
which are supposed to render such a restriction
necessary. A completely equal democracy, in a
nation in which a single class composes the numerical majority, cannot be divested of certain evils;
but those evils are greatly aggravated by the fact
that the democracies which at present exist are not
equal, but systematically unequal in favor of the
predominant class. Two very different ideas are
usually confounded under the name democracy.
The pure idea of democracy, according to its defini-
tion, is the government of the whole people by the
whole people, equally represented. Democracy, as
commonly conceived and hitherto practiced, is the
government of the whole people by a mere majority
of the people, exclusively represented. The former
is synonymous with the equality of all citizens; the
latter, strangely confounded with it, is a government
of privilege in favor of the numerical majority, who
alone possess practically any voice in the State.
This is the inevitable consequence of the manner
in which the votes are now taken, to the complete
disfranchisement of minorities.

The confusion of ideas here is great, but it is so
easily cleared up that one would suppose the slightest
indication would be sufficient to place the matter in

its true light before any mind of average intelligence. It would be so but for the power of habit,
owing to which, the simplest idea, if unfamiliar, has
as great difficulty in making its way to the mind as
a far more complicated one. That the minority
must yield to the majority, the smaller number to
the greater, is a familiar idea; and, accordingly, men
think there is no necessity for using their minds any
further, and it does not occur to them that there is
any medium between allowing the smaller number
to be equally powerful with the greater, and blotting
out the smaller number altogether. In a representative body actually deliberating, the minority must
of course be overruled; and in an equal democracy
(since the opinions of the constituents, when they
insist on them, determine those of the representative body), the majority of the people, through their
representatives, will outvote and prevail over the
minority and their representatives. But does it
follow that the minority should have no representatives at all? Because the majority ought to prevail
over the minority, must the majority have all the
votes, the minority none? Is it necessary that the
minority should not even be heard? Nothing but
habit and old association can reconcile any reasonable being to the needless injustice. In a really
equal democracy every or any section would be represented, not disproportionately, but proportionately.
A majority of the electors would always have a
majority of the representatives, but a minority of
the electors would always have a minority of the
representatives. Man for man they would be as
fully represented as the majority. Unless they are,

there is not equal government, but a government of inequality and privilege. One part of the people rule over the rest. There is a part whose fair and equal share of influence in the representation is withheld from them, contrary to all just government, but, above all, contrary to the principle of democracy, which professes equality as its very root and foundation.

The injustice and violation of principle are not less flagrant because those who suffer by them are a minority; for there is not equal suffrage where every single individual does not count for as much as any other single individual in the community. But it is not only the minority who suffer. Democracy thus constituted does not even attain its ostensible object—that of giving the powers of government, in all cases, to the numerical majority. It does something very different; it gives them to a majority of the majority, who may be, and often are, but a minority of the whole. All principles are most effectually tested by extreme cases. Suppose then that, in a country governed by equal and universal suffrage, there is a contested election in every constituency, and every election is carried by a small majority; the parliament thus brought together represents little more than a bare majority of the people. This parliament proceeds to legislate, and adopts important measures by a bare majority of itself; what guarantee is there that these measures accord with the wishes of a majority of the people? Nearly half the electors, having been outvoted at the hustings, have had no influence at all in the decision; and the whole of these may be, a

9

majority of them probably are, hostile to the measures, having voted against those by whom they
have been carried. Of the remaining electors,
nearly half have chosen representatives who, by
supposition, have voted against the measures. It is
possible, therefore, and even probable, that the
opinion which has prevailed was agreeable only to
a minority of the nation, though a majority of that
portion of it whom the institutions of the country
have erected into a ruling class. If democracy
means the certain ascendency of the majority, there
are no means of insuring that but by allowing every
individual figure to tell equally in the summing up.
Any minority left out, either purposely or by the
play of the machinery, gives the power not to a
majority but to a minority in some other part of
the scale.

The only answer which can possibly be made to
this reasoning is, that as different opinions predominate in different localities, the opinion which is in a
minority in some places has a majority in others;
and, on the whole, every opinion which exists in the
constituencies obtains its fair share of voices in the
representation. And this is roughly true in the
present state of the constituency. If it were not,
the discordance of the house with the general sentiment of the country would soon become evident.
But it would be no longer true if the present constituency were much enlarged; still less if made coextensive with the whole population; for in that
case the majority in every locality would consist of
manual laborers; and when there was any question
pending on which these classes were at issue with

the rest of the community, no other classes could succeed in getting represented anywhere. Even now, is it not a great grievance that in every parliament a very numerous portion of the electors, willing and anxious to be represented, have no member in the house for whom they have voted? Is it just that every elector of Marylebone is obliged to be represented by two nominees of the vestries, every elector of Finsbury or Lambeth by those (as is generally believed) of the publicans? The constituencies to which most of the highly educated and public-spirited persons in the country belong, those of the large towns, are now, in great part, either unrepresented or misrepresented. The electors who are on a different side in party politics from the local majority are unrepresented. Of those who are on the same side, a large proportion are misrepresented, having been obliged to accept the man who had the greatest number of supporters in their political party, though his opinions may differ from theirs on every other point. The state of things is, in some respects, even worse than if the minority were not allowed to vote at all; for then, at least, the majority might have a member who would represent their own best mind, while now the necessity of not dividing the party for fear of letting in its opponents, induces all to vote either for the person who first presents himself wearing their colors, or for the one brought forward by their local leaders, and these, if we pay them the compliment which they very seldom deserve, of supposing their choice to be unbiased by their personal interests, are compelled, that they may be sure of mustering their

whole strength, to bring forward a candidate whom
none of the party will strongly object to—that is, a
man without any distinctive peculiarity, any known
opinions except the shibboleth of the party. This
is strikingly exemplified in the United States,
where, at the election of President, the strongest
party never dares put forward any of its strongest
men, because every one of these, from the mere fact
that he has been long in the public eye, has made
himself objectionable to some portion or other of the
party, and is therefore not so sure a card for rallying all their votes as a person who has never been
heard of by the public at all until he is produced as
the candidate. Thus the man who is chosen, even
by the strongest party, represents perhaps the real
wishes only of the narrow margin by which that
party outnumbers the other. Any section whose
support is necessary to success possesses a veto on
the candidate. Any section which holds out more
obstinately than the rest can compel all the others
to adopt its nominee; and this superior pertinacity
is, unhappily, more likely to be found among those
who are holding out for their own interest than for
that of the public. Speaking generally, the choice
of the majority is determined by that portion of the
body who are the most timid, the most narrow-
minded, and prejudiced, or who cling most tena-
ciously to the exclusive class interest, and the electoral rights of the minority, while useless for the
purposes for which votes are given, serve only for
compelling the majority to accept the candidate of
the weakest or worst portion of themselves.

That while recognizing these evils many should

consider them as the necessary price paid for a free
government is in no way surprising. It was the
opinion of all the friends of freedom up to a recent
period; but the habit of passing them over as ir-
remediable has become so inveterate that many persons seem to have lost the capacity of looking at
them as things which they would be glad to remedy
if they could. From despairing of a cure there is
too often but one step to denying the disease, and
from this follows dislike to having a remedy proposed, as if the proposer were creating a mischief
instead of offering relief from one. People are so
inured to the evils that they feel as if it were unreasonable, if not wrong, to complain of them. Yet,
avoidable or not, he must be a purblind lover of
liberty, on whose mind they do not weigh, who
would not rejoice at the discovery that they could
be dispensed with. Now nothing is more certain
than that the virtual blotting out of the minority is
no necessary or natural consequence of freedom;
that, far from having any connection with democracy, it is diametrically opposed to the first principle
of democracy—representation in proportion to numbers. It is an essential part of democracy that minorities should be adequately represented. No real
democracy, nothing but a false show of democracy,
is possible without it.

Those who have seen and felt, in some degree,
the force of these considerations have proposed various expedients by which the evil may be, in a
greater or less degree, mitigated. Lord John Russell, in one of his reform bills, introduced a provision that certain constituencies should return three

members, and that in these each elector should be
allowed to vote only for two; and Mr. Disraeli, in
the recent debates, revived the memory of the fact
by reproaching him for it—being of opinion, ap-
parently, that it befits a conservative statesman to
regard only means, and to disown scornfully all fel-
low-feeling with any one who is betrayed, even once,
into thinking of ends.   Others have proposed that
each elector should be allowed to vote only for one.
By either of these plans a minority equalling or exceeding a third of the local constituency would be
able, if it attempted no more, to return one out of
three members.   The same result might be attained
in a still better way if, as proposed in an able pamphlet by Mr. James Garth Marshall, the elector retained his three votes, but was at liberty to bestow
them all upon the same candidate.

[The author proceeds to state his preference for the plan of
personal representation propounded by Mr. Hare, over other
plans of reform, as more effectual and complete, as securing
more fully the objects and avoiding the mischiefs mentioned in
his preceding remarks.   He expresses regret, however, that
none of those other plans had " been carried into effect, as any
of them would have recognized the right principle and prepared
the way for its more complete application."
His preference for personal representation arises from the
fact that it would provide for all local minorities of less than a
third in a constituency, and for all minorities made up from
several constituencies.   His views appear to be, to some extent,
affected by the peculiar character of British districts, and the
absence of great State organizations in the kingdom affording
free play for the cumulative vote.   As personal representation
is a question not proposed for examination in the present
report, or for exposition in the papers which accompany it, his
remarks upon it are here omitted.   But two additional ex-

tracts, relating to general considerations connected with reform in representation, are added below.]

The natural tendency of representative government, as of modern civilization, is toward collective mediocrity; and this tendency is increased by all reductions and extensions of the franchise, their effect being to place the principal power in the hands of classes more and more below the highest level of instruction in the community. But, though the superior intellects and characters will necessarily be outnumbered, it makes a great difference whether or not they are heard. In the false democracy which, instead of giving representation to all, gives it only to the local majorities, the voice of the instructed minority may have no organs at all in the representative body. . . . In the American democracy, which is constructed on this faulty model, the highly-cultivated members of the community, except such of them as are willing to sacrifice their own opinions and modes of judgment and become the servile mouthpieces of their inferiors in knowledge, do not even offer themselves for Congress or the State legislatures, so certain is it that they would have no chance of being returned. . . . In every government there is some power stronger than all the rest, and the power which is strongest tends perpetually to become the sole power. Partly by intention and partly unconsciously it is ever striving to make all other things bend to itself, and is not content while there is anything which makes permanent head against it—any influence not in agreement with its spirit. Yet, if it succeeds in suppressing all rival influences, and moulding every-

thing after its own model, improvement in that
country is at an end, and decline commences. Human improvement is a product of many factors, and
no power ever yet constituted among mankind includes them all. Even the most beneficent power
only contains in itself some of the requisites of
good, and the remainder, if progress is to continue,
must be derived from some other source. No community has ever long continued progressive but
while a conflict was going on between the strongest
power in the community and some rival power—
between the spiritual and temporal authorities, the
military or territorial and the industrious classes,
the king and the people, the orthodox and religious
reformers. When the victory on either side was so
complete as to put an end to the strife, and no other
conflict took its place, first stagnation followed, and
then decay. The ascendency of the numerical
majority is less unjust and, on the whole, less mischievous than many others, but it is attended with
the very same kind of dangers, and even more certainly, for when the government is in the hands of
one or a few, the many are always existent as a rival
power which may not be strong enough ever to control the other, but whose opinion and sentiment are
a moral and even a social support to all who, either
from conviction or contrariety of interests, are opposed to any of the tendencies of the ruling authority. But when the democracy is supreme there is
no one or few strong enough for dissentient opinions
and injured or menaced interests to lean upon. The
great difficulty of democratic government has hitherto seemed to be how to provide, in a democratic

society, what circumstances have provided hitherto
in all the societies which have maintained themselves ahead of others—a social support, a *point
d'appui* for individual resistance to the tendencies
of the ruling power, a protection, a rallying point
for opinions and interests which the ascendant public opinion views with disfavor. For want of such
a *point d'appui* the older societies, and all but a
few modern ones, either fell into dissolution or became stationary (which means slow deterioration)
through the exclusive predominance of a part only
of the conditions of social and mental well-being.
. . . The only quarter in which to look for a supplement, or completing corrective to the instincts
of a democratic majority, is the instructed minority,
but in the ordinary mode of constituting democracy this minority has no organ.—*Considerations on
Representative Government,* chapter vii., *Harper's
Edition,* 1862.

[March 2, 1869, the foregoing Report (with Appendix) upon
being presented to the Senate was ordered to be printed. The
following day it was further ordered that 2000 additional copies
should be printed for the use of the Senate. Two editions of
it were subsequently published by the Personal Representation
Society of Chicago, for distribution at home and abroad.]

AN ADDRESS

ON

PROPORTIONAL REPRESENTATION BY THE FREE VOTE.

DELIVERED BEFORE THE SOCIAL SCIENCE ASSOCIA-
TION, PHILADELPHIA,

TUESDAY EVENING, OCT. 25, 1870.

Gentlemen of the Association:—I desire my remarks to-night to be understood as made in con-
tinuation of what was said and written by me on
former occasions on the subject of Electoral Reform.
In a speech in this city on the 19th of November,
1867, in a speech in the Senate on the 11th of July
of the same year, and in a report from the Senate
Committee on representative reform, 2d of March,
1869, I discussed the Free Vote in its proposed application to Federal Elections and stated the general
arguments in favor of its adoption. I do not propose to go over again the ground covered by those
speeches and by that report, but to present additional views, the product of further reflection upon
this question of reform, and to mention the steps
which have been taken in this State and in other
States, looking toward the submitting of the plan
of reformed voting to practice.

THE FREE VOTE.

The Free Vote may be applied to elections whenever two or more persons are to be chosen together to the same office for the same term of service, and it consists in allowing the voter to distribute his votes among candidates as he shall think fit, or to concentrate them upon one. It is here assumed that the voter shall have the same number of votes as the number of persons to be chosen, and that the candidates highest in vote shall be declared elected.

ITS EFFECT ON SINGLE ELECTIONS.

It will be observed that the free vote is inapplicable to the election of a single person; it can be applied only where two or more are to be chosen. But it will be a great mistake to assume that it will have no effect upon single elections because it cannot be applied to them in form and directly. Due reflection and a careful examination of the subject will convince any intelligent man—any man well acquainted with the practical workings of our political system—that while its direct operation must be confined to plural elections its indirect effects upon single ones will be very great, and very salutary also, whenever it shall come to be established. For the advocates of the new plan assert with confidence and upon fair grounds of reason, that it will secure absolutely to political parties their just representation in all ordinary cases of Presidential, Congressional, Legislative and other elections to which it shall be applied, and will therefore greatly weaken the tendency toward violent and corrupt party action in the elections to which it shall *not* apply.

The election of Governor in a State is mainly interesting because of the influence which the result will exert upon the next elections in the State for Presidential electors, members of Congress and members of the Legislature; such an election is hotly contested, money is expended upon it and all possible means to control it brought into active play, because elections which are to follow will be powerfully influenced if not determined by the issue of the contest. In like manner and for the same reason other elections of single officers are assailed by evil influences and become degraded and of evil report. In my opinion, our remedy, and a very effectual one, will be to make all our Congressional and Legislative elections plural and then apply to them and to Presidential elections the free vote or some other device by which just representation of the people shall be secured. Then Gubernatorial and other single elections will be purified and improved; they will no longer exert any considerable, much less controlling, influence upon Federal or Legislative elections and will not therefore invite or provoke those corrupt and evil influences by which they are now assailed.

ITS OBJECTS—JUST REPRESENTATION AND PURE ELECTIONS.

Two capital objects are sought to be accomplished by the free vote considered as an instrument of reform: *First*, the just representation of the people in government, and *Second*, the purification of popular elections.

How to secure the proportional representation of

political parties or interests in government is certainly a question of high importance, and we have reason to rejoice that it is now receiving earnest attention in our own country and in Europe. We must all agree that the majority vote—as I shall call the old plan to which we have been accustomed—is both insufficient and unjust in the case of many elections to which it is applied, and that in unchecked operation it is positively pernicious and hurtful. Observe, I am not speaking of the majority or plurality rule of elections which in its proper application to returns is a necessity, but of the *majority vote*, of that instrument of oppression by which government is made unsatisfactory because it is made unjust. The law has said to the citizen, "You shall distribute your votes singly among candidates although by doing so you will lose them all and stand deprived of all voice in the government. You and your neighbor shall be made to struggle constantly, each to deprive the other of his equitable right in the very attempt to maintain his own. And if you shall not choose to vote in this exact manner and to grasp at more than belongs to you, you shall not vote at all; you shall stand aside disfranchised and ignored." No wonder that our people, instructed by experience and scourged by many evils, are beginning to complain of the law and to inquire whether there is not some possible remedy for electoral injustice—some plan of amendment by which all the people can have their votes counted and obtain by them appropriate power and influence in the government.

Yes, there *are* remedies for this injustice, and one

of them I advocate to-night; a remedy convenient of application and effectual for all our purposes of reform. But it is not proposed in antagonism to other plans of reform, nor as a finality in the art of government. It may stand simply for what it is—a good, useful, workable plan for the improvement of elections and for securing justice to the whole body of our electoral population.

The second great object of reformed voting—the purification of elections—invites to a more elaborate exposition of an existing evil and of the remedial character of the new plan, than my space and time will permit; but I cannot pass it wholly unnoticed. Certainly when you shall cheapen elections by taking away the motive or the main motive for spending money upon them, you will purify them also. They will be cleansed and elevated in character by being made cheap and inexpensive to parties and candidates who are now compelled to expend money upon them profusely as the indispensable condition of success. Now beyond all question the free vote will cheapen elections. It will take away from parties almost entirely two powerful motives which now operate upon them—a greed for unjust representation and a fear of unjust disfranchisement —by the conjoint operation of which desperate and expensive struggles are produced. When a party shall be made secure in its just representation *by its own votes* it need not buy a majority in the corruption market as a measure of necessary defence. When it cannot by the aid of corrupt votes rob the opposite party and take to itself *more* than its just share of representative power, it will become frugal in its expenditures and honorable in its conduct. Thus the free vote destroys or checks corruption by taking away the motives which produce it, and in this respect vindicates itself as a most powerful instrument of moral improvement and progress.

THE APPLICATION OF THE FREE VOTE.

The free vote is proposed for application to the following elections:

1. To the choice of Electors of President and Vice-President of the United States.

2. To the choice of members of Congress.

3. To the choice of Senators and Representatives to the Legislatures of the several States.

In Pennsylvania it should be further applied to the election of the following officers:

1. Judges of the Supreme Court.

2. Law Judges of all Common Pleas and District Courts composed of more than one Law Judge.

3. Associate Judges of Counties.

4. Aldermen and Justices of the Peace in wards, boroughs, and townships.

5. County Commissioners and County Auditors.

6. Directors for the Poor for counties or for Poor districts whenever their election shall be authorized.

7. Councilmen of cities and boroughs.

8. Assessors of taxes whenever two are to be chosen, and Assistant Assessors triennially.

9. Constables whenever two are to be chosen.

10. Supervisors of Roads and Overseers of the Poor in townships.

11. Borough and Township Auditors.

12. Directors and Controllers of Common Schools in all the School Districts of the Commonwealth.

The new plan should also be applied throughout the country to stockholder elections for the choice of officers of incorporated companies. One of the amendments to the Illinois constitution, adopted in July last, provides, that in all elections in that State for directors or managers of incorporated companies the free vote shall be allowed, so that stockholder minorities in such companies may always be represented in their management, and abuse and wrong be detected or prevented. And all corporations require and should have this fundamental and most salutary check in their constitution.

But there is still another application of the free vote, heretofore unnoticed, which I believe to be in the highest degree important; I mean its application to primary elections or to the nomination of candidates. In fact when reform shall have accomplished its work in the legal elections and shall have invigorated and purified *them*, it will be required more than ever in the primary ones. For as all nominated candidates will commonly be elected under the new plan, their nomination must be made upon sound principles and with all possible guards against corruption and abuse. But here it is evident that the same remedy which will improve the one class of elections can be used to improve the other also; in other words, that the free vote can often be applied directly to the nomination of candidates and always to the choice of delegates to nominating bodies. Give it such application freely, to the fullest possible extent, and you will find that you have

reached and mastered the ultimate difficulty in the
way of electoral reform.

CONCERNING THE USE OF FRACTIONAL VOTES—THEIR UTILITY AND CONVENIENCE.

In the Bloomsburg act fractional votes are allowed
when three, four, or six persons are to be chosen,
and they may be allowed with advantage in other
cases. Most commonly they will be convenient and
desirable to majorities rather than minorities, and
there can be no question that their allowance will
popularize the free vote, render its reformatory action more effectual and facilitate its extension generally to popular and corporate elections. Fractional
votes have been used with approval many times in
recent local elections in Pennsylvania, they have
also been used in national political conventions for
the nomination of candidates for President and
Vice-President of the United States, and their use
will be found essential to the smooth working of
representative elections under the amended constitution of Illinois. It is evident that when a voter has
three votes and shall desire to bestow them equally
upon two candidates, he must divide one of his
votes; in other words, in order to give one vote and
a half to each of two candidates he must break one
of his votes into two equal fractions. When four
persons are to be chosen and the majority of the
voters shall desire to vote for three candidates, (giving an equal support to each,) fractions of one-third
should be created; that is, each majority voter
should divide one of his votes into three equal
parts, so that he can give one vote and one-third to

10

each of the three candidates. And when six persons are to be chosen and the voter shall desire to vote for four, he must (in order to render them an equal support) divide two of his votes into four halves and give one vote and a half to each of the four candidates he votes for.

Some other numbers involved in elections are less adapted than the numbers three, four, and six for the application of fractional voting; but many others are as much so, and nearly all admit of such application to a useful extent. For instance, the number five admits of the giving of two and a half votes to each of two candidates, or one and one-fourth to each of four; and the number nine admits of one and a half votes to each of six candidates, or two and one-fourth to each of four. But as it seems necessary or highly desirable on grounds of convenience to avoid fractions of which the numerator exceeds unity or one, we cannot very well divide five votes equally among three candidates, nor seven among five, etc. There is, however, more than one resource in such cases of difficulty. Terms of official service may be arranged with reference to the new plan of voting, or the body of electors in a State or district, united by party association, may divide themselves for the purpose of casting votes. Take the case of a court of five judges, chosen for ten-year terms: Instead of electing them all together it would be well to elect a part of them every fifth year, say two at one time and three at another, and so on at successive quinquennial elections. And so to a court of seven judges, four might be chosen at one time and three at another. Again, take the case of a State entitled to eight members of Congress in which the political majority is entitled, by its numbers, to elect five.   In a party convention or by a State committee it might be easily arranged that while the great mass or principal part of the majority voters of the State should vote for four candidates, (giving two votes to each,) a district containing one-fifth of their strength should be set off or set apart in which the voters of the party should give all their votes to one candidate.   And so in Pennsylvania, entitled to twenty-four members of Congress, and where political parties are nearly equal in strength, either party that supposed itself in the majority could vote for a thirteenth member by a district vote, while the general mass of its voters in the State would vote for twelve.   No law would be necessary to authorize these and other like arrangements; they would be made by the voluntary action of parties whenever their expediency became evident.

· In fact, by the means mentioned, and by others, the use of fractional votes can be dispensed with altogether in our plan of electoral reform, and whole votes alone retained.   But I would not dispense with them in all cases, but would authorize them whenever their utility should be evident and their inconvenience slight.   At present I am prepared to say that I would allow fractional votes of one-half, one-third, or one-fourth, whenever their use shall be necessary to enable voters to give an equal support to the candidates they vote for under the new plan.

The counting of fractions in making up election

returns is a very simple performance as shown at recent elections in this State. Fractions being always attached to whole votes on the tickets may even be disregarded in scoring down votes upon the tally-paper and be added at the end of the score. For instance, when two candidates have been voted for as follows:

John Jones, 1½ votes,
William Brown, 1¼ votes,

the first ticket drawn from the box may be copied upon the tally-paper, (omitting the word "votes,") and then that and succeeding tickets marked down in scores of five toward the right according to the common practice. To the sum of the scores for a candidate fifty per centum will be added at the end of the line. Thus if 80 such tickets have been voted, the count for each candidate will be carried out—80 + 40 = 120 votes. In this case the figures "1½" attached to a candidate's name become a sign of value for the strokes which follow, and may be conveniently enclosed in a circle with a pen. If whole votes alone shall be voted on other tickets for the same candidate, they should be scored on a separate line above or below the other and be carried out and added at the proper place on the right.

THE FILLING OF VACANCIES.

Upon a careful reading of speeches made by John Bright in 1867, at Manchester, at Birmingham, and in the House of Commons, in hostility to cumulative voting and to the limited vote as embodied in the Cairns amendment to the Reform Bill, I became thoroughly convinced of the utter weakness of all

possible objections to minority representation, (as it
was then called.)   A first-class man, laboring with
great earnestness on repeated occasions, was unable
to make good a single objection to reform, and was
compelled in the final debate on the 8th of August,
to plant himself upon purely conservative ground
and insist upon the *novelty* of the proposition before
the House. So far as I can remember, there was
but one point made by him which reached the dignity of appearing plausible, or which seemed to call
for explanation or reply. That was that the new
plans were defective in regard to the filling of vacancies that might happen pending terms of official
service. Supposing, for instance, that the seat of a
member of Parliament from a triangular district—
a district of three members—should become vacant
from any cause pending his term, neither the cumulative or limited vote could be applied at a special
election to the choice of his successor. I admit the
fact in the case supposed, but I deny the objection
based upon it. That objection is wholly misconceived and will disappear upon being submitted to
examination. Mr. Bright did not desire the third
member for Birmingham to be taken by the Tories,
and therefore opposed reform; but his best point,
like all his others, was unworthy of his genius and
his fame. Party interest misled him as it has often
misled other men of equal distinction and mental
power.

  Now as the question of filling casual vacancies,
under reformed voting, has never been discussed in
this country, nor, so far as I know, been examined
abroad, (unless in connection with schemes of repre-

sentation which do not come within the scope of my present discourse,) I shall proceed to speak upon it briefly, and shall incidentally dispose of the Bright objection just mentioned.

In the first place I have to remark that if hereafter casual vacancies shall be filled by popular election and by the majority vote, we shall be in no worse condition than we are now; we shall simply continue, as to such occasional election, the existing rule. In the next place it is to be considered that whenever two or more vacancies shall exist at the same time, the free or limited vote can be applied to an election held for the purpose of filling them. Again, it is evident that most vacancies that will happen, will be of majority members or officers, and that the application of the majority vote to the choice of successors will be perfectly proper and in complete harmony with our plan of reform. But I will take the comparatively rare or unusual case of a minority vacancy standing alone, or the still rarer case of two or more such vacancies (without majority ones) existing at the same time. How shall such minority vacancies be filled? I answer, they can be filled and filled properly either by election or appointment. In many if not most cases appointments may be made for unexpired terms, but whenever possible in any case an appointment should be made from among the voters who shall have voted for the officer or person whose place is to be filled. As an illustration I will read the provision concerning the filling of vacancies contained in the County Commissioner bill introduced into the Senate of Pennsylvania at its last session. After providing for the election of three County Commissioners and three County Auditors, respectively, for three year terms, the fourth section provides as follows :

"Sec. 4. Vacancies in the office of County Commissioner or County Auditor occurring otherwise than by the expiration of a regular term of service, or occasioned or continued by a failure to elect under this act, shall be filled by appointments to be made by the Courts of Quarter Sessions of the Peace of the several counties in which such vacancies shall occur, which appointments shall be for the remaining part or time of any unexpired term to be filled. In the filling of any such vacancy the following rules of selection shall be observed, to wit: *First*, The appointment shall be made from among the qualified electors of the county who shall have voted for the Commissioner or Auditor whose place is to be filled, and *Second*, The Judges of the Court by whom the appointment is to be made shall receive and consider any respectful petition from qualified electors of the county who shall have voted for the Commissioner or Auditor whose place is to be filled, and shall appoint such fit persons so recommended as shall, in their opinion, be most acceptable to the greater part of the electors by whom the Commissioner or Auditor whose place is to be filled was chosen."

The power of appointment for the filling of vacancies may be variously lodged according to the nature of the case or the character of the office to be filled, but no matter where lodged it should always be exercised under a rule of selection similar to that contained in the bill just cited, so that the just division of offices between parties shall be at all times maintained.

But when an appointment cannot well be made to fill a vacancy on account of the magnitude of the office, the long duration of the unexpired term, or because it is difficult in the given case to select a proper appointing power, a popular election to fill the vacancy may be provided for. In such case I would call only upon the voters who had previously voted for the officer or person whose place is to be filled and would confine the right of choice to them. The other voters of the constituency or district ought not to participate in such election for evident reasons and should be excluded. But at this point an objector may say that it will be difficult to distinguish the proper voters from others and to confine the electoral privilege to them. I do not think so. The party position of most men is fully known in their own election districts, and in doubtful cases the right of challenge will guard against improper votes. The official lists of voters taken down at a former election can be referred to for the prevention of fraud, and any one offering to vote may be called upon to prove by his own oath or by other testimony that he voted at such former election for the officer or person whose place is to be filled. Besides, as there will be no struggle between political parties for a majority at such elections, the most fertile of all causes of fraud will be wholly excluded from them. In fact where there shall be but one candidate at such an election, (which will be the ordinary case,) there will be no motive at all for fraud and its existence will be rendered impossible.

But I am quite certain that when the free vote or some similar plan of reform shall come into general use, secret voting will be entirely dispensed with because it will no longer be necessary to the protection of the voter against intimidation and other forms of improper influence. The ballot may remain to us, but it will be an open one—probably in the slip-ticket form—and a large amount of mystery, intrigue, deception and meanness will be expelled from elections. And, by numbering the ballots when voted, or by other means easily applied, it will be possible to prove afterwards beyond dispute for whom any voter cast his votes. Possibly we may come at last to a plan of registering votes which will still more completely or conveniently enable us to classify voters and determine for whom they voted. At all events, by dispensing with the secret vote we shall possess greater facilities than now for the proper polling of votes at special elections.

LOCAL USE OF REFORMED VOTING.

The free vote was first used in an election at Bloomsburg, in this State, on the 12th of April last, when six persons were to be chosen members of the town Council for the ensuing year. The result was that three Democrats and three Republicans were elected. It was again used in the same town on the second Tuesday of the present month in the choice of Constables, Assessors, Assistant Assessors, School Directors, and Town Auditors. Altogether, at the two town elections, seventeen officers have been chosen under the new plan, and they are all good men and are fairly divided between parties. Not one person among the whole six hundred voters of the town is known to have expressed himself against the change, or is believed to be desirous of returning to the old and unfair majority vote. In short, the change has been completely satisfactory and is strongly endorsed by public opinion.

Directors of the Poor for the Bloom Poor District in Columbia county (the district containing one thousand two hundred voters) were also chosen at the October election under the new plan and in a satisfactory manner. The majority elected two and the minority one.

In the county of Northumberland, in Sunbury, Northumberland and other boroughs, the new plan was also tried at the recent election (principally in the choice of Councilmen) and with good and satisfactory results.

Certain advantages of the new plan not foreseen or not foreseen distinctly, appeared in these local elections. In the first place, they showed that the number of candidates at an election will be greatly reduced by the new plan; that in most cases no more persons will run than can be elected, because each party will nominate only the number it has votes to elect. Next, it was shown that blunders in nomination, either as to the number of candidates to be supported or as to individual nominations, could be readily and certainly corrected by the voters at the legal election. Also, that bolting (as it is called) is deprived to a great extent of its mischievous character, bolters being only able to represent themselves by their own votes when their number is adequate, without being able to turn an election upside down or prevent a just division of the offices between parties. It was also clearly shown at those elections that the preparation, polling, counting, and return of fractional votes, in cases where their use was found desirable, was quite simple and convenient, occasioning no difficulty, uncertainty or confusion.

PROGRESS OF REFORM.

The State of New York a few years since used the limited vote in choosing thirty-two delegates at large to her Constitutional Convention. No voter was allowed to vote for more than sixteen. More recently she chose the six Associate Judges of her highest court on the same principle; no voter was allowed to vote for more than four. But though these were steps in the right direction and resulted in fuller representation of the people, it must be acknowledged that the limited vote is an imperfect contrivance and not fitted for extensive use. More wisely instructed, the State of Illinois the present year has adopted the free vote, not only for the election of directors or managers of incorporated companies, as before mentioned, but also for the election of Representatives in her Legislature. They will be chosen biennially, commencing with the year 1872, three being elected together from each senatorial district. In this State, in August last, a respectable convention in favor of minority representation was held at Reading. It adopted proper resolutions and organized committees for future work. The men concerned in that convention and the friends of reform generally in this State, look forward to a Constitutional Convention as the means for securing the main objects they have in view. And they particularly desire that the members of such convention, if one should be called, shall be elected upon a plan of reformed voting, so that the whole people shall be represented in the convention.

Without a convention, however, much can be done. The Legislature has complete power over municipal elections and can reform them at pleasure, and it can also largely improve the representation of the people in the Legislature itself.

In conclusion I will say to all friends of reform, be confident and hopeful of the future. It is well for us "to labor and to wait." Great changes are best made when made deliberately and with due caution; not in passionate heat, but upon cool conviction. Electoral reforms may come slowly, but they are sure to come, for their necessity grows every year more evident.

A SPEECH

DELIVERED IN THE SENATE OF PENNSYLVANIA, ON
MONDAY EVENING, MARCH 27, 1871, UPON
THE BILL ENTITLED

"AN ACT FOR THE FURTHER REGULATION OF BOROUGHS."*

MR. SPEAKER:—I came to this Senate to serve
during my present term with the intention of de-
voting myself particularly to the subject of Electoral
Reform. I thought that the attention of the Representatives of the people assembled in the Legislature should be directed to some fundamental and
searching changes in our electoral system, by which
existing abuses shall be checked or prevented in
future.

Now, sir, in the first place, I propose to call attention to what has been done heretofore in this
State upon this subject of reform, in the direction
indicated by the present bill.

INSPECTORS OF ELECTION.

In the Constitutional Convention of 1837–8, Mr.
Thomas Earle, of the county of Philadelphia, sub-

* The bill upon which the above speech was delivered passed and became a law. Those sections of it which relate to the election of Councilmen, in boroughs, to the support of which the argument of the speech
was directed, will be found at page 229 of this volume.

157

mitted propositions on two occasions, with reference
to the choice of election officers by the people, upon
the plan of what is now known as the limited vote.
On the 27th of June, 1837,* he addressed that Convention at some length in support of his second
proposition. It was then submitted to a vote and
rejected very strongly; by a vote of, I think, over
three to one, and the majority comprised most of the
strong men of the Convention—such men as Woodward, Sergeant, Forward and others. The Convention passed off and nothing was done. At the session of the Legislature in 1839, the Governor of the
Commonwealth called attention in his message to
the subject of electoral reform. He pointed out to
the two Houses that extensive changes had become
necessary in our election laws by reason of the
amendments to the Constitution. He pointed out
the fact that great frauds had taken place at elections in various parts of the Commonwealth, and, in
short, that our electoral system had fallen under reproach and needed amendment. During the course
of the session, Mr. Senator Brown, of Philadelphia
county, turned his attention to this subject, and, in
a Committee of Conference upon the General Election bill of that year, obtained the insertion substantially of the proposition which had been advocated by Mr. Earle, in the Constitutional Convention
the year before, and for which Mr. Brown himself
had voted, he being a member of that Convention.
Well, sir, that proposition will be found among our
statutes as one of the most important and useful provisions of the election act of 1839. It provides that

* 3 Convention Debates, 173.

each voter, at the time when election officers are to be chosen, shall vote for but one person for Inspector of elections during the coming year, and that the two candidates highest in vote shall be declared elected. Then follows a provision that each Inspector, so chosen, shall appoint a clerk. The Judge of the election; the only additional officer, is chosen under the old plan of the majority vote. That was in 1839, and it is to be noted that upon debate, this reform was carried in the Senate by a vote of only fifteen to eleven.

But this law as to the manner of choosing election officers has continued to the present time, a period of over thirty years, and it is well known that it is most salutary in operation and most satisfactory to the people. I do not know what the whole number of election districts in the State is at the present time; in 1838 the number a little exceeded one thousand. I suppose the number now exceeds two thousand, and it happens under this law that in nineteen-twentieths of the election districts of the Commonwealth, each of the two political parties into which our people are ordinarily divided, has an Inspector in the Election Board, and also a Clerk, and that the majority has the Judge. Sir, it is this provision of the law that has preserved our elections from degeneracy and disgrace. If it were recalled from our statute book, and we should apply to the choice of election officers our ordinary plan of voting, we might expect an enormous increase of fraudulent voting throughout the State, with consequent degeneracy of our political system, and to a great extent discredit would be cast upon the political institutions under which we live.

JURY COMMISSIONERS.

Some years since, complaint began to be made in various parts of the State that jurymen were not fairly selected by County Commissioners and Sheriffs to whom the law committed their selection. In some counties they were taken, it was alleged, exclusively from the majority party in the county— the County Commissioners and Sheriffs representing the majority and selecting their political friends almost exclusively, from year to year. Appeals were made to the Legislature, and several local acts were passed for particular counties, providing a new arrangement, an election by the people of two Jury Commissioners in the same manner in which Inspectors of Election are chosen under the election act of 1839. Finally the Governor recommended the extension of this plan to the whole Commonwealth. This recommendation was made, I believe, by Governor Curtin. A general statute was passed and approved by Governor Geary in April, 1867, applying this plan of Jury Commissioners to the whole State, and every Senator present is familiar with it. Since that time throughout the State we have had elections for those officers upon the plan of the limited vote. The statute assigns to President Judges some duties in connection with the Jury Commissioners. In many of the judicial districts, the President Judges declined to act, or did not act for some time after the law was passed. They thought, and I suppose thought properly, that they ought to have no part in the selection of men who were to serve in their courts as jury-men; that it was a duty which ought not to be charged upon them, because it was to some extent inconsistent with their judicial duties and with that entire independence which ought to exist between the Judges and jury who are to try the disputes and differences of the citizen. But presently it came to be understood that in all cases under that law jury-men would be divided equally between political parties; that in a county where there was nearly a two-thirds majority the minority would have an equal number, which seemed unfair; and so, from time to time appeals have been made to President Judges to take part and assist their political friends to get their full share, or perhaps more than their share of jurymen.

One of the President Judges described to me the performance on one occasion when he first attended to select jurors. It was in a county with the inhab-itants of which he was not very familiar, he having previously resided in an adjoining county; but he was told that he must assist in filling the wheel and he did so. He found a Democratic and a Repub-lican Jury Commissioner sitting on each side of a table, and each of them with a hat full of names. The proceeding was after this fashion: The Demo-cratic Commissioner reached into his hat and took out a name, and put it into the box or wheel; the Republican Commissioner did the same from his hat, and then the Judge, who happened to be a Repub-lican, reached into the Republican's hat and took out a name and put it into the wheel; and at the end

11

of the proceeding the Judge did not know a single
name that he had put into the wheel, but the duty
charged upon him under the law had been, after a
fashion, discharged.

What ought to have been done in 1867? Why,
I insist that the bill which is lying upon your table,
introduced early in the session, ought to have passed
instead of the Jury Commissioner act. That provides that in the election of County Commissioners
all the voters of a county shall be enabled to represent themselves by their own votes; that in all ordinary cases the majority shall be enabled to elect
two Commissioners and the minority one, and then
that the board, so made up, shall be charged with
this duty of selecting jurymen, as formerly. We
would, by that arrangement, be enabled to dispense
with two unnecessary officers—the Jury Commissioners—and we would also be enabled to dispense
with this clumsy provision in relation to the participation of President Judges in the selection of jury-
men. We would have the people fairly represented
in courts of justice whenever issues of fact were to
be tried, and every object designed to be obtained
by the act of 1867 would be fully accomplished.
That, by the way, is only one of the advantages, as
I think, of this County Commissioner bill which is
upon your files. But I proceed:

LOCAL ACTS.

At the last session the two houses of the Legislature passed ten or twelve local bills, at my instance,
applying reformed voting to certain municipal elections in the counties of Columbia and Northumber-

land. A proposition and arrangement which you
have in the third section of the pending bill in relation to boroughs, was applied to the eight boroughs
in Northumberland county, to the town of Bloomsburg and the borough of Berwick in Columbia
county, and to two poor districts in those counties.
Substantially the free vote was applied to them, and
it has had successful operation.

BILLS PROPOSED.

This constitutes the legislation which has heretofore been had in this particular line of reform. At
this session the Senate has passed a bill applying
the free vote to the choice of Directors of Common
Schools, and now it is asked to pass this bill in relation to the election of Councilmen of boroughs
throughout the Commonwealth. The provision is
that in all boroughs incorporated under or pursuant
to general laws, and in all boroughs heretofore established by special acts which may come under the
general laws, there shall be six Councilmen, and in
selecting them each voter may distribute or concentrate his six votes according to his own judgment,
without legal restraint. Now, comparatively described, this provision amounts to this : That, whereas, the existing law, after assigning to the voter
his six votes, compels him to distribute them singly
among six candidates, this bill will withdraw that
limitation, and allow him to distribute them according to his own judgment, without legal compulsion.
Now, sir, the fundamental principle of our government is that men, or at least American men, are
competent to self-government. Our system is said

to be a system of self-government—that the citizen is able to choose and determine for himself in all matters of discretion where strong reasons of public interest do not interpose to demand legal regulation. What the supporters of this bill ask is, not that the law shall be extended, not that legal regulation shall be increased, not that the law-making power shall interfere, and do more than it has heretofore done, but that it shall withdraw itself from the citizen, and allow him a larger measure of freedom and of choice, in strict accordance with the fundamental principles of our government.

OBJECTIONS CONSIDERED—CHOICE OF MEMBERS OF CONGRESS.

Now, sir, what objections are there to this plan of voting? Why the Senator from Greene [Mr. Purman] the other day went over some of those that may naturally occur to a candid and reasonable mind upon first approaching this subject. · He stated them, and he stated them in a fair and proper manner, suggesting the line of argument which it is necessary for me to pursue in vindication of this bill. He suggests that if this plan of voting were applied to the choice of members of Congress there would be no districting of this or any other State; that the members would be elected by general ticket throughout the whole Commonwealth; and he seemed to apprehend that there would be some difficulty in executing such a plan. To this I make two replies: I say, in the first place, that the districting of States is not at all incompatible with this plan of voting; it comports with it perfectly. You

might have a plan of plural though not of single
districts. But there would be no difficulty if members were elected by general ticket in the whole
State. Representation of different localities in the
State even could be easily secured. The reasons for
this opinion I have stated upon another occasion.

CHOICE OF MEMBERS OF THE LEGISLATURE.

Again, the Senator seems to suppose that it would
be necessary, if this plan of voting were applied to
the choice of members of the Legislature, that the
State should be divided into four Senatorial districts
for the choice of Senators, and into four Representative districts for the choice of Representatives.
Well, sir, I never heard that suggested before. It
never occurred to me that such arrangement would
be selected if this plan were applied. The Senator
will find, by referring to the present constitution of
the State of Illinois, that it provides that each Senatorial District in that State shall select three Representatives upon the plan of the free vote. The result is that in that State the Legislature will form
fifty-one Senatorial districts, and then their duty of
apportioning members of the Legislature will be
concluded. By the Constitution, while each Senatorial District chooses one member of the Senate, it
also chooses three members of the House, and each
voter may give his three votes to one, two or three
candidates for representative, so that the majority
will have two and the minority one. Probably, as
the result, the Democratic representation in Northern
Illinois will be largely increased, while in Southern
Illinois the Republican voters will be emancipated;

they will send their share of members to the Legislature. That case illustrates the manner in which a State may be districted, or in which representatives to the Legislature may be chosen by districts under this plan of voting.

If the Senator had referred to Mr. Medill's amendment, introduced into the convention of Illinois, with reference to the election of Senators, he would have ascertained that a very convenient method could have been applied to their election by the free vote. The Senator's suggestion of this difficulty about districts reminds me of what occurred in 1869. About the month of October, of that year, I had occasion to address a gentleman in the State of Illinois, and mentioned to him this subject of reformed voting as one that would possess interest for their convention which was soon to meet. He answered by saying that he did not see how they could possibly apply such a plan to the election of members of the Legislature. [Their Legislature was to be composed of a large number of members; as it meets only every second year, they can very well afford to have large numbers in each House; there are advantages, or supposed advantages, in large numbers of members in legislative bodies.] He did not see, he could not understand how a plan of reformed voting could be applied to the choice of fifty-one Senators, and to the choice of one hundred and fifty-three Representatives. He was at that time laboring under the same doubts which occurred to the Senator from Greene [Mr. Purman]. Now, sir, that same gentleman went down to the convention in Springfield shortly afterwards, and made a

motion to appoint a Committee on Electoral and
Representative Reform, of which he was made
Chairman; and he was the leading man concerned
in putting into the constitution of the State the very
provision in reference to the choice of Representatives to which I have referred, and also other important provisions applying the same plan to the
election of directors of incorporated companies, and
to the election of judges in the city of Chicago.
This supposed difficulty of districting a State for the
purpose of applying a reformed plan of voting in
Legislative elections is quite illusory. Districts to
which this plan shall be applicable are more easily
made than districts in ordinary apportionment laws,
and if we were compelled, under the constitution, to
so district our State that all the people should have
representation by this plan of voting, we would not
have as much difficulty as we have now under our
present system of gerrymandering and disfranchisement. Let me say to the Senator that we get rid of
the great difficulty and evil of gerrymandering by the
free vote; we cut it up by the roots, or, at least, we
reduce it to its smallest dimensions.

THE MAJORITY SHOULD RULE.

The Senator says the majority should rule. Well,
that is true. Mr. Jefferson said so—that absolute
acquiescence in the will of the majority, fairly pronounced, was a vital principle of our system, or one,
at least, which must be applied and carried out constantly, or our experiment of free government would
end in failure. To that I assent most fully. But
Mr. Mill long ago pointed out the fact that the

majority vote, as heretofore existing in Great Britain and in the United States, does not secure the will of the majority—that, in point of fact, the rule which we get from it, as we apply it, is a rule of the majority of the majority, or often of a small portion only of the people. In the first place, at the popular elections you count out all the minority voters; you count or allow only majority votes and put aside the rest. A large part of the people, then, are virtually disfranchised; they have no further voice in the government beyond the giving of fruitless votes, which, after being scored down, are in effect scored out again. Then the representatives so chosen, meet in a legislative body, and when any measure of policy is to be voted upon, the majority rule is applied again, and the minority of the legislative body ignored; so that the majority of the legislative body pronounces the rule of law for the citizen.

Besides, in practice in this country, legislative majorities, upon all measures of a political character at least, and many others, act under a system of consultation—that is, under what we call the caucus rule. The representatives of the majority in the representative body meet together, and subject their wills to the decision of a majority of themselves; and that caucus decision, concocted and settled in secret, becomes the law of the State. The caucus is in the third degree removed from the people, and there are three eliminations of popular power before the law is enacted. Therefore I say you do not necessarily secure the rule of the majority under your majority vote, because the majority of the legislative body, made up as I have described it, and acting as it does, may very likely represent only a minority of the people out of doors, and such, in point of fact, is frequently the case.

Under reformed voting what do you do? You do not destroy votes given at the popular elections; you count them all; you take them and respect them; you consider them as sacred and inviolate and give to them full and complete effect. And what is the result? Substantially that all the electors are represented and obtain due voice and influence in the enactment of the laws. Then, in the legislative body you have all the people represented. Each voter, except in rare cases, has his representative in place on whose attention he has a claim and to whom he can speak as to a friend. There is thorough representation; all your people are heard. How widely different is the case now! and because it is different this evil of local or private legislation is beginning to be exclaimed against all over the State; and if you do not take steps to correct it, there will be a movement of popular power that will reach over you and beyond you, and through a change of the fundamental law will effectually correct the evil.

The rule of the majority! I agree to the principle; we propose to apply it in this bill. We take the vote in the legislative body, and there, the will of the majority is appropriately pronounced, and it can be properly pronounced nowhere else. It will take effect with a sanction that it does not now possess, because when all the people have been heard in the enactment of a law or regulation, they will very likely be satisfied with it; and besides, there will be greater security for the fairness and wisdom of such law or regulation in the fuller consideration to which it will be subjected.

BALANCE-OF-POWER PARTIES.

The Senator says that under this plan of voting all the little side parties of the country would be represented and heard. As it is now under the old majority vote they are kept out of Congress, out of Legislatures, and out of other positions in the Government. Because they are a small number in any given constituency, you apply to them the majority vote, and you extinguish them or push them away from the high places of power, and do not allow their voices to be heard there. The Senator seems to think that this is an advantage; he seems to think it was proper in the case of the Abolitionists, who were continually repressed by the control and discipline of the old political parties, and were kept down in that way. He might have extended his remark to the South and have said that Union men there were kept out of the local Legislatures and kept out of Congress, by the discreet handling of the majority vote in the hands of the extreme leaders of the South. The minority elements in the North and South were kept down by the majority vote; but, sir, you did not destroy the fire of sectionalism by your repression; it burned and glowed underneath the hollow system of your majority, until it burst out into an uncontrollable flame in which we were all involved. How would it have been, if, instead of repressing them, you had allowed

them to be represented in proportion to their numbers, and allowed everybody in the country to see
the growth of opinion, and your statesmen to prepare securities against it? But you pushed that
danger out of sight as much as possible, and shut
your eyes to it as long as you could. Nevertheless
it was irrepressible; in spite of your majority vote,
the war came and ran its terrific course for four years.

How is it? Here you have a small body of men
in a State, whose single issue, whose single object is
very important to them, so that they will vote with
reference to it as the Abolitionists did. They make
their single issue superior to all others that engage
the public mind. After a time they get strength
enough to hold the balance of power between parties, as the Abolitionists did in many States. When
they get to that stage of growth what do they do?
They say to a political party, " do our work and we
will give you power; affiliate yourselves with us
and you shall triumph; repel us, reject us, and you
go into a minority or remain in a minority in the
State; your leading men will be struck down at all
elections." Why, in Massachusetts, the Democrats
allied themselves with the free soil element and
elected Charles Sumner to the Senate of the United
States; that element held the balance of power, and
the Democracy were seduced into that act of folly.

The Whig party in State after State was seduced
into a similar kind of alliance subsequently, until it
became utterly debauched and eventually gave up
its own organization and took a creed in which this
balance-of-power party had its choice principles inserted, and thus the movement went forward until

war came. I insist then, that the best thing you
can do in order to secure the peace of the country,
is to give all your citizens just representation in the
government. If I had time I would go on and
prove, as I think I could, that our late war would
never have occurred if there had been an honest,
fair, and wise system of electoral action in this
country—if all the people had been enabled to represent themselves thoroughly in government by
their own votes, after the fashion or upon the principle of a free-handed and just exercise of their
electoral power.

CORRUPTION OF ELECTIONS.

There was one other point of objection mentioned
by the Senator from Greene [Mr. Purman] to which
I must refer. It was that in cases that might arise
under this bill, there would be greater opportunities
or facilities for corruption than under the old plan
of voting; that a corrupt man or one desirous of
corrupting electors, when he purchased a voter,
would get his whole six votes instead of getting but
one vote, and that the tendency of this new plan
would be to increase corruption instead of diminish-
ing it. Let me answer this point by a few figures.

The town of Bloomsburg polled in 1868 six hundred and forty-six votes for President, of which
Seymour had three hundred and twenty-nine, and
Grant three hundred and seventeen, being a Democratic majority of twelve votes. That town elects
six members of a town Council under the plan of
reformed voting. Upon the vote of 1868 three
Democratic town Councilmen would be elected.

each receiving six hundred and fifty-eight votes,
and three Republican Councilmen would be elected,
each receiving six hundred and thirty-four votes—
that is, each party can obtain three of the six as a
matter of course under this plan of voting, and
voting as the people do in that town, the political
candidates would have the respective numbers
which I have mentioned. Suppose a volunteer candidate desires to interrupt the regular course of an
election in that town, and proceeds to debauch voters
in order to appropriate their votes to himself. If
he takes his votes from the majority or the Democracy of the town, he is required, in order to
succeed, to purchase eighty-three voters; if from
the minority, he must obtain eighty; if he obtain
his votes equally from both parties, it would be
necessary for him to get ninety-two voters; if he is
to obtain his votes in that corrupt manner as against
the regular parties running a joint ticket, he must
obtain ninety-three voters. Now, observe two
things. In the first place, the supposed corruption
of the voters can only extend to the election of *one*
Councilman out of six. The man who buys these
voters can only affect the election to the extent of
one-sixth of the general result. Again, in no ordinary
case, and hardly in any case, can he be expected to
obtain so many voters by corrupt or improper means.
The number is too great to be seduced, particularly as
they are to be taken away from their party allegiance
and party associations. They must break over party
lines and desert party nominations in order to prostitute themselves to the purpose of the volunteer.
When you come to look into this point you must per-

ceive that the danger of seduction is infinitely small
and worthy of but little consideration. What I have
always said and now say is, that reformed voting
reduces the evil of corruption at elections to its
minimum. Of course it will not take hold of
human nature and change it; it will not reorganize
the hearts or intellects of the people. I assign to it
no such complete renovating power; but what I do
insist upon is that it will reduce this evil of corrupting voters to its lowest possible quantity, or to use
the scientific term, to its minimum.

Now take the old plan of voting in the same town
and with the same vote given to each party respectively. Suppose this volunteer desires to defeat some
man nominated by the majority; he has some private job of his own; he wants a street laid out
through his property or wants a street closed, or
water-works established; he desires something done
that will promote his interests, and aims to defeat a
certain candidate to that end. What has he to do?
Buy thirteen majority voters and it is done! There
is a majority of twelve in this case—in the case
taken. He has only to corrupt thirteen men and
his object will be accomplished. Under the majority vote thirteen taken from the majority will
change the result of the election, and he may easily
draw off that small number as a volunteer. Suppose
again, that this man is a member of the minority in
the town, and he desires to be elected to the Council
for some selfish purpose; he says to his party
friends, "nominate me and I will spend money
enough on this election to secure my success, and
not only my own but also the success of five other

candidates to be placed on our ticket, and we will take away from the opposite party their whole representation in the local legislature of the town." His party friends assent; the ticket of six is made up as proposed, the proposer himself being one. What has he to do under the majority vote in order to elect himself and his colleagues? Buy seven votes only! The democratic majority in the town is but twelve. Cannot seven or more loose voters be found in any party out of a total of two or three hundred? He seduces seven voters, and he puts himself into the council, with colleagues to assist him in his ulterior designs. If they put the town in debt, you cannot help it; if they persecute their political enemies in the town, the injustice must be borne; a little money in the hands of a base man has secured immunity to the evil. Such elections as this are occurring continually throughout the State in boroughs and other municipalities, under the majority vote. Under the free vote in Bloomsburg you must seduce eighty to a hundred men, in order to affect the choice of councilmen to the extent of one member in six! Under the old plan seven corrupted voters may change the whole election.

But there is an additional consideration. The party assailed by the corrupt scheme just mentioned come together and say, "Are we to be cheated? No! We have money also. We must 'fight fire with fire.'" And so both parties spend money on the election. Year by year this evil goes on and increases. Your political system is becoming cankered at the very core, and gentlemen stand here hesitating and doubting whether electoral reform is necessary, and whether a man who talks for it and works for it is not a little visionary or at least somewhat ahead of the times.

There is another thing that is sometimes done. Coalitions are common; we have what are called "Citizens'," "People's" or "Union" tickets set up. They are very well in some cases, but are often set up in the interest of some man, or of a few. A man of the majority is offended at what his party has done; perhaps they have done him nothing but sheer justice; they have declined to put him into office, and he has a dozen men subject to his influence, or he has money, and he goes to the opposite party—the minority—and he says to them, "Put me on your ticket, and I will elect it." Or if he does not ask to be put upon the ticket himself, he asks that some personal friend of his shall be put on, and that pledges shall be given in favor of something he wants done. Then by turning over a small number of voters from his own party to the other, the coalition is made to succeed.

I insist, therefore, that these points of objection, or of doubt rather, in reference to this new plan, do not condemn it or render its adoption unwise or improper.

REFORM IN NOMINATIONS.

[Mr. B. proceeded to speak upon the application of reformed voting in the choice of delegates to nominating bodies, and particularly to County Conventions, describing the various plans upon which such bodies were chosen, and insisted that the same remedy which would purify and improve the legal elections should be extended to the voluntary or primary ones also. He strongly condemned the Crawford County plan of nomination, and expressed his preference for that recently adopted in the County of Columbia, under which there was representation of election districts in proportion to their party vote, and complete freedom to the electors in casting their votes for delegates. He concluded by stating that he regarded the bill under consideration as a step in the course of reform— as one well calculated to have a considerable effect in the improvement of municipal government and to familiarize the people with a new but effectual and necessary plan for the renovation of popular elections.]

CONCLUDING DEBATE.

In Senate, March 29, 1871.—Agreeably to order the Senate resumed the third reading and consideration of Senate bill entitled " An act for the further regulations of boroughs."

Mr. Buckalew. Mr. Speaker, if any gentleman desires to make remarks upon this bill I will give place to him; if not, I desire to say a few words and then have the vote taken. I desire to explain that this bill does not apply to any borough in the State established by special law. It only applies to those that have been or may be incorporated under the act of 1851, or the prior act of 1834. Nor does it apply in many cases where, by special legislation, particular arrangements have been made in boroughs for the selection of Councilmen. There are a large number of laws which provide, for instance, that where there are one, two, three or more wards, each ward shall be entitled to elect a member of Council, or more members than one, for one, two or three year terms; so that it often happens that only one Councilman is voted for by the same body of electors. This bill does not disturb such arrangements or affect the manner of voting in such cases. It

12

applies only to those boroughs which exist under general laws, and to those hereafter established or brought under those laws.

I desire to add another explanation, and that is, that this plan of voting is very different from that proposed by Mr. Hare, in a work of some celebrity. He proposes a plan of personal representation by means of preferential voting, as it is called, and he announces his leading object to be to emancipate voters from the domination or control of party organization; to enable them to vote without reference to those associations heretofore known in Great Britain and in this country as political parties. I am not for his plan; and I desire it to be distinctly understood that the free vote points to an object quite different from his. This plan now before us, assumes the existence in political society of political parties, and it assumes that they will exist hereafter. It is simply a proposition by which political parties can represent themselves conveniently and justly by their own votes. It does not strike at party organization. In fact, Mr. Speaker, I agree entirely with the main portion of the argument submitted by yourself [Mr. Wallace] to the Senate the other evening, in which it was insisted that political parties were a necessity in free governments—at least that they were inevitable wherever free play was permitted to the political activity of the citizen. This doctrine was laid down by Mr. Madison perhaps as briefly and clearly as it ever was, in the forty-ninth number of the *Federalist*, in which he said that "an extinction of parties necessarily implies either a universal alarm for the public safety, or an absolute extinction of liberty." Now, sir, I think that reformers who, in the present stage of civilization, look to political arrangements independent of party organization, must necessarily be visionary and their schemes impracticable; and I am one of the last men who would assent to the adoption of any new system based upon their ideas. I take political parties as I find them; I take political society, divided fundamentally upon great government issues, and I assume that so long as free play is permitted to the human mind in political affairs there will be parties, and government must be organized and administered with reference to them, and that all attempts based upon an assumption that it is possible to conduct public affairs without parties, are idle and vain; in fine, that all attempts based on that idea must result in complete and disastrous failure. No such object has been proposed by persons in this country, or beyond the ocean, who have supported this plan of the free vote or cumulative voting. All they propose is to put into the hands of political parties an instrument by which they can act justly at elections, by which they can obtain for themselves a fair share of power by their own votes and by which it will be impossible for them to take from their fellow-citizens any portion of political power which belongs to *them;* by which the principle of gambling (as I call it) shall be extracted from elections, and by which the motive for spending money in order to obtain the majority at elections shall be taken away.

I think this explanation was due to the Senate, and to those who pay attention to our debates, be-

cause some distrust or question has been created in
the minds of gentlemen who imagine that the new
plan proposed here is identical with or similar in
principle to the reform proposed by Mr. Hare, which
is so complicated, and so far beyond the convenience
of political society that there is good reason for opposition to it; or at least for distrusting it as an expedient in the management of elections.

Mr. Speaker, I shall not pursue the discussion of
this subject any further, as it seems to be admitted
that this particular bill is but a reasonable experiment—a reasonable experiment by which the merits
and true character of this plan of voting can be ascertained and settled before the people.

[NOTE: Upon the conclusion of Mr. Buckalew's remarks,
Mr. White and Mr. Osterhout addressed the Senate in support
of the bill, which then passed the Senate without a call of the
yeas and nays.

Subsequently, upon its consideration in the House of Representatives, the following letter in strong indorsement of the
change proposed to be made by it in the manner of electing
Councilmen in boroughs, was presented by Mr. Strang, a leading member of the House, and read by the Clerk:

BLOOMSBURG, May 8, 1871.

HON. B. B. STRANG:—DEAR SIR: Observing that on your
motion the session of the House on Wednesday evening of this
week is to be devoted to the consideration of the Borough Supplement bill, which among other useful changes provides for
the introduction to a certain extent of the free vote into borough elections, we are induced to address to you a few earnest
words recommendatory of the bill. In our judgment the passage of that bill will secure more of reform and improvement
in boroughs than any other measure which the Legislature can
enact, while it will familiarize the people with the new plan of
voting, which has been so successful and satisfactory in our re-

cent Bloomsburg elections. After having carefully observed
the working of the new plan when put into practical operation,
as it has been here at three elections, we are ready to approve
it and to declare our opinion that it possesses great merit.
It is readily comprehended by voters when they come to de-
posit ballots. It is of complete convenience in all cases, and it
is just in its operation, giving to every considerable interest
representation according to its relative strength. In addition
to these valuable qualities possessed by no other system ever
adopted in this State, the tendency of the new plan is to check,
if not wholly prevent, improper combinations and corrupt
practices at elections, and its certain effect must be to produce
reformed administration in municipal affairs. These, with
many other considerations which have, no doubt, suggested
themselves to your mind, induce us to hope that your efforts to
procure the passage of the bill through the House will be
crowned with success.

With great respect yours, &c.,

WILLIAM ELWELL,

President Judge.

D. A. BECKLEY,

Editor *Republican.*

H. L. DIEFFENBACH,

Editor *Columbian.*]

LETTER TO SECRETARY JORDAN.

THE REPRESENTATION OF SUCCESSIVE MAJORITIES.

To FRANCIS JORDAN, *Secretary of the Commonwealth of Pennsylvania.*

SIR:—In a letter of yours recently published you enumerate the several subjects which will be proper for consideration in the approaching Constitutional Convention of this State, and among others " Minority Representation" as one. This term "Minority Representation" is inaccurate and misleading as applied to the several plans of electoral reform which have been proposed in this country and partially applied by statutory enactments in this and in other States and notably by Constitutional amendment in the State of Illinois. No one proposes the representation of minorities by the limited, cumulative, or free vote, or by list or preferential voting, as those several plans have been explained, advocated, and partially applied in Europe and in the United States. They are all plans for the representation of successive majorities in plural elections, and all of them are intended to apply the majority principle of government more completely and justly than ever before. Let us not be misled by words ill understood, or perverted from their true signification, nor by reasoning which while pertinent to the election of a single person may be quite inapplicable to the election of several or many.

It is said, and the remark is quite true in a general sense, that ours is a system of self-government, but no plan of representation ever devised can make it such completely and beyond the possibility of a disfranchisement of some members of the electoral population. We must content ourselves with an approach to a standard of absolute perfection, without indulging hopes of ever reaching it by the utmost exertion of our powers. But we must approach it as nearly as we can, or we will be false to the principles we profess and subject ourselves to just reproach from the friends of free government in all lands. Our country is new and our experiment and trial of free institutions is being made not only upon a grand scale, but under conditions more favorable for success than ever before existed in the whole history of the human race.

The more complete representation of the people in government is, simply stated, the object of those who advocate electoral reform upon either of the plans before mentioned; but it is an entire mistake to assume that they intend to subordinate the greater to the less in any of the arrangements they propose, or to subvert or impair any principle heretofore accepted as sound and just in republican government. On the contrary, they adhere to the principle of majority government with admirable fidelity and give to it new, useful, and extended operation and effect. They represent more persons—disfranchise fewer ones—and cut off the main source of electoral corruption, by carrying the majority principle further than it has ever been carried and placing a power for its effectual enforcement in the hands of the people themselves.

The force of these general remarks will be best exhibited by an illustration of the principle of extended representation to which they refer, and for such illustration I will take the case of Bloomsburg—my own town—where four elections have been held under the plan of the free vote. The town contains, say, 612 voters, 312 of whom are Democrats and 300 Republicans. (These are not far from the exact numbers as shown at recent elections.)

A President of the town Council is to be elected annually who is the principal executive officer of the town as well as President of the Council. If the 312 Democratic voters unite in support of a candidate he will be elected, and properly elected, upon the sound principle that a greater number shall be preferred to a less in the assignment of representation. A very few voters in this case turn the scale, but the result is perfectly just. There is but one majority to be considered and that in favor of the successful candidate.

Next, two Assessors of taxes are to be elected annually, and here the free vote comes into play and secures their division between parties. Each voter is permitted to give one vote to each of two candidates, or two votes to one. Each party, of course, will run but one candidate, because they can elect no more, and the second majority in the town is represented as well as the first. The figures are as follows: Divide 612 (the whole vote) by 2, (the number of assessors,) and we obtain a ratio, or number of voters for an assessor, of 306. Give the first assessor to the first majority of 312 Democrats and deduct the ratio; we have then left, unrepresented, but 6 Democrats to 300 Republicans, and the free vote carries the second assessor to this second, or Republican majority. How much better this is than giving both the assessors to the first majority! Here but 6 voters are unrepresented instead of 300. And in practical government a clear advantage is gained; for the possible spite, partiality or incompetency of one assessor is checked or corrected by the other, and the chances of fair play in the valuations of property in the town are increased.

A similar and salutary division of officers takes place annually in the choice of two school directors and two constables, and triennially in the choice of two assistant assessors.

But in the election of three persons the improvement introduced by the new plan is still more evident than in the case of two. The numbers will run: Ratio, 204; first Dem. majority 312; second Rep. maj. 300; third Dem. maj. 108, and the general result will stand 2 to 1 in favor of the party having the preponderance upon the total vote. The disfranchisement of Republican voters will be reduced from 300 to 96, and this by simply permitting each voter to cast his three votes for one, two or three candidates as he shall think fit. In Bloomsburg three town Auditors are elected together every third year.

Take next the case of the annual election of six

Councilmen. The ratio for a Councilman will be 102 and the five successive majorities after the first will all be represented by the free vote. Although no calculation of them will be made at the election such will be the inevitable result; for as each voter may bestow his six votes upon any number of candidates less than six, each party will run but three, all of whom will be elected and but six voters in the whole population will be unrepresented instead of 300. Here we have a very nearly complete representation of all the voters of the town by following the majority principle at each successive stage of the distribution.

The exclusive representation of first majorities at plural elections is a stupid misapplication of a just principle—a crude, unjust and pernicious rule, the inevitable effect of which, if continued, will be the destruction of republican government. For it produces violent struggles between parties and candidates for a preponderance of vote, with constantly increasing corruption at elections and demoralization of the people. These evils cannot be cured or corrected by mere preachment while their cause is left in full operation. We must take away or greatly reduce the *motive* for corrupting voters in order to introduce reform which shall be effectual and lasting, and this will be accomplished when we provide that all interests in political society, of any considerable magnitude, may represent themselves in government by their own votes and in proportion to their numbers, without resort to corruption or other means of undue influence.

Nov. 30, 1871.

THE CHOICE

OF

PRESIDENTIAL ELECTORS.

A SPEECH DELIVERED IN THE SENATE OF THE UNITED STATES, FEBRUARY 17, 1869.*

[In Senate, January 28, 1869, Mr. Buckalew, by unanimous consent, introduced a Joint Resolution (Sen. Res. No. 209) proposing an amendment to the Constitution of the United States in relation to the manner of choosing electors of President and Vice-President of the United States, which on his motion was referred to the select Committee on Representative Reform. On the following day Mr. Morton reported the Joint Resolution without amendment, stating that the report of the Committee in its favor was unanimous. (*Globe*, 674–704.) That Resolution will be found at length in this volume, *ante*, page 104, in the general report of the Committee on Representative Reform as made to the Senate on the second of March following. February 9, House Joint Resolution No. 402, proposing the Fifteenth Amendment to the Constitution of the United States in relation to colored suffrage being under consideration in the Senate in Committee of the Whole, Mr. Morton moved to amend by adding the above amendment, reported by him as an additional amendment to the Constitution to be numbered xvi. His motion was lost, yeas 27, nays 29. Afterward, however, the same day, the House Resolution having been reported to the Senate and being under further consideration, he renewed his amendment and it was carried after debate by a vote of 37 to 19. A motion to reconsider it

* *Congressional Globe*, 3d Sess. 40th Cong., 1287.

was lost, and the Joint Resolution was returned to the House
with that and other amendments. (*Globe*, pp. 1041 to 1044.)
Subsequently, on the 17th February, the House having non-
concurred in the Senate Amendments, those amendments
underwent further consideration and debate, when the following speech was delivered by Mr. Buckalew against receding
from the Morton amendment.]

Mr. BUCKALEW. The Senator from Massachusetts [Mr. Sumner] on a former occasion pronounced a strong denunciation of electoral colleges
for the choice of President and Vice President of
the United States. In that he uttered the voice of
public opinion everywhere, long formed, about
which there is no dispute. These colleges are badly
constituted; they do not operate well nor to accomplish the purpose of their original institution.
With reference to all that I think there is a general
agreement. But the Senator went on to make another remark, and that was that he preferred a direct vote by the people of the United States for
candidates for these great offices of President and
Vice President.

Sir, he followed the lead of great men in expressing that opinion or desire. President Jackson made
a recommendation of a change of the Constitution
to secure such a popular vote, I think, in six annual
messages. It was a favorite question of reform with
the late Senator Benton. I believe you, sir, [Mr.
Wade,] also a few years ago introduced the question
in the Senate, and had a formal proposition for
amending the Constitution of the United States considered here.

Now, Mr. President, theoretically it is understood

through the country that the people do choose their President themselves, that they vote for him, and the machinery of the Electoral College is looked upon as surplusage, unnecessary—as the Senator from ·Massachusetts expresses it, "a sham." It is thought to be a thing superfluous, a piece of machinery established by the Constitution which the people have outgrown; that it is in point of fact obsolete, and that the people themselves do, after a fashion, vote for the candidates for President and Vice President of the United States.

Sir, this is a very incorrect opinion. The people do not vote for President and Vice President of the United States, and the votes they cast for electors to perform that function to cast actual votes for the election of President and Vice President do not accomplish necessarily the object for which they are given. I showed some days since, when this subject was before the Senate, some startling statistics to prove this. Among other facts then shown were the facts that in 1860 it required 114,596 popular votes to obtain an elector for Mr. Douglas, who was one of the candidates for President, while it required only 15,144 to obtain an elector for Mr. Bell, one of the other candidates. The figures also show that Mr. Douglas, who was the second candidate · before the people, who received 1,375,157 votes, was the lowest of all the four candidates in the electoral colleges, so that if there had been a slight disturbance of the actual vote as it was given in a few States, by which the election would have been sent to the House of Representatives—it came nearly going there anyhow—Mr. Douglas, the second can-

didate before the people in the number of votes
polled, would have been ruled out of the House altogether, and the choice of that House would have
been between Mr. Lincoln, Mr. Breckinridge, and
Mr. Bell; Breckinridge receiving 847,953 popular
votes, (independent of South Carolina,) Bell
590,631, and Douglas 1,375,157. What would
have been the result? Why, sir, that House would
have chosen—

Mr. WILSON. Will the Senator explain how it
would be that Mr. Douglas would have been ruled
out? The Constitution, if I understand it, requires
the House to choose from the four highest candidates.

Mr. BUCKALEW. The three highest candidates.

Mr. WILSON. Four.

Mr. BUCKALEW. Three. So, in 1824, Mr. Clay
was ruled out of the House because Jackson, Adams,
and Crawford were above him; he was the fourth
man. Infallibly that House in 1860, if by a mere
accident there had been a few votes changed in a
few States, would have made John Bell or John C.
Breckinridge President of the United States. They
could not have elected Mr. Douglas if they had
desired.

Mr. EDMUNDS. Will the Senator permit me to
ask him, for information, a question?

Mr. BUCKALEW. If it relates to this precise
point.

Mr. EDMUNDS. I should like to have him explain how that happened—whether it was in connection with the fact that in the slave States a much
fewer number of votes, on account of the slaves being

represented in the result, accomplished the election of an elector, and whether, therefore, Bell and Breckinridge, carrying more of the slave States than Douglas got votes in the Northern States, did not come in on that theory?

Mr. BUCKALEW. Undoubtedly that affected the question to a certain extent, but it does not account for the great part of the discrepancy.

Mr. EDMUNDS. It accounts for just what would make the difference.

Mr. BUCKALEW. Just for the difference it caused; and I will say to the Senator that it is not a very considerable element in the calculation, although it is a just one to be considered. And it did not affect the vote between Lincoln and Douglas.

How did the electoral vote run in 1864? The result was right that year; the voice of the people was executed, but not by any necessary operation of our system. Mr. Lincoln's electors were chosen of a ratio of 10,292; those of McClellan by a ratio of 86,274. I repeat, the result was right, but that was not the merit of the system, it was a mere accident. So in 1824, when Jackson had one-half more votes than Mr. Adams from the people. The return does not show his full popular vote, because South Carolina chose by her Legislature. He had one-half more than Mr. Adams; he had more than Mr. Adams and Mr. Crawford combined before the people; and what was the result? Why, sir, he was left in a large minority in the electoral colleges. Adams and Crawford together obtained 26 more electors than belonged to them, changing the result by 52 electoral votes. The election was thrown into the House of Representatives, and there a great mistake was made, an affront was given to the American people—or at least they accepted it as such—and it had an effect to a large extent upon subsequent elections.

I will not dwell upon this point further than simply to refer to the numbers at two other elections. Take the election of 1832. The Jackson electors had a ratio of 3139; the Clay electors 11,228. In 1852 the Pierce electors had a ratio of 6242; the Scott electors of 32,846. In 1824 the plurality candidate for President was beaten because of the machinery of the electoral colleges. In 1860, that great election which touched the depths of the popular heart throughout the country, the candidate second in the choice and hearts of the American people by the machinery of the electoral colleges had no possibility of ever entering the House of Representatives as a competitor for the result. It required one hundred and fourteen thousand American freemen to give him one vote in the electoral colleges, when twelve thousand could give Breckinridge one vote; and if you made all allowance for the counting of the three-fifths of slaves in the South, it would not have disturbed the ratio more than a few thousands.

You see, sir, that this old machinery, then, is not a mere sham; it is an instrument of injustice, and, I will add, of peril also to the future of this country. Any time at the next presidential election, in 1872, or at any other future election, a large majority of the American people may vote without avail and without result for their choice for the office of President; and a minority man, a man largely in the minority before the people, may obtain a majority of presidential electors. It depends upon the accident of how majorities happen to run in particular States.

Mr. President, during three years that I resided in one of the Spanish American republics there were revolutions in thirteen out of fourteen of those republics. Those republics are scourged and desolated by revolutions, beginning with Mexico and going south to the Argentine Confederation and to Chili. What produces these revolutions ordinarily? A disputed presidential election. That is the cause three times out of four, and has been ever since 1825, when those republics began to take their present organizations. Three times out of four, and perhaps oftener, a dispute about a presidential election causes revolt and civil war, and desolates all those portions of the New World.

Mr. President, the very point upon which I am now speaking is a tender and delicate point of our Constitution, and it has contained in it perhaps more danger to our country than all other political causes combined. You have no mode of deciding a contested election of President and Vice-President, no machinery provided, no clear grant of power in your Constitution. It is not even positively certain how you shall count electoral votes in case of dispute. A surging and rampant House of Representatives turns itself into a mob even now when your Constitution is about being executed by the presiding officer of the Senate, and it requires days of heat—I had almost said of indecorous debate—in

13

that House to compose the waves of passion which are roused upon a mere technicality, with no actual change of the result of the election depending upon the decision.

It is the point of danger in our political institutions, this point of presidential elections. Will you wait until the danger is upon you; will you wait until civil war is again let loose; will you continue the old and defective machinery, always unjust, always full of peril and danger, until the crisis shall come? Slavery is gone—the great question which divided our communities of the North and South. It is buried in the tomb of the past; no voice will be sufficiently loud or powerful in all the centuries of the future to wake it or to speak it again into life. It will no more return to vex the councils of this Government or to inflame the hearts of our people; no blood will be shed to settle the great issues which it raises and which it inflames. But here in the very heart of your Constitution is a defective and weak point. I call your attention to it. I ask you to consider it, and now, in the days of quiet and of peace, before trouble has come, fortify yourselves against future danger; take hold upon these electoral colleges, which are not merely shams, as the Senator from Massachusetts says, but boxes of Pandora from which may issue demons of discord and violence to trouble and scourge your country and your people in future years. Give the opportunity to men of statesmanship and of wisdom to reform these colleges by regulating the manner in which the electors shall be chosen. That is one proposition contained in the Senate amendment which went to the House, which that House will adopt if you insist upon it.

Mr. President, why is it that the recommendations of President Jackson were unheeded, and that other men having the ear of Congress and having the ear of the country since have been unable to secure the adoption of a proposition for the amendment of our Constitution to dispense with our electoral colleges? Why is it? Why cannot you submit at once a proposition that the people shall vote directly for President and Vice-President and expect its adoption? It is my business to answer that, and I have a complete and satisfactory answer.

Under the scheme of electoral colleges each State has two senatorial electors, as they are called—that is, has two electors as a State; and then it has an additional number equal to the number of Representatives from the State. When you provide that the people shall vote directly for President and Vice President you virtually strike off from each of the States the equal power which they now have in choosing senatorial electors. You give to each State, then, in point of fact, in substance, a power proportioned to the number of Representatives which they select to the lower House of Congress. What is the effect? Why, that Rhode Island and other of the small States lose a large portion of their political power in the presidential election. Draw an amendment and send it down to the States to-morrow proposing this change, and how would it present itself to their reflections? Here are Delaware, Florida, Kansas, Nevada, Nebraska, and Oregon, six States with three electors each, two senatorial and one representative. Your amendment would mean that each of these States should give up two-thirds of its political power in the election of President and Vice President. Instead of having three electors as at present to count in an electoral college, they would have a popular vote, equivalent to only one to count upon the general result. Then take the States which elect two members, Rhode Island and Minnesota. Each of these has four electors, and under the amendment suggested they would have what would be equal to two; they would lose one-half of their power. The State selecting three Representatives and having five electors are New Hampshire, Vermont, California, and West Virginia. They would lose two-fifths of their political power in a presidential election. Connecticut, South Carolina, and Texas each elect four Representatives and have six electors. They would lose one-third of their power. Louisiana, Maine, Maryland, Mississippi, and New Jersey would lose two-sevenths. Alabama, Iowa, Michigan, and Wisconsin would lose one-fourth, as they are now entitled to eight electors each.

Here are twenty-four States which would each lose one-fourth of their political power or more up to two-thirds by adopting such an amendment to the Constitution. Twenty-four States out of thirty-seven interested by that large percentage of power against the adoption of such a change to the Constitution! Ten States can defeat an amendment when all the States are counted. These figures are exactly accurate, except we are to take into account that the large States would lose their senatorial electors, although the percentage of loss to them would be very small; it would affect the result only to a very small extent.   That is, the loss of power to the States I have enumerated would not be quite as large as these figures make it, although it would be nearly that.   If, then, you have twenty-four out of the thirty-seven States largely interested in rejecting such an amendment to the Constitution, nobody can doubt that, instead of such an amendment receiving the three-fourths vote of the States necessary to its ratification, it would be rejected by a majority of the whole number, and that whenever submitted.   In other words, it is impossible to procure an amendment to the Constitution of the United States by which the people of our country shall vote directly for President and Vice President.   It is against the interests of too many States, it is against the interest of too many State interests, to permit it to take place at all, and therefore it will never be accomplished.

This reform, then, of a direct choice by the people being out of the question, what can be done?   Why, sir, you can do what this amendment proposes: you can give to Congress the power to prescribe the manner in which electors shall be chosen, and thus you can introduce reform, and in no other way whatever. At present the power to prescribe the manner in which electors shall be chosen rests with the Legislatures of the several States.   In former times in South Carolina the Legislature prescribed that they themselves should choose electors, and that arrangement continued until recently.   The new Constitution of South Carolina, formed under the reconstruction laws, provides that the people shall select them by popular vote. That provision in that Constitution is a nullity undoubtedly. It is impossible for South Carolina by an amendment of her Constitution to take away from her Legislature a power imposed upon it by the Constitution of the United States. The provision therefore is a mere nullity. The Legislature of South Carolina will be at any time competent to resume her former practice of choosing electors of President and Vice President. The Legislature of Alabama recently proposed to take this power into its own hands, and it was only checked by an executive veto. Hereafter this mode of choosing electors may be resorted to by Legislatures of other States, and thus great trouble and difficulty may be introduced. It is a thing which ought not to be permitted. Now, Mr. President, in point of fact, if the Legislatures of the States do not assume to themselves the power to choose electors, they cannot reform the present system of choosing by general ticket, and that will be seen in a moment by any one who will bestow due reflection upon this subject. In all the States, Florida alone excepted, and perhaps Louisiana also, electors are chosen by general ticket—that is, each voter of the State votes for as many electors as the State is entitled to in her electoral college, and the majority obtain the whole number for that State.

It is impossible to change this system as the power is now located; and why? Take the case of the State of New York; you propose in the State of New York that electors shall be chosen by single districts or according to some other plan of reform, and what will be the answer? "Why, we cannot afford to do that in this State; we shall only break up our own political power; our party will lose nearly one-half its strength in this State; therefore we cannot afford to do it, and will not do it. Besides that, if we were inclined to do it, we could not, because other States not doing the same thing we should lose a portion of our political strength in this State, while the opposite party to us in another State electing by general ticket would hold the whole of its power, and thus we should inflict injury on ourselves as a political organization without any compensation whatever."

The political majority in any Legislature anywhere in the United States would say this to itself and to you if you proposed to it any reform whatever in the mode of choosing presidential electors. They would give the conclusive answer, "We cannot afford to do it and weaken our own power; we cannot control other States; and as long as they do not adopt the same mode of choosing electors you simply ask us to make a sacrifice; we cannot do it, and we will not do it." The result is that although the old general ticket system for choosing representatives was changed twenty or thirty years ago because it was intolerable, the choice of presidential electors is still according to the old plan, because there is no power here in Congress to amend it. The power which does exist in the State Legislatures cannot be exercised, and I venture to say it never will be. Therefore you have fixed in the Constitution the electoral colleges, an institution which three-fourths of the States will not change, which

is imbedded in the Constitution firmly, and then
you have a system of election by general ticket of
the members of those colleges in the respective
States which cannot be changed and will not
be changed by the Legislatures, who have theoretically the power to do it. There will be no
change, and what is the result? Here I come to
the point which touches us to the quick; which
should make our blood bound through our veins
when we think of it. By general ticket your presidential election is poised upon the vote of two or
three of the larger States, Pennsylvania particularly: and the year of a presidential election into
those States are poured all the corrupt influences
which elections can invite. We are deluged with
evils because our large States have an unjust or
badly-arranged power in the electoral colleges.
Money is poured into our States in a profuse stream
to corrupt and to degrade the elections held among
our people. It was because the voice of Pennsylvania, under an electoral college system, was likely
to rule or influence the result throughout the
country that half a million of dollars perhaps were
poured out in that State in 1868.

On behalf of my people; on behalf of our
republican institutions put in peril; on behalf of
justice and honesty in elections; on behalf of the
American people, whose voices ought to be heard
and counted fairly, I appeal to you to support this
amendment, which will permit reform and will
secure it. The road of reform is now closed up.
The patriot and the honest man must now work and
labor in vain. They can do nothing. Here is the

golden opportunity. An amendment relating to
suffrage is sent here from the House respecting the
persons who shall vote in the United States, and
here is an amendment proposing that the people
shall have secured to themselves the right of choosing presidential electors; that it shall not be taken
or snatched from them by intrigue or corruption
in the Legislatures; that their honest voices shall
always be heard in the choice of electors; and next,
that reform in the manner in which elections shall
be held may be introduced by the Congress of the
United States upon due cause shown. Congress
can introduce reform, and will do it. It did introduce reform in electing Representatives to the lower
House. It ordered the States to break themselves
up into single districts; and when New Hampshire
and one or two other States resisted enforced its
will, because it spoke by virtue of the power of this
Federal Constitution of ours. Give to Congress
identically the same power over the choice of presidential electors; say, as this amendment says, that
Congress may prescribe the manner in which they
shall be chosen. Congress is not obliged to do it; it
only permits it; and by a simple statute here you can
divide the States, or order the Legislatures to divide
the States, into single districts for choosing presidential electors, or you can provide what far-sighted and
just men now contemplate, and which eventually
all will seize upon as a measure of more complete
and perfect justice, that the people in each State,
according to their party divisions, may so vote that
each shall get a due share of power in the electoral college, by simply voting for the number of

men for which they have an adequate number of
votes; that in my State, with six hundred thousand
voters, each party holding three hundred thousand
of them, each or either may vote for twelve instead
of twenty-four electors, and by uniting their vote
upon that smaller number elect them. This is what
I hope may eventually be reached. But nothing is
commanded; the future is left open; and the men
who represent the people of the United States, and
who represent the States of this Union here assembled in council in these two Houses, may reach out
their hands to this system of election and reform it
so as to secure popular rights, so as to secure honest
elections and a just voice and expression by the
American people in these great elections of President; and thus you will have a guarantee of ines-
timable value against future disturbance, difficulty,
and possibly revolution and war in this country
from a disputed presidential election. Justice and
public safety appeal to you,

Is there any objection to this? None at all, except a mere prejudice. Some men say, " Why, you
are giving more power to Congress; you are taking
power away from the States; you are increasing
Federal power, and the tendency of this measure is
toward consolidation." Now, sir, of all the people
in the world with whom I have least patience, give
me the man of stupidity; the man who is fighting
against his own purpose and object without knowing
it; the man who with good and sincere motives is
doing bad and evil work and does not know it.
Those people who are shouting State rights and
State privilege and State immunity and authority,

and doing the work of mischief at the same time, are persons with whom we should have least patience; perhaps no patience at all.

The choice of presidential electors is properly a Federal question, rather than a State question. It relates to this Government, and not to the government of the States. It will therefore be properly lodged in this Government, because it belongs and pertains to it legitimately. In the next place, as I have already shown to you, the location of this power in Congress is a necessity. Located as it is now it will never be exercised; you can introduce no reform. Being, therefore, Federal in its nature, being necessary to the introducing of any reform in the regulation of the choice of presidential electors, it should be located in the two Houses of Congress, where, if it should at any time be exercised improperly, you can introduce change and amendments afterward.

Mr. President, I will read one single passage from one of the best printed and best edited newspapers in the United States, although my opinions are as wide from it as the poles are asunder. In speaking of this proposed amendment it says:

"It will prevent the entire vote of such a State as New York, for instance, being cast for a particular candidate through the rascality of its chief city."

I am not indorsing that statement. I am reading what this paper says:

"It will give more nearly than now the sense of the people for President in the electoral colleges, because each district will have its own representative. If anything was to be done at all with the electoral vote, we should prefer to have had the colleges abolished, that the untrammeled will of the people should be expressed directly upon the question of the fitness of the candidate for President."

I have already spoken to that point and shown that it is impracticable. This article concludes by saying:

"However, this question will not embarrass the suffrage proposition, as the two articles are to be voted on separately."

Mr. EDMUNDS. What paper is that?

Mr. BUCKALEW. The Boston Commonwealth.

From what I have said, Mr. President, it will be discovered that I have very strong opinions, possibly strong feelings also, in favor of this proposition for amending the Constitution of the United States in regard to the choice of presidential electors. I have imperfectly, and without much preparation, stated to the Senate a few of the leading considerations which, in my judgment, demand this reform. It is now within our reach. We can seize upon it; we can secure it; we can appropriate it, not to ourselves only, but to the whole American people, and all this can be done without embarrassment in regard to the other proposition of amendment of suffrage. It is distinct in its nature and it is to be submitted distinctly for the action of the several States. One proposition can be acted upon without embarrassing the other in any way whatever. We have now a golden opportunity for presenting this proposition, and presenting it in connection with an amendment which invites it, because it is an amendment for the extension of suffrage, while this is for the regulation of suffrage.

One point more, sir, and I will leave the subject. Can anything be more evident than that now, when we are extending suffrage in the United States, and extending it largely, extending it as it was not contemplated it ever could be extended until within a few years past, it becomes us to improve our machinery, to improve our constitutional arrangements by which suffrage is to be worked in future? In calling upon the people of the United States to adopt an amendment which shall make this extension, which shall allow the casting into the ballot-boxes, North, South, and West, of hundreds of thousands of votes from a new and hitherto disfranchised class, will you not present to them some proposition of reform with regard to the manner in which this suffrage shall be exercised, so that it shall have just operation and fair effect, so that the corruption of a few votes in a State shall not turn the whole scale and change elections? In my judgment, therefore, in addition to all the other considerations, this proposition is most timely. It never could have been presented at a juncture when in point of time it was more appropriate and more deserving of adoption by Congress and by the American people.

[Eventually the Senate, with some reluctance, receded from its amendments by a vote of 33 to 24, Mr. Morton accompanying his concession to the House with the declaration that his amendment could not at that time receive due consideration in the House, but that it was not of a party character, and he believed it would be submitted and adopted at a future time. It commended itself to the good judgment of the American people, and he believed that hereafter men of all parties would support it. (*Globe*, 1295.)

On a prior occasion, on the 9th of February, when the Morton Amendment was under consideration in the Senate, Mr. Buckalew submitted some statistics of Presidential elections, the republication of which, in connection with the foregoing speech, appears necessary or proper to à full view of the important question discussed. We quote below a liberal extract from his remarks as contained in the *Globe*, p. 1043.]

UNEQUAL REPRESENTATION OF THE PEOPLE IN PRESIDENTIAL ELECTIONS.

In the Presidential election of 1824, between Jackson and Adams, Jackson, with a popular vote one-half greater than Adams, received fourteen electoral votes less than his due share, making a difference or change of twenty-eight in the electoral colleges between them. He received more votes from the people than Adams and Crawford combined, and yet they outnumbered him twenty-six in electoral votes.

In the Presidential election of 1828 the Jackson electors were chosen by an average of 3652 votes each, and the Adams electors by 6170 votes.

In 1832 the result was:

	Popular vote.	Electors.	Ratio.
Jackson	687,502	219	3,139
Clay	550,189	49	11,228
Wirt		7	
Floyd		11	

The total popular vote of Jackson and Clay was 1,237,691, and their electoral votes combined 268. A common ratio for them therefore was 4618, from which it results that Clay should have had 119 and Jackson 149 electoral votes. Clay lost 70 electors, making a change of 140 in the result as between them. Jackson should have had 30 electoral majority, but he had 170, or more than five times his true majority.

I will now cite more recent cases.

PRESIDENTIAL ELECTION 1852.

	Popular vote.	Electors.	Ratios.
Pierce	1,585,545	254	6,242
Scott	1,383,587	42	32,846
Hale	157,296		
	3,126,378	296	

Six thousand Pierce voters obtained an elector, while 32,000 were required for a Scott elector! Now, dividing the whole popular vote by the whole number of electors we obtain the average or common ratio of votes to each elector of 10,562. If electors then had been obtained by the several candidates in proportion to the reported popular vote for each, the result would have been: Pierce 150; Scott 131; and Hale 15. By the defective plan upon which electors were chosen, it appears then that Pierce had 104 more electoral votes than his due share, that Scott had 89 less than his share, and that Hale was deprived entirely of electors. And it is to be remembered that the 104 electoral votes to Pierce in excess of his due share really count 208 upon the result in the electoral colleges, because they are deducted from the other candidates.

Take next the Presidential election of 1860.

	Popular vote.	Electors.	Ratios.
Lincoln	1,866,452	180	10,369
Douglas	1,375,157	12	114,596
Breckinridge	847,953	72	11,777
Bell	590,631	39	15,144
Total	4,680,193	303	

Common ratio, 15,446. Lincoln should have had 121 electors, Douglas 89, Breckinridge 55, and Bell 38. Douglas obtained less than one-seventh of the

electoral vote which belonged to him upon the popular vote. Though second in choice with the people, he was the lowest in the electoral vote of the
four candidates. If, by a slight change of votes in
a few States, the election had gone to the House of
Representatives, he would have been ruled out, as
the House must choose from the three candidates
highest in electoral vote, and Breckinridge or Bell
would probably have been elected by the House.

I might refer to several other Presidential elections. For instance, in 1864, the ratio of the Lincoln
electors was 10,292, and for the McClellan electors
86,274. In 1868 the difference between the ratios
of Grant and Seymour electors was somewhat less,
but still very remarkable. In both these elections
the popular majority secured the result they desired.
But this was fortunate or accidental rather than a
certain result under our electoral system as now
constituted. . The election of 1824 proves that a
plurality as well as a minority candidate may suffer
heavy loss of electoral votes, and in fact be defeated.
And the subsequent cases must convince us that
there is danger of defeat in future elections even to
majority candidates.

The conclusion to be drawn from the facts in our
political history is that at any time a candidate
with a minority of votes given to him by the people
of the United States may have a majority in the
electoral colleges." *

* In the figures given above of popular votes at Presidential elections, no vote for South Carolina is included, as her electors were chosen
by the Legislature. But the unavoidable omission of any popular vote
from that State does not materially affect the exhibit or argument. A
single remark may be added in this place. Can any one doubt, in view

THE ELECTORAL COLLEGES, THEIR DEFECTS AND FAILURE, AND REMEDIES PROPOSED.*

BY COL. JOHN H. WHEELER, STATISTICAL BUREAU, TREASURY DEPARTMENT.

This nation has recently passed through an exciting election for President, and the electors have met at the capitals of each State and cast their votes.

We propose to show that the present mode of election of President and Vice President does not guarantee "a republican form of government," or carry out the intentions of the framers of the Constitution, or the will of the people, which is the foundation of our form of government.

We are aware of the reluctance which exists to disturb the provisions of the Constitution or the customs of the nation. But this very Constitution has been amended again and again, and once in regard to this very question.

Under the second article of the Constitution, the electors, appointed in such manner as the Legislatures of the States may direct, meet in their respective States and vote by ballot for two persons; the person having the majority of the whole number of electors appointed shall be President, and the person having the next greatest number of votes shall be Vice President.

By this mode the first President (Washington) was elected twice, (1788 and 1792,) and John Adams (in 1796) once.

In consequence of the violence to the popular will attempted to be done through this mode, this article was amended in 1804, (Sept. 25,) and the electors required to name in their ballots the person voted for as President, and in distinct ballots the

of the facts shown, that reformed voting is imperatively demanded in Presidential elections to secure the just representation of the people, to check political corruption, and to avoid the fearful danger of a disputed Presidential succession? Doubtless the electoral colleges are admirably adapted to the workings of a plan of electoral reform. Useless or worse than useless at present, they may be made available and efficient in improving our political system and securing to us the just ends of popular government, whenever the free vote or some other appropriate instrument of reform shall be applied to utilize and invigorate them.

* This Essay by Col. Wheeler was contained in the Appendix to Senate Report on Representative Reform, of 2d March, 1869, (ante,) but is now inserted here as its proper position in this work.

14

person voted for as Vice President. They are to make a list of all the persons voted for, and the number of votes for each, which they are to transmit to the President of the Senate, who, in the presence of the Senate and House of Representatives, shall count the votes and declare who is chosen. Thus the matter now stands. We propose to show, as previously stated, that this mode as now used does not carry out the intention of the framers of the Constitution; that it is not a faithful indication of popular will, and, therefore, is subversive of the principle that lies at the foundation of our government—that the will of the people lawfully expressed should be inviolate. If this is so, this mode should be abolished.

As to the intent of the framers of the Constitution we are not left in doubt. Alexander Hamilton, of New York, a member of the convention which formed the Constitution, in No. 68 of the Federalist, acknowledged that the mode as prescribed for the election of the President by electors chosen by the people *was objectionable.* He says:

The convention which formed the Constitution did not desire the appointment of President to depend on pre-existing bodies of men, who might be tampered with beforehand to prostitute their votes.

The mode was suggested by the practice of the Germanic Confederation; and this was that the electors or people should choose as their representatives or electors men of high·character, capable and honest, above influences of place or power, (for no person holding an office of trust or profit under the United States can be an elector,) and these electors, unbiased by party partialities and prejudices, unawed by power, impervious to the seductions of place, but guided only by patriotism and virtue, should select some citizen of the nation, eminent for his services, virtues, and talents, as Chief Magistrate.

If this be the true intent of the framers of the Constitution, how widely does the practice differ from the intent! Any one who has ever witnessed the assembling of the electors of any State can but have felt the ridiculous mockery with which, as mere automatons, they carry out the edict which a caucus or convention has already dictated; and for any elector to vary therefrom, or dare to follow the convictions of his judgment, would be political suicide, although it is his constitutional right so to do. One case only occurs to our memory in the history of our government where an elector has ventured to exercise this unquestioned right. In 1820 Mr. William Plummer, elected in New Hampshire as an elector to choose a President, voted for John Quincy Adams (who was not then a candidate or the nominee of any party) against James Monroe.

He was doomed to political death. This incident was the more singular as it was the only vote cast in any electoral college against Mr. Monroe. This gave occasion to the caustic remark of John Randolph, of Virginia, in Congress, that "Mr. Monroe came in by *unanimous consent* and went out of office by *unanimous consent.*"

That the mode now used may be no indication of the wishes of the people, may fail in many instances to carry out their will, and, in fact, be at variance with and in opposition thereto, the examples in our political history, as we will presently show, abundantly prove.

In 1800 this mode had nearly placed in the Presidential chair Aaron Burr, for which high position it is well known he did not receive a single electoral or popular vote.

In 1824, under this mode, John Quincy Adams was placed in the Presidential chair against the declared wishes of a majority of the people, for he was in a minority in both the electoral and popular vote. We have prepared a table of the popular and electoral vote. The electoral vote is given from the organization of the government; the popular vote is only from 1824. This vote has no constitutional existence, and no federal record officially presents it. Prior to the adoption of the amendment in 1804 the mode of choosing electors was so heterogeneous, by the legislatures, by districts, and by the people, that no accurate or perfect compilation concerning it is extant worthy of confidence. Even after the adoption of this amendment very many States continued to choose electors by the legislature, (notably New Jersey, North Carolina, South Carolina, and occasionally Connecticut, Massachusetts, New York, and Vermont.) In the election of 1824 the electors for President and Vice President in Delaware, Georgia, Louisiana, South Carolina, New York, and Vermont were chosen by the Legislatures of those States. Of the election of 1820, back to which the table of popular vote extends, *Niles's Register*, of

18th November, 1820, has this item : "In Maryland and Virginia the election of electors excites so little interest because there was no thought of opposition that very few votes were cast, only 17 at Richmond." Hence of the popular vote, as before stated, no complete record is extant. The table on the next page is as complete as possible and worthy of careful study.

(It is to be remembered that the State of South Carolina continued to choose electors by her Legislature down to the time of the late rebellion in 1861; so that no popular vote from her is included in the above returns. As she is, however, a State of the third or fourth rank in population, the absence of her votes does not greatly affect the completeness or accuracy of our exhibit.)

An examination and analysis of this table, and a comparison of the electoral with the popular vote, will prove the positions we have laid down, that the mode of the electoral vote, as now used, does not carry out the popular vote, and is not a faithful reflex of public opinion; and that therefore it should be modified or discontinued.

Take the first case that occurs in this table, where the popular vote appears—the vote in the election of 1824: General Jackson received 152,899 reported votes, and John Quincy Adams only 105,321; yet by this mode of machinery the public will was violated and Adams chosen.

The next election (1828) while the popular majority for Jackson was 137,870, in a total vote of 1,162,180, his electoral majority was 95, in a total of 261; that is, the popular ratio was as 1 to 8; the electoral majority was as 1 to 2¼, a ratio three times greater.

In the next election (1832) this disparity appears still more glaring. While Jackson's popular majority was 137,313, in a total vote of 1,237,691, or as 1 to 9, his electoral majority was 170, a ratio seven times greater.

In the next election (1836) the popular majority for Van Buren was but 2608, in a total vote of 1,541,318, while the electoral majority was 124, in a total vote of 294; that is to say, the ratio of the majority of the popular votes was but as 1 to 600, while the ratio of the electoral majority was less than 1 to 6, a ratio 100 times as great.

Popular and electoral vote of the United States from 1788 to 1869.

Year.	Term.	Candidates.	Party.	Electoral vote.	Total number of electors.	Popular vote.
1788	1	George Washington............	Unanimous	69	69	
1792	2	"	"	132	132	
1796	3	John Adams............	Federalist..............	71	} 139	
		Thomas Jefferson............	Republican	68		
1800	4	"	"	73	} 138	
		John Adams............	Federalist..............	65		
1804	5	Thomas Jefferson............	Republican	162	} 176	
		C. C. Pinckney............	Federalist..............	14		
1808	6	James Madison............	Republican	122	} 175	
		C. C. Pinckney............	Federalist..............	47		
		George Clinton............		6		
1812	7	James Madison............	Republican	128	} 217	
		De Witt Clinton............	....	89		
1816	8	James Monroe............		183	} 217	
		Rufus King............	Federalist..............	34		
1820	9	James Monroe............	Republican	231	} *235	
		John Quincy Adams............		1		
1824	10	Andrew Jackson............	Democrat..............	99		152,899
		John Quincy Adams............	Federalist..............	84	} 261	105,321
		William H. Crawford............	Caucus	41		47,265
		Henry Clay............	Whig............	37		47,087
1828	11	Andrew Jackson............	Democrat..............	178	} 261	650,028
		John Quincy Adams............	Federalist..............	83		512,158
1832	12	Andrew Jackson............	Democrat..............	219		687,502
		Henry Clay............	National Republican...	49	} †288	550,189
		William Wirt............	Anti-Mason............	7		
		John Floyd............	Anti-Jackson............	11		
1836	13	Martin Van Buren............	Democrat	170		771,963
		William Henry Harrison....	Whig............	73		
		Hugh L. White............	"	26	} 294	769,350
		Daniel Webster............	"	14		
		Willie P. Mangum............	"	11		
1840	14	William H. Harrison............	"	234		1,274,203
		Martin Van Buren............	Democrat............	60	} 294	1,128,303
		James G. Birney............	Abolitionist	......		7,609
1844	15	James K. Polk............	Democrat............	170		1,329,023
		Henry Clay............	Whig............	105	} 275	1,231,843
		James G. Birney............	Abolitionist	......		66,304
1848	16	Zachary Taylor............	Whig............	163		1,362,242
		Lewis Cass............	Democrat............	127	} 290	1,223,795
		Martin Van Buren............	Free-soil............	......		291,878
1852	17	Franklin Pierce............	Democrat............	254		1,585,545
		Winfield Scott............	Whig............	42	} 296	1,383,537
		John P. Hale............	Free-soil............	......		157,296
1856	18	James Buchanan............	Democrat............	174		1,838,229
		John C. Fremont............	Free-soil............	114	} 296	1,342,864
		Millard Fillmore............	Whig............	8		874,625
1860	19	Abraham Lincoln............	Republican............	180		1,866,452
		Stephen A. Douglas............	Democrat............	12	} 303	1,376,957
		John C. Breckinridge............	"	72		847,953
		John Bell............	Whig............	39		590,631
1864	20	Abraham Lincoln............	Republican............	212	} ‡233	2,223,035
		George B. McClellan.........	Democrat............	21		1,811,754
1868	21	Ulysses S. Grant............	Republican............	214	} §317	3,016,353
		Horatio Seymour............	Democrat............	80		2,706,637

* In this election (9th term) Pennsylvania, Mississippi, and Tennessee did not cast their full electoral vote.

† In this election (12th term) Maryland did not cast her full vote.

‡ In this election (20th term) Alabama, Arkansas, Florida, Georgia, Louisiana, Mississippi, North Carolina, Tennessee, Texas, South Carolina, and Virginia cast no electoral votes. ¸

§ In this election (21st term) Mississippi, Texas, and Virginia did not vote, and in Florida electors were chosen by the Legislature, and not by popular vote.

In the election of 1840 Harrison's popular majority was 145,900, in a total poll of 2,402,506, a ratio of 1 to 16, while his electoral majority was 174, in a vote of 294, or nearly ten times greater than the popular majority.

In the next election (1844) Polk received but 31,000 majority in a total of 2,626,950, or 1 in 900, while his electoral vote was 170 out of 275, or 1 to 4; 200 times the popular vote.

In 1848 General Taylor was in a minority of the popular vote; his vote being 1,362,242, and Cass and Van Buren had 1,515,173; and yet he received a majority of the electoral votes.

In 1852 Pierce's popular majority was 202,008, in a total vote of over 3,000,000, a ratio of 1 to 15, while his electoral majority was 192, out of 296 votes, a ratio ten times as great.

In 1856 Mr. Buchanan was in a minority of the popular vote; he received 1,838,229, while the vote of Fremont and Fillmore was 2,216,789; and yet he received a majority of the electoral votes.

In 1860 Mr. Lincoln was in a minority of nearly a million of popular votes. He received a total vote of 1,866,452, while the vote of Douglas, Breckinridge, and Bell combined was 2,813,741; and yet Mr. Lincoln received a majority of 123 in an electoral vote of 303. This election demonstrates in a most conclusive manner the fallacy of the electoral mode, and the possible misrepresentation under it of the popular will. Lincoln received 180 votes, and Douglas only 12, out of 303 electoral votes. In the popular vote Lincoln received 1,866,452, while Douglas received 1,375,157 votes.

In 1864 Lincoln received 2,223,035 and McClellan received 1,811,754 of the popular vote, while in the electoral college Lincoln received 212 votes, and McClellan received 21. A ratio of 22 to 18 in one case to 10 to 1 in the other.

In the last Presidential election (1868) Grant received a popular majority of 309,716 in a total of 5,722,990, a ratio of about 10 to 9, while his majority of electoral vote was 134 in in a total of 294, a ratio of 13 to 5.

This analysis, carefully made, proves beyond all cavil and error that there is no analogy or community between the vote as expressed by the electoral college and the will of the people as expressed at the polls. In every case they differ. Hence, the mode by electors is unfair, since it misrepresents the popular will.   Justice and truth demand its modification or abolition.   By this cumbersome and circumlocutory process the electors may be compelled to elect a candidate rejected by the people, or reject a candidate accepted by the people.   The defeat of General McClellan was complete, for he carried only three States—Delaware, Kentucky, and New Jersey.   The whole electoral vote was 233, of which a majority necessary for a choice was 117.   Now a change in the popular vote of 35,000 from Lincoln's would have changed the vote of every State mentioned below, and carried their full electoral vote.   These added to the vote he had received would have elected General McClellan.

States.	Lincoln's popular majority.	Electoral vote.
New Hampshire	3,530	5
Rhode Island	5,632	4
Connecticut	3,407	6
New York	6,750	33
Pennsylvania	20,076	26
Maryland	7,415	7
Indiana	20,190	13
Oregon	1,432	3
Nevada	3,236	3
Kentucky.		
New Jersey	....	21
Delaware		
Total	70,665	121

The change of 50,000 popular votes in New York in 1848 from Taylor to Cass, or giving one-half of the votes thrown away upon Van Buren to Cass, would have thrown the 36 electoral votes of New York to Cass, and elected him.

We have shown that, by the present electoral system, a person may be made President by receiving a majority of the electoral votes, who is in a minority before the people.   We have shown that Lincoln, in 1860, in a popular minority of more than a million of votes, swept the electoral college by an overwhelming majority; that Douglas, who received a popular vote equal to two-thirds of Lincoln's, received only one-fifteenth of his electoral vote; that Breckinridge, who was 500,000 votes behind Douglas, received six times as many votes in the electoral college, and Bell, who was 800,000 votes of the people behind Douglas, received thrice his number of electoral votes.

Can any demonstration be more complete and satisfactory as to the utter uselessness and impolicy, if not injustice and iniquity, of the present mode of election by electoral colleges?

This defect in the machinery of our government has been long seen by the statesmen of the nation. General Hamilton, one of the framers of the Constitution, acknowledges of this mode that it was objectionable, and when the amendment of 1804 was adopted, he proposed another, as follows:

To divide each State into districts equal to the whole number of senators and representatives from each State in the Congress of the United States, and said districts to be as equal in population as possible, and, if necessary, of parts of counties contiguous to each other, except where there may be some detached portion of territory not sufficient of itself to form a district, which then shall be annexed to some other district.

Thomas H. Benton, during his 30 years in the Senate, again and again brought this subject before Congress.

General Jackson, in his first annual message, urged an amendment to the Constitution, to secure the election of the President by a direct and immediate vote of the people. This he repeated in five subsequent messages. In his message of 1829, he says: "*To the people belongs the right of electing their Chief Magistrate.* It never was designed that their choice in any case should be defeated, either by the intervention of electorial colleges, or by the agency confided in certain contingencies to the House of Representatives. I, therefore, would recommend such an amendment to the Constitution as may remove all intermediate agency in the election of President and Vice President."

President Johnson, in 1845, when a member of the House, and in 1860, when a Senator in Congress, urged similar views. As President, in a message to Congress, dated July 18, 1868, he fully sets forth the injustice and inequality of the present mode, "as virtually denying the right of every citizen of the United States possessing the constitutional qualification to become a candidate for high office, and also denying the right of each qualified voter in the nation to vote for the person he deems most worthy and well qualified."

Senator Wade, of Ohio, now President of the Senate, at a recent session brought this question as to a direct vote of the people for President before the Senate, and defended the position by an able argument. In a recent debate on Senator Buckalew's amendment, the present mode of electors was denounced by Senator Sumner and others " as cumbersome, effete, and inconvenient." The scene which occurred recently in the counting of the electoral votes in the joint convention of both houses of Congress shows that the system must be altered. Mr. Miller, of Pennsylvania, introduced recently (February 8, 1869) an amendment to the Constitution to allow the qualified voters of the respective States to vote directly for President. The amendment to the Constitution (Article XVI.) of Senator Morton, adopted by the Senate February 9, 1869, is a proposition in the right direction—that the people shall select electors, (and not the Legislatures,) and that Congress shall have the power to prescribe the manner in which such electors shall be *chosen by the people.*

Connected intimately with this subject, as a useful remedy for the evils of the present system, is the reform proposed by Senator Buckalew, of cumulative voting; which is, that where there are more persons than one to be chosen, the voter shall possess as many votes as there are persons to be chosen, and the voter may bestow his votes at his discretion upon the whole number of persons to be chosen, or upon a less number, cumulating his votes upon one, two, three, or any number less than the whole. The plan introduced into Parliament as early as 1854, by Lord John Russell, is nearly similar; that in certain constituencies which return three members to Parliament, each voter should be allowed only to vote for two. This plan was adopted in 1867, and is now the law of England. Still another plan is urged by John Stuart Mill in his work on " Representative Government," (proposed originally by James Garth Marshall,) that the elector, having his three votes, should be at liberty to give all to one candidate, or two to one and one to another. This is similar to the plan introduced in the Senate (January 13, 1869) by Senator Buckalew, and commended by Earl Grey in his work on " Parliamentary Reform." The more these works are studied, the more clearly will appear the perfect feasibility of the plan and its transcendent advantages.

The allied plan of personal representation has also been highly commended. As presented by Mr. Hare in an elaborate work, it contains another great idea; that those who did not like the local candidates may fill up their ticket by voting for persons of national reputation. This is sometimes done in our country on important occasions of deep interest. In 1835, a convention was called in North Carolina to reform her constitution. It was the first convention for this purpose since 1776, and deeply excited the public mind. The ablest men of the State were chosen without regard to their location or politics.

The natural tendency of representative governments, in the opinion of Mr. Mill, is to *collective mediocrity*. This will be increased the more the elective franchise is extended. Edmund Burke was repudiated by the electors of Bristol, in 1780, for Parliament, for his advocacy of the cause of the American colonies. He was, however, returned by another constituency, and continued during life in Parliament, contributing to its debates and to the glory of the nation. In contrast to this, William R. Davie, who had been a gallant and successful officer in the war, governor of the State, (1798,) envoy extraordinary to France, (1799,) was defeated in popular elections in North Carolina, when a candidate for Congress and for the Legislature, [illegible] individuals without extraordinary merit or talent.

There is hardly a State of our Union in which the congressional districts are not gerrymandered in the interest of party. This adds to the deterioration of our public service, so that Mr. Mill declares "it is an admitted fact that in the American democracy, which is constructed on this faulty model, the highly cultivated members of the community, except such as are willing to sacrifice their own judgment and conscience to the behests of party and become the servile echo of those who are inferiors in knowledge, do not allow their names as candidates for Congress or the Legislature, so certain it is they would be defeated."

February, 1869.

Constitutional Amendment in Illinois.

A Convention authorized to frame and submit to
the people, amendments to the Constitution of Illinois, met at Springfield in December, 1869, and concluded the performance of its duties and adjourned
finally on the 13th of May, 1870. The amended
constitution for the State, as formed by the convention, was submitted to a popular vote for adoption
or rejection on the first Saturday in July following,
at which time also eight additional propositions of
amendment were submitted severally to a like vote.
An ingenious and convenient plan was provided by
the Convention for taking the sense of the people
upon all the questions submitted, by means of a
single ticket. The tickets or ballots properly prepared were to be distributed by the Secretary of
State through the County Clerks, and upon their
face were to indicate clearly and separately an affirmative vote for each of the propositions to be passed
upon—first, the new or amended Constitution, and
next, in their order, the several separate amendments proposed. Whenever the voter should strike
off or erase from his ballot either one of the propositions, his vote was to be counted as given against
it, otherwise in its favor. Thus *nine* distinct questions were passed upon by the people, though pre-

cisely the same form of ticket was furnished to each voter.

The work of the Convention is of peculiar interest outside of Illinois, because it included several provisions well calculated to secure electoral reform in that State, which were by strong majorities adopted by the people. These will now be given in the order in which they appear in the amended Constitution, accompanied by some observations which they respectively invite.

ELECTION OF REPRESENTATIVES IN THE LEGISLATURE.—The Seventh Section of the Fourth Article of the amended Constitution is as follows:

" The House of Representatives shall consist of three times the number of the members of the Senate, and the term of office shall be two years. Three Representatives shall be elected in each senatorial district at the general election in the year A. D. 1872, and every two years thereafter. In all elections of Representatives aforesaid, each qualified voter may cast as many votes for one candidate as there are Representatives to be elected, or may distribute the same or equal parts thereof among the candidates as he shall see fit, and the candidates highest in votes shall be declared elected."

Under this amendment a minority of voters in a district exceeding in number one-fourth of the whole vote, can elect one of the three Representatives from a district. The principle applied is simply this: that each voter shall be allowed to distribute or concentrate his three votes as he shall think proper, and that candidates highest in vote shall be declared elected. Practically, whenever one party is clearly in a majority in a district, but not able to poll a three-fourths vote, its members

will nominate and vote for two candidates only, and
the minority will nominate and vote for one, and all
the candidates voted for will be elected. No candidate will be beaten and both classes of voters will
be fairly represented. This will be the ordinary
case, but exceptional cases are fully provided for.
When the majority shall be strong enough to poll a
three-fourths vote they will vote for and elect three
candidates, or the whole number to be chosen.
When parties are about equal in strength, or each
may indulge the expectation of obtaining a majority
vote, each will nominate and support two candidates
and whichever one shall poll a majority of votes will
elect both its candidates, while the minority will
elect but one. In this case it will be certain from
the outset that each party will carry one of its candidates, and there will be a fair test of strength between them upon the election of a second one.
Only one candidate will be beaten and both parties
will be represented as nearly as may be in proportion to their respective numbers. Again, when
there shall be three parties or interests in a district
struggling for representation, it will probably happen that each will obtain one Representative, or that
one of them will obtain two and another one Representative, whereas under the old plan of voting one
party or interest would be likely to obtain the whole
three *upon a mere plurality vote;* in other words, a
minority of voters might, in many cases, elect their
whole ticket and the majority of voters be left without any Representative whatever. Finally, the new
plan allows the voter to discriminate between candidates in giving them his support. He can in voting

for two candidates express the relative strength of
his desire for the election of each, by giving one of
them two votes and the other one. In some cases
this will be a valuable and convenient privilege, and
its exercise will tend· to the certain success of the
best men among candidates where all cannot be
elected.

The allowance of *half-votes* in the new plan is
one of its best features, and will secure its convenient working and promote its ultimate popularity.
This feature, however, is rather for the convenience
of the majority than of the minority, and is not indispensable to the new plan. The majority can
vote in either one of three ways:

1st. Give single votes to each of three candidates,
which is the old plan;

2d. Give one and a half votes to each of two; or,

3d. Have one-half their voters give two votes to
A and one to B, and the other half two votes to B
and one to A.

Whenever their vote shall not exceed three-
fourths of the whole vote of the district, they cannot reasonably or safely support three candidates.
If with a weaker vote than three-fourths they shall
attempt to elect the whole three Representatives, the
minority may take advantage of the dispersion of
their vote and carry a second Representative. In all
ordinary cases, therefore, the majority will support
but two candidates. They will not run a third candidate simply that he may be beaten, and incur at
the same time the danger of losing one of the two
Representatives to which they are entitled and have
power to elect.

Assuming, then, that in all ordinary cases, guided by reason and self-interest, the majority will support but two candidates, the question remains, In which one of the two ways above mentioned shall they vote for them? It will be quite possible for the majority to divide their votes territorially or otherwise into two equal or nearly equal divisions and use two forms of ticket at the election. Half their voters giving A two votes and B one, and the other half giving B two and A one, the whole strength of the party will be economized and distributed equally to the two candidates. No strength will be wasted or misapplied. But this plan will be inconvenient to the majority even when the proper result shall be secured, which will not always be entirely certain. We think, therefore, that this particular mode of majority voting will be found much less satisfactory in practice than the other, above referred to, which involves the use of half-votes. When every majority voter shall divide his three votes equally between two candidates, giving a vote and a half to each, there can be no doubt that the object aimed at—the full and economical use of party power in the election—will be reached, and reached too without trouble or inconvenience. The preparation of a ticket reading as follows:

John Jones, 1½ votes,

William Brown, 1½ votes,

will be within the competency of any person who can read and write, and its intelligent use by voters a matter of course. As to counting such votes, (as elsewhere explained in the present volume,) the question of convenience is equally clear. The election officers can copy upon their tally-papers from the first ticket drawn from the box, the names of the candidates with the figures attached (it will be convenient to enclose the latter in small circles with a pen) and will then take down that and successive tickets in scores of five towards the right according to the common practice. The figures $1\frac{1}{2}$ will thus constitute a sign of value for the strokes which follow, and after summing up the latter, fifty per cent. will be added to make up the true total of votes. Thus, if eighty such tickets are counted to a candidate, the score will be carried out—$80 + 40 = 120$ votes, which will be placed to the credit of such candidate upon the return.

CHOICE OF DIRECTORS AND MANAGERS OF INCORPORATED COMPANIES.— The Third Section of the Eleventh Article is one of the most important ever introduced into a constitution, and is as follows:

"The General Assembly shall provide by law, that in all elections for directors or managers of incorporated companies, every stockholder shall have the right to vote, in person or by proxy, for the number of shares of stock owned by him, for as many persons as there are directors or managers to be elected, or to cumulate said shares and give one candidate as many votes as the number of directors multiplied by his number of shares shall equal, or to distribute them on the same principle among as many candidates as he shall think fit; and such directors or managers shall not be elected in any other manner."

There are, probably, several thousand corporate companies in Illinois to the elections of which this important amendment will apply; for it searches out all such bodies in the State, without exception, and applies to them the hand of reform. Hereafter, a mere majority, a clique or a combination of stock-holders in an Illinois corporation, will not be allowed to exclude their co-stockholders from all voice in the management of the corporation, nor will a minority of stockholders holding a majority of stock be allowed to do so. The mismanagement of corporate bodies, and secresy, intrigue or corruption in the proceedings of their officers, will receive an important and necessary check. All the stockholders will be able to represent themselves in the board of managers, thus securing to themselves at all times full knowledge of the corporate proceedings and of the administration of the funds which they have invested. They will be enabled more perfectly to protect their own interests in the corporations and to prevent the growth of abuses.

ELECTION OF JUDGES IN COOK COUNTY.—By the twenty-third section of the sixth article of the Constitution, as amended, the Circuit Court of Cook County (in which Chicago is situate) was made to consist of five Judges, who are to hold their offices for six-year terms. This provision required the election of three new Judges, and their first election was provided for in the seventh section of the schedule to the amendments, upon the plan of the limited vote. That section contained the injunction "That at said election in the County of Cook no elector shall vote for more than two candidates for Circuit Judge." The election held under this provision on the first Saturday in July, 1870, resulted in the choice of two Judges by the political majority and one by the political minority of Cook County. The

15

provision was found to be satisfactory on trial, and the Judges elected under it were all competent and fit men.

The men of the Illinois Convention and the people of Illinois deserve the thanks of the whole country for their action in behalf of electoral reform. But special credit is due to Mr. Medill, (formerly of the Chicago *Tribune* and now Mayor of Chicago,) who, as Chairman of the Committee on Electoral and Representative Reform in the Convention, took the lead in argument and labor to secure the passage of those propositions of amendment to which we have referred. He had the cordial assistance of Mr. Browning, former Secretary of the Interior in the Government of the United States, and of other able and worthy colleagues in the Convention; but to him above others the principal honor is due of the good and timely work accomplished in his State.

WEST VIRGINIA AMENDMENTS.

The Constitutional Convention of West Virginia, which met January 16, 1872, agreed upon two amendments for the introduction of electoral reform into that State, which were subsequently adopted by the people, along with other amendments of the Convention. One of these was borrowed from Illinois, and constitutes section four of article eleven of the new Constitution of the State. It is exactly like the Illinois provision, already given, for the free vote in all elections of directors or managers of incorporated companies.

The other amendment referred to is section fifty of article six of the new Constitution, and is as follows:

" The Legislature may provide for submitting to a vote of the people at the general election to be held in 1876, or at any general election thereafter, a plan or scheme of proportional representation in the Senate of this State, and if a majority of the votes cast at such election be in favor of the plan submitted to them, the Legislature shall at its session succeeding such election rearrange the Senatorial Districts in accordance with the plan so approved by the people."

Utah Amendment.—In the new Constitution of Utah, adopted March 18, 1872, (preparatory to her application for admission into the Union as a State,) appears the following provision:

ART. iv., SEC. 25: "At all elections for Representatives each qualified elector may cast as many votes for one candidate as there are Representatives to be elected in the county or district, or may distribute the same among any or all the candidates, and the candidates receiving the highest number of votes shall be declared elected."

PENNSYLVANIA STATUTES

REFORMED VOTING.

I. GENERAL LAWS.

CHOICE OF INSPECTORS OF ELECTION: *Act of 2d July*, 1839, *entitled "An Act relating to the Elections of this Commonwealth."—Pamphlet Laws*, 519, *sections 3 and 4.*

"SEC. 3. The qualified citizens of the several wards, districts, and townships, shall meet in every year, at the time and place of holding the election for Constable of such ward, district, or township, and then and there elect, as hereinafter provided, two Inspectors and one Judge of Elections.

"SEC. 4. Each of such qualified citizens shall vote for one person as Judge, and also for one person as Inspector of Elections, and the person having the greatest number of votes for Judge shall be publicly declared to be elected Judge; and the two persons having the greatest number of votes for Inspectors, shall, in like manner, be declared to be elected Inspectors of Elections."

228

ELECTION OF JURY COMMISSIONERS: *"An act for the better and more impartial selection of persons to serve as Jurors in each of the Counties of this Commonwealth,"* section 1; passed 10th April, 1867.—*P. Laws,* 62.

"SEC. 1. That at the general election to be held on the second Tuesday of October, A. D. 1867, and triennially thereafter, at such election, the qualified electors of the several counties of this Commonwealth shall elect, in the manner now provided by law for the election of other county officers, two sober, intelligent, and judicious persons to serve as Jury Commissioners in each of said counties, for the period of three years ensuing their election; but the same person or persons shall not be eligible for re-election more than once in any period of six years: *Provided,* That each of said qualified electors shall vote for one person only as Jury Commissioner, and the two persons having the greatest number of votes for Jury Commissioner shall be duly elected Jury Commissioners for such county."

BOROUGH SUPPLEMENT: *By an Act, entitled "An Act for the further regulation of Boroughs,"* approved 2d June, 1871, (*P. Laws,* 283,) it was provided as follows:

"SEC. 2. The number of members of any town council of a borough where the number is now fixed at five shall be hereafter six, and in boroughs hereafter incorporated under general laws the number of such councilmen shall be six; but the several courts of the Commonwealth having jurisdiction to incorporate boroughs may, on granting an incorporation or upon application made to them for the purpose, fix or change the charter of any borough so as to authorize the burgess or chief executive officer thereof to serve as a member of the town council, with full power as such, and to preside at the meetings thereof.

"Sec. 3. In elections for members of town councils each voter may at his option bestow his votes singly upon six candidates, or cumulate them upon any less number, in the manner authorized by the fourth section of the act to define the limits and to organize the town of Bloomsburg, approved March fourth, one thousand eight hundred and seventy; and vacancies in any council shall be filled in the manner provided in the fifth section of the same act; but nothing herein contained shall be held to regulate or affect the manner of choosing the burgess or other principal executive officer of a borough even where he shall be authorized to serve as a member of town council."

CONSTITUTIONAL CONVENTION ACT OF 1872: "*An act to provide for calling a convention to amend the Constitution;*" approved 11th April, 1872.—*P. Laws*, 53.

"Sec. 1. That at the general election, to be held on the second Tuesday of October next, there shall be elected by the qualified electors of this Commonwealth delegates to a convention to revise and amend the Constitution of this State; the said convention shall consist of one hundred and thirty-three members, to be elected in the manner following : Twenty-eight members thereof shall be elected in the State at large, as follows : Each voter of the State shall vote for not more than fourteen candidates, and the twenty-eight highest in vote shall be declared elected; ninety-nine delegates shall be apportioned to and elected from the different senatorial districts of the State, three delegates to be elected for each Senator therefrom ; and in choosing all district delegates, each voter shall be entitled to vote for not more than two of the members to be chosen from his district, and the three candidates highest in vote shall be declared elected, except in the county of Alleghany, forming the twenty-third senatorial district, where no voter shall vote for more than six candidates, and the nine highest in vote shall be elected, and in the counties of Luzerne, Monroe, and Pike, forming the thirteenth senatorial district, where no voter shall vote for more than four candidates, and the six highest in vote shall be elected; and six additional delegates shall be chosen from the city of Philadelphia, by a vote at large in said city, and in their election no voter shall vote for more than three candidates, and the six highest in vote shall be declared elected. .

"Sec. 2. The following regulations shall apply to the aforesaid election to be held on the second Tuesday of October next. . . .

" *First.* The said election shall be held and conducted by the proper election officers of the several election districts of the Commonwealth, and shall be governed and regulated in all respects by the general election laws of the Commonwealth, so far as the same shall be applicable thereto, and not inconsistent with the provisions of this act.

"*Second.* The tickets to be voted for members at large of the convention shall have on the outside the words, 'delegates at large,' and on the inside" the names of the candidates to be voted for, not exceeding fourteen in number.

"*Third.* The tickets to be voted for district members of the convention shall have on the outside the words, 'district delegates,' and on the inside the name or names of the candidates voted for, not exceeding the proper number, limited as aforesaid; but any ticket which shall contain a greater number of names than the number for which the voter shall be entitled to vote, shall be rejected; and in the case of the delegates to be chosen at large in Philadelphia, the words, 'city delegates,' shall be on the outside of the ticket. . . .

"Sec. 8. That in case of vacancies in the membership of said convention, the same shall be filled as follows: If such vacancy shall be of a member at large of the convention, those members at large who shall have been voted for by the same voters, or by a majority of the same voters who shall have voted for and elected the member whose place is to be filled, shall fill such vacancy; if such vacancy shall be of a district or city member of the convention, those members at large of the convention who shall have been voted for by the same or by a majority of the same voters who shall have voted for such district or city member, shall fill such vacancy; in either case, the appointment to fill a vacancy shall be made by the members at large aforesaid, or by a majority of them, in writing; and all such written appointments shall be filed among the convention records."

Among the other additional provisions of the Convention Act appears the following proviso in the fourth section :

"*Provided*, That one-third of all the members of the convention shall have the right to require the separate and distinct submission to a popular vote of any change or amendment proposed by the convention."

II. LOCAL LAWS.

THE BLOOMSBURG ACT: "*An act to define the limits and to organize the town of Bloomsburg;*" *passed 4th March,* 1870.—*P. Laws,* 343.

"SEC. 4. To the end that the electors of Bloomsburg may exercise their right of suffrage freely and without undue constraint, and may obtain for themselves complete representation in their local government, the plan of the free vote shall be lawful, and is hereby authorized in the elections for officers of said town and for all officers to be chosen by them exclusively : In any case where more persons than one are to be chosen in said town to the same office, for the same time or term of service, each voter duly qualified shall be entitled to as many votes as the number of persons to be so chosen, and may poll his votes as follows, to wit :

"*First.* When two persons are to be chosen, he may give one vote to each of two candidates or two votes to one.

"*Second.* When three persons are to be chosen, he may give one vote to each of three candidates, two votes to one candidate and one to another, one vote and a half to each of two candidates or three votes to one.

"*Third.* When four persons are to be chosen, he may give one vote to each of four candidates, one vote and one-third to each of three, two votes to each of two or four votes to one.

"*Fourth.* When six persons are to be chosen, he may give one vote to each of six candidates, one vote and a half to each of four, two votes to each of three, three votes to each of two or six votes to one.

" In every case the candidates highest in vote shall be declared elected. Whenever a voter shall intend to give more votes than one or to give a fraction of a vote to any candidate, he shall express his intention distinctly and clearly upon the face of his ballot, otherwise but one vote shall be counted and allowed to such candidate. This section shall apply to the choice of School Directors and of all officers to be chosen exclusively by the electors of said town, whenever its application shall be possible.

" SEC. 5. Vacancies in any of the offices of said town may be filled by appointments to be made by the Court of Quarter Sessions of the Peace of Columbia County, except as herein otherwise provided; but any appointment so made shall be of an elector of the said town who shall have voted for the officer or person whose place is to be filled. . . . This section shall apply to vacancies in all the offices before mentioned except those of Justice of the Peace and Director of Common Schools."

By the second section of the same act a Town
Council is to be elected annually, consisting of six
members chosen by the free vote, and a President
chosen by a majority vote ; and by the third section
two Constables and two Assessors of Taxes annually, and three town Auditors every third year.
By general laws two Assistant Assessors of taxes
are to be chosen triennially, and two Directors of
Common Schools each year for three year terms.
To the choice of all the foregoing officers, except
the President of the Town Council, the new plan of
voting applies, and it will also apply to the election
of Justices of the Peace of the town whenever the
two authorized by law shall happen to be electable
at the same time for the constitutional term of five
years.

BOROUGH COUNCILMEN IN NORTHUMBERLAND
COUNTY: *"An Act relating to the extension of
borough limits in Northumberland County;"*
passed 6th April, 1870.—P. Laws, 1000.

"SEC. 1. That the number of town councilmen
in each of the several boroughs of Northumberland
County, to be hereafter chosen, except in the borough of Sunbury, shall be six; and they shall be
chosen according to the provisions of the fourth
section of the act to define the limits and to organize the town of Bloomsburg, approved March 4th,
1870; and vacancies in their number shall be filled
by the Court of Common Pleas of Northumberland
County in accordance with the provisions of the
fifth section of the same act."

COUNCILMEN IN BOROUGH OF MILTON: *"An Act relative to elections in the borough of Milton;"* approved 14*th April*, 1870.—*P. Laws*, 1177.

"SEC. 2. That the members of the town council of said borough shall be chosen annually, commencing with the next election, and three thereof shall be chosen from each ward upon the principle of the free vote as defined and fixed in the fourth section of the act to define the limits and to organize the town of Bloomsburg, approved March 4th, A. D. 1870, and all acts and parts of acts inconsistent herewith are hereby repealed."

OFFICERS IN BOROUGH SUNBURY: *"An Act relating to elections in the borough of Sunbury;"* approved 14*th April*, 1870.—*P. Laws*, 1178.

"SEC. 1. That in elections hereafter held in the borough of Sunbury for borough or ward officers, whenever two or more persons are to be chosen to the same office for the same term of service, each voter may at his discretion bestow his votes upon one or more candidates less in number than the whole number of persons to be chosen in the manner provided in the fourth section of the act to define the limits and to organize the town of Bloomsburg, passed at the present session, and the candidates highest in vote shall be declared elected: *Provided*, That inspectors of election shall be chosen as heretofore, and that directors of common schools shall be considered and held to be borough officers within the meaning of this act."

BOROUGH OFFICERS IN BERWICK: *"An Act supplementary to the several acts relating to the borough of Berwick in the County of Columbia;"* approved 13*th May*, 1870.

"SEC. 1. That the number of town councilmen to be hereafter chosen at elections in the borough of Berwick, Columbia County, shall be six; and that all elections in said borough for the choice of borough officers and for the choice of directors of common schools, and all appointments and elections to fill vacancies in the offices of said borough, shall be according to the fourth and fifth sections of the act to define the limits and to organize the town of Bloomsburg, approved 4th March, 1870: *Provided, however,* That this section shall not apply to the choice of inspectors of election for said borough."

DIRECTORS FOR THE BLOOM POOR DISTRICT: *"An Act to regulate the election of directors of the poor for the Bloom district in Columbia County;"* approved 28*th March*, 1870.—*P. Laws*, 611.

"SEC. 1. That on the second Tuesday of October next, and every third year thereafter at the time of township elections under general laws, the qualified electors of Bloomsburg and of the several townships which shall have become a part of the Bloom district for the support and maintenance of the poor, shall elect three persons to be directors of the poor for said district, whose terms of service shall commence upon the first day of April next following their election, and continue for three years.

"SEC. 2. In all elections of said directors, whether

for regular terms or to fill vacancies, each voter may
distribute his votes to and among candidates as he
shall think fit, or may bestow them all upon one
candidate; and where three directors are to be
chosen he may give one vote and a half to each of
two candidates; in all cases the candidates highest
in vote shall be chosen. . . .

"SEC. 3. Whenever a single vacancy shall occur
or exist in said board of directors, the Court of Quarter
Sessions of the Peace of Columbia County shall
fill the same for the whole remaining part of the unexpired term in question, by appointing some fit and
competent person from among the electors of said
poor district who shall have voted for the director
whose place is to be filled."

SCHOOL DIRECTORS IN CERTAIN DISTRICTS.—By
an act approved 10th February, 1871, (P. Laws, 41,)
it was provided, "That hereafter in the election of
School Directors in the Twenty-second, Twenty-
fourth, and Twenty-seventh Wards of the City of
Philadelphia, each elector shall vote for four persons, and the six having the highest number of votes
shall be declared duly elected to serve for three
years from the first day of January next succeeding
their election."

By another act, approved 2d June, 1871, (P.
Laws, 1351,) entitled, "An Act to change the mode
of electing school directors in certain townships in
the counties of Bradford and Susquehanna," it was
provided—

"That from and after the passage of this act,
school directors in Smithfield township, in the

county of Bradford, and Apolorous and Franklin townships, Susquehanna County, shall be chosen by the electors of said districts in the manner following : Whenever an even number is to be chosen, each elector shall have the right to vote for one-half the number to be elected, and whenever an odd number is to be chosen, each elector may vote for a majority of the number to be elected, and the persons who shall receive the highest number of votes to the number to be chosen, shall be declared elected, and of those persons elected, the ones receiving the highest number of votes shall hold their office for the longest term of years."

RIVERSIDE BOROUGH : " *An Act to incorporate the village of Riverside, in the County of Northumberland, into a borough;*" *approved 4th May, 1871.—P. Laws, 1120.*

" SEC. 10. The election of councilmen and other officers of said borough, including school directors and justices of the peace, shall be upon the plan of the free vote, and according to the provisions of the fourth section of the Bloomsburg act of 4th of March, 1870, so far as the same can be applied ; and the filling of vacancies in the offices of said borough shall be, according to the fifth section of the same act, by the court of common pleas of Northumberland county."

UNIONTOWN BOROUGH : " *A supplement to the several acts relating to the borough of Uniontown, Fayette County;*" *approved 11th May, 1871.—P. Laws, 748.*

" SEC. 2. That at the next election in said borough,

and annually thereafter, there shall be chosen by vote at large in said borough, six members of council, two assessors of taxes and two constables; and the said councilmen, assessors, and constables shall be elected under the provisions and in the manner prescribed by the fourth section of the act of March fourth, one thousand eight hundred and seventy, entitled " An Act to define the limits and to organize the town of Bloomsburg;" and vacancies in said offices shall be filled, pursuant to the provisions of the fifth section of the same act, by the court of quarter sessions of Fayette County.

"SEC. 3. At the next election, and annually thereafter, the voters of said borough shall also elect at large two school directors, who shall hold their offices for three-year terms; and at said next election, and every third year thereafter, there shall be elected three auditors who shall annually settle and adjust all accounts of said borough; and the said school directors and auditors shall be voted for and chosen in the same manner as the officers mentioned in the second section of this act."

SNYDERTOWN BOROUGH: "*An Act to erect Snydertown, in the county of Northumberland, into a borough;*" approved 26th May, 1871.—*P. Laws,* 1225.

"SEC. 5. That whenever two or more persons are to be chosen to the same office in said borough, for the same term of service, they shall be voted for and chosen according to the provisions of the fourth section of the Bloomsburg act of 4th of March,

1870: *Provided, however,* That this section shall not apply to the choice of inspectors of election."

SHAMOKIN BOROUGH: *"An Act for the division of the borough of Shamokin into two wards, and for the better government of the same;"* approved 19th of May, 1871.—*P. Laws,* 958.

"SEC. 7. In the election of all borough and ward officers in said borough, (except inspectors of election,) whenever two or more persons are to be elected to the same office, for the same term of service, they shall be voted for and chosen under the provision of the 4th section of the Bloomsburg act of fourth of March, Anno Domini one thousand eight hundred and seventy; and vacancies in said offices, when the manner of filling them shall not be otherwise provided for by law, shall be according to the fifth section of the same act by the court of quarter sessions of Northumberland County; the manner of voting herein provided for shall apply to the election of justices of the peace and directors of common schools."

HULMEVILLE BOROUGH: *"An Act to incorporate the borough of Hulmeville, in Bucks County;"* approved 8th March, 1872.

"SEC. 6. That all elections in said borough for the choice of councilmen, town auditors, assistant assessors and justices of the peace whenever two or more are to be chosen at the same time and for the same term of service, shall be according to the provisions of the 4th section of the Bloomsburg act of 4th March, 1870, and vacancies in the said offices, except that of justice of the peace, shall be according to the 5th section of the same act; and all elections held in said school district of Middletown township and said borough of Hulmeville for the choice of school directors shall also be subject to and according to the provisions of the aforesaid fourth section of the Bloomburg act."

SCHOOL DIRECTORS IN CONYNGHAM TOWNSHIP, CO-LUMBIA COUNTY: *"An Act relating to the election of school directors in Conyngham township, Co-lumbia County;" approved 8th March,* 1872.

"SEC. 1. That the provisions of the fourth section of an act, entitled ' An Act to define the limits and to organize the town of Bloomsburg,' approved 4th March, 1870, be and the same are hereby extended to the township of Conyngham in the county of Columbia, so far as the same relates to the election of school directors, from and after the passage of this act."

BOROUGH OF CHAMBERSBURG: By an act approved 9th April, 1872, (P. Laws, 1011,) Chambers-burg was divided into four wards, and the second section of the act makes provision for the election of councilmen therefrom as follows:

"SEC. 2. The town council shall consist of two members from each ward, who shall hold their offices for the term of two years; and in their election each voter may give his two votes to one candidate, and candidates highest in vote shall be declared elected. . . ."

III. A SPECIAL STATUTE.
A CONTESTED ELECTION COMMITTEE.

A remarkable case occurred of the application of the limited vote to the choice of an election committee, at the legislative session of 1872. By an act approved 21st February, of that year, supplementary to the general election act of 2d July, 1839, provision was made for selecting in a new manner a committee of seven members of the Senate to try the important contested election case of McClure vs. Gray. The act was as follows, omitting matter irrelevant to the present purpose:

"Sec. 1. . . . That in any case of contested election now pending in the Senate the committee for the trial of the contest shall be selected and formed by the Senate . . . by choosing six members thereof viva voce, each Senator voting for no more than three members, and the six highest in vote shall be declared selected; the remaining member of the committee shall be chosen by lot in manner following, to wit: The names of all the remaining Senators present except those of the Speaker and sitting member shall be written on distinct pieces of paper as nearly alike as may be, each of which shall be rolled up and put into a box or urn by the Clerk of the Senate or some person appointed by the Senate to act in his stead, and the box or urn shall be placed on the Speaker's desk; the Clerk of the Senate, or person appointed to act in his stead, having thoroughly shaken and intermixed said papers, shall draw them out one by one, and the names of the Senators so drawn shall be written down on a separate list by one of the clerks until thirteen names shall have been drawn; a separate list of the thirteen Senators so drawn shall be given to each of the parties to the contest, who shall, accompanied by the Clerk or other person appointed to act in his stead, immediately withdraw to some adjoining room, where they shall proceed to strike off alternately the names upon said list until but one name shall be left thereon; and the Senator whose name shall remain shall be the seventh member of the committee.

"Sec. 3. Any vacancy occurring in said committee shall be filled as follows: If such vacancy shall be of a member chosen by the votes of Senators, it shall be filled by a new appointment made in open Senate, by the same or by a majority of the same Senators who shall have voted for the member whose place is to be filled; if such vacancy shall be of the seventh member of the committee chosen as aforesaid by lot and challenge, his place shall be filled in the same manner as that in which the said seventh member shall have been chosen, all the names of the qualified members present being first placed in the box or urn for the purpose of selection; and any member chosen to fill a vacancy shall be duly sworn, and shall perform all the duties and possess all the powers of an original member of the committee from the time of his selection: In no case of the selection of a committee or of the filling of a vacancy shall the sitting member be permitted to vote, and in case of the absence or refusal to act of the contestant or of the sitting member, the Senate shall appoint some proper person to act in his stead."

The foregoing plan for selecting an election committee is believed to be much superior to the Grenville plan, borrowed from parliamentary practice, which has heretofore obtained in Pennsylvania, and is prescribed by the general election law of 1839. By the latter, all the members of a committee are drawn by lot and challenge, and it may happen that all of them will be members of one political party, thus excluding all certainty of thorough investigation in the trial, as well as an impartial decision. So, too, the very extended allowance of challenge by the old plan makes it probable in any given case that the ablest members of the body upon both sides will be excluded from service on the committee, leaving the committee to be composed of weaker and less independent members.

LOCAL ELECTIONS IN PENNSYLVANIA UNDER REFORMED VOTING.

UNDER the Pennsylvania statutes for reformed voting, just given, there have been numerous elections held within the last two or three years. From among these a few are selected to illustrate the practical working of the new plan. They are cases in which there were disturbing influences, interfering with regular party action, but yet all of which resulted in fair representation of the people. They furnish evidence of the practicability of the new plan under any combination of circumstances likely to occur, and they further prove that not only does the new plan give to every respectable interest its due representation, but it also eliminates from election contests most of the soreness and bad blood which commonly attend them. It has this latter effect, because under it there are but few beaten candidates, no party or interest usually putting up more persons to be voted for than it has votes to elect.

If the subjoined cases prove that the new plan works justly and well in the turmoil and excitement of irregular or exceptional election contests, it is manifest that its operation in all ordinary cases must be still more satisfactory and complete.

BLOOMSBURG TOWN ELECTION FOR COUNCILMEN : The first election held in Bloomsburg under the new plan of voting was on April 12, 1870, and the following was the result :

For President of the Council :

	Votes.
Elias Mendenhall	213
Robert F. Clark	202
Majority	11

For Councilmen :

William B. Koons	393½
Frederick C. Eyer	362½
Stephen Knorr	297
Joseph Sharpless	392
Caleb Barton	364
Charles G. Barkley	429
Simon C. Shive	260½
Scattering	35½

Republicans in *italic*. The regular Democratic ticket had upon it the names of Koons, Eyer and Knorr, with two votes to each, and was successful, although votes were diverted from the two latter to Shive and Barkley, Democrats, originally named upon the Opposition People's ticket. For originally the People's ticket was formed with the four names upon it of *Sharpless, Barton,* Barkley and Shive, or two from each party.

But as in the course of the voting it appeared probable that a fourth man could not be carried upon the 'People's ticket, there was a partial dropping of Shive and concentration upon Barkley, which accounts mostly for the ultimate disparity of votes between those two candidates. The formation of a people's ticket in the manner above mentioned, with *Mendenhall* for President of the Council, no doubt resulted in the election of the latter, although it was unsuccessful in defeating any of the regular candidates for Councilmen nominated by the Democratic majority in the town; but as the President is a member of the Council, the general result was exactly right as between parties, the political majority in the town having four and the minority three in the Council, representing fairly the political opinions as well as the personal preferences of the citizens. In the case of this election the new plan was subjected to a severe test by reason of irregular party action in the formation of a combined or people's ticket, but it vindicated itself in a just and proper result. The weakest candidate only upon the combined ticket was beaten, and each party obtained ultimately its appropriate measure of representation in the government of the town.

A SECOND ELECTION IN BLOOMSBURG: A second election in the town for the choice of other town officers beside Councilmen, was held on the second Tuesday of October, 1870, in connection with the general election. There were to be chosen two Constables;

two Assessors of taxes; two assistant Assessors;
two School Directors and three Town Auditors, beside the usual officers of election for the two districts of East and West Bloomsburg, and a Justice
of the Peace to fill a vacancy. Omitting the latter
officers from further notice, as they were electable
under former laws, we proceed to explain how those
chosen under the Bloomsburg Act were voted for
and elected.

Each party nominated a ticket in the same form.
The Democratic ticket was as follows:

Constable—Martin C. Woodward, 2 votes.

Assessor—John K. Grotz, 2 votes.

Assistant Assessor—Frederick C. Eyer, 2 votes.

School Director—Charles W. Miller, 2 votes.

Town Auditors—John B. Casey, 1½ votes, B.
Frank Zarr, 1½ votes.

The Republican ticket being arranged in the
same manner, with other names, it was certain from
the outset that *all* the candidates of both parties
would be elected except one of those for Auditor.
The majority would carry two Auditors and the
minority but one. There was, therefore, very
smooth work in the election of local officers; an absence of animosity and sharp management; no
trading of votes and no necessity to struggle for a
majority in order to avoid defeat and virtual disfranchisement. *Each party obtained its share of
the town offices by its own votes.*

We append the vote for the several candidates.

Constables.

Martin C. Woodward.. 753

Baltzer T. Laycock.. 368

Assessors.

John K. Grotz	498
Joseph Sharpless	654

Assistant Assessors.

Frederick C. Eyer	494
Samuel Shaffer, Sr.	640

School Directors.

Charles W. Miller	502
Jacob K. Edgar	628

Town Auditors.

John B. Casey	367½
B. Frank Zarr	366
F. P. Drinker	490½
Ephraim P. Lutz	481½

All the above were elected except the one lowest in vote for Auditor; the Republicans in *italic*.

The very large vote given to Mr. Woodward for re-election as Constable was intended as a compliment to an officer of unusual merit, whose vigilance in the preservation of order in the town, and fidelity in the performance of his other duties, had attracted to him a large measure of public confidence and approval. It will be observed that at the foregoing election the ordinary political minority of the town had in fact the majority of the votes polled, as the general election which accompanied the town election at that time was not an exciting one, and there was a sluggish vote of the majority party. It is evident therefore that under the old plan of voting the party ordinarily in the minority in the town would have swept all the offices voted for except one constable, and would have deprived their opponents almost entirely of representation, so far as representation was dependent upon that election. But at the very next election, on the old plan of voting, a similar injustice would have been inflicted, though in exactly the opposite direction; the Republican minority would have lost every office voted for, and the majority have seized them all, whereas under the new plan, at both elections, each party obtained its just share.

SUNBURY ELECTION OF OCTOBER, 1870: At that election most of the borough and ward officers being electable under the new plan of voting, there was a partial division of them between parties. The Chief Burgess and the Second Burgess were respectively voted for at large, under the majority rule, and were of course carried by the Republican majority of the town. But to most of the other officers the new rule applied. Each of the two wards elect annually two assistant Burgesses and four members of the Town Council, beside their proper Ward officers. We give some results in the West Ward from the election returns, which show, however, only the votes given to candidates who were elected; (Republicans in *italic*:)

WEST WARD.

Republican, 247; Democratic, 110.

ASSISTANT BURGESSES, (2).—*John Bourne*, 277; George Hill, 217.

COUNCILMEN, (4).—*N. F. Lightner*, 306; *J. W.*

Friling, 293; *Jacob Renn,* 273; Thomas M. Pursell, 219.

OVERSEERS OF THE POOR, (2).—*Fred. Merrill,* 237; P. F. Zimmerman, 210.

STREET COMMISSIONERS, (2).—*Chas. Gossler,* 252 Charles F. Martin, 236.

In the East Ward, (Republican, 210, Democratic, 107,) the minority carried one of the four Councilmen and one or two of the other officers.

In the voting given above, the Democrats in each case generally gave two votes to one candidate, but in the case of four Councilmen, the Republicans gave one vote and one-third to each of three, and the Democrats four votes to one.

ELECTION OF COUNCILMEN IN NORTHUMBERLAND BOROUGH.—In Northumberland Borough, at the October election, 1870, there was a Republican majority of 10 for Burgess. Very properly each party nominated only three Councilmen, although six were to be chosen, because the free vote applied to the election of those officers. The result was that the Democrats, giving each two votes to each of their three candidates, elected them, but one of the Republican candidates was beaten by a Republican Volunteer. As this case illustrates the working of the free vote, the facts will be stated as they are understood to have occurred. At the Republican meeting to nominate Councilmen, a gentleman who expected to be nominated was defeated by the arts or influence of a personal enemy, who immediately afterwards boasted of the achievement. The friends of the beaten man became indignant and concluded to rectify the injustice done, by electing him as an independent candidate. The free vote afforded them the ready means of accomplishing their purpose, and they proceeded at the election to vote plumpers of six votes for their friend and carried him through the contest triumphantly. Without disturbing the results of the election generally, they carried their man and secured representation for themselves in the council according to their desire.

Bolting a nomination under the new plan means, then, that commonly the bolters can obtain their due share of power and no more, and that the whole election cannot be turned upside down or changed throughout by them. One-sixth of the voters of Northumberland can elect one Councilman, but they cannot disturb the other voters of the town in choosing the remaining five. Under the old majority rule the bolters would have been compelled to form a combination with the opposite party, or to trade or buy votes, in order to succeed; the whole election would probably have been muddled or disgraced, and one party or the other would have carried more than its share of the officers to be elected. The new plan insures justice to all, prevents intrigue and corruption, preserves the orderly action of parties, cuts off the main mischiefs of bolting, and encourages the selection of good men as candidates.

We append the vote for Councilmen in full:

Wm. T. Forsyth...................................... 328
James Tool.. 301
A. H. Stone.. 291

Wm. H. Leighow.. 319
Benj. Heckert... 224
James McClure.............. 207
Hiram Young, Ind...................................... 561

Republicans in *italic*. McClure being the lowest, was the defeated candidate.

ELECTION OF DIRECTORS OF THE POOR FOR THE BLOOM POOR DISTRICT.—At the election held in October, 1870, for three Directors of the Poor, under the special act of March 28th of that year, the voting was as follows:

	Miller.	Kramer.	*Ikeler.*	*Schuyler.*
Bloomsburg, East...232½	222	226½	163½
Bloomsburg, West...132	123	223½	180
Greenwood 227	235½	346½	127½
Sugarloaf..............180	180	12	10½
Scott......... ....115½	145½	364½	12
	923	906	1173	493½

Stephen H. Miller and William Kramer, *Democrats*, and Johnson H. Ikeler, *Republican*, were therefore elected for three-year terms commencing on the first day of April following. These officers being chosen on the plan of the free vote, it was inevitable that they would be divided between the two political parties according to a just principle of representation; the majority in the district would be able to elect two and the minority one. The Democrats therefore voted tickets in the following form:

"Stephen H. Miller, 1½ votes;
William Kramer, 1½ votes."

The Republicans nominated two candidates also, and tickets for them were prepared in the same form; but as they had not votes enough to elect both they finally concentrated their vote mainly upon Ikeler, as shown in the above return. The election at last became to them a question of choice or preference between their own candidates, and the result proved that they preferred Ikeler. It is here shown that the free vote not only divides offices fairly between parties, but enables voters of either party, in certain cases, to choose between their own nominees and to correct any blunder made in their nomination. The truth is, that the new plan of voting is so flexible as well as just that it readily adapts itself to any state of facts at an election, and gives to the voter that complete freedom of action which is necessary to his judicious exercise of the right of suffrage. In this case, where three Directors of the Poor were to be chosen, allowing each voter to give his three votes to one, two, or three candidates, as he might think fit, enabled each party to take what belonged to it and to handle its votes in the most convenient and effectual manner to that end; and it also afforded the ready means of correcting a blunder made in the selection of candidates. This election also furnishes evidence of the convenience and accuracy with which fractional votes may be polled, counted, and returned in all cases where their use shall be found desirable.

Scoring of Fractional Votes.—An ordinary and convenient mode of tallying or counting tickets containing fractional votes which has obtained in the local elections above referred to, and in others, may here be properly presented.

When tickets containing one and a half votes to each of two candidates are to be counted by election officers, the fraction may be disregarded in the first instance, and the tickets only scored upon the tally lists, the sum of the fractions being added at the end of the score, as already explained in another place. In a given case of forty such tickets polled, the score will stand as follows:

John Jones,　$(1\frac{1}{2})$ 〜〜〜〜 =40+20=60 votes.

William Brown, $(1\frac{1}{2})$ 〜〜〜〜 =40+20=60 votes.

If in addition to tickets containing fractional votes, a candidate shall have polled for him tickets containing whole votes alone, the latter may be scored separately above the line containing the fractional votes, and be carried out and added at the right. Thus if he shall receive, in addition to votes scored as above, twenty whole votes unconnected with fractions, the score or tally may be made as follows:

〜〜 20

John Jones, $(1\frac{1}{2})$ 〜〜〜〜 =40+20=60=80 votes.

Other modes of keeping the tally lists may be resorted to at the discretion of election officers, but those above are given because they have some sanction from practice, and because by their use economy of space is consulted in the making up of returns.

NOMINATIONS TO OFFICE.

Good plans for nominating candidates to office are almost as important, and deserve consideration almost as much, as good plans for electing them. In this place it is therefore proposed to notice two recent plans of nomination which have been applied in Pennsylvania to the selection of nominees for county offices. They are both popular-vote plans, and the purpose of both is to avoid the evils which ordinarily attend upon representative conventions. The one is known as the "Crawford County System," and the other as the "Columbia County Plan;" so named from the counties in which they respectively originated and were first put in force.

By the Crawford County plan, the voters at primary elections vote directly for candidates for nomination; from each election district a return judge conveys the return of his district to a joint meeting of return judges for the county; in the joint meeting of those judges the returns are cast up and candidates highest in vote for each office are declared the nominees. Of all bad plans, accepted in recent practice, this is unquestionably the worst, and yet to men of little reflection and narrow experience, it seems fair, reasonable, judicious and just. Hence it has been adopted in many counties in place of the old convention plan. The main objections to it are these: That it produces, inevitably, expensive contests for nomination; that it tends strongly to fraudulent voting and fraudulent returns; that it makes success very often dependent upon intrigue between candidates whereby voters are deceived; that it shamefully disregards and puts open contempt upon the doctrine that the majority shall rule; that it leads to embarrassment of voters and to blunders in voting by reason of ignorance among voters of the relative strength of candidates, and lastly, that it substitutes a feeble body of return judges (who hardly bear a representative character) for a regular, strong convention, for the transaction of other party business beside the making of nominations. Of course it multiplies candidates, exasperates popular passions, and degrades the whole tone of party action.*

But the Columbia County plan of nomination is a popular-vote plan of a different character, and challenges attention and respect, because it retains

---

* The working of the "Crawford County system" as a nominating plan was well shown in the Democratic nominations for Northumberland County, in 1871. It was in force there, at that time, and exhibited some of its worst features. Hundreds of false or unpolled votes were reported to control results, and were, almost of necessity, received and counted at the meeting of the return judges; for one imperfection of the plan is that it provides no means for the investigation and correction of the frauds which it invites. Upon the face of the returns of votes for the respective candidates for the several offices, at the primary elections, it further appeared that each of the nominees (save one) had less than one-half the total vote and one of them less than one-third.

Analyzing the vote we get the following exhibit:

President Judge.—For nominee, 1408, for other candidates, 2399.

Representative.—For nominee, 1585, for other candidates, 2275.

Associate Judge.—For nominee, 1349, for other candidates, 2219.

Treasurer.—For nominee, 983, for other candidates, 2461.

Commissioner.—For nominee, 1273, for other candidates, 2074.

This is indeed minority representation with a vengeance! But it was unavoidable under the plurality rule.

It only remains to state, that the whole ticket set up in this very objectionable way was beaten, and that the plan of nomination which produced the disaster was forthwith abolished, and the convention plan restored with proportional representation of districts.

17

the feature of a convention well constituted for work, and because it applies the principle of reformed voting very thoroughly to the nomination of candidates. The rules which embody and give form to this plan are not supposed to be perfect—in fact, it is evident that they might be improved in construction, and made much more comprehensive and complete—but as the first formal attempt to secure proportional representation in a nominating body chosen by popular votes, they may claim a place in this volume, and justify the comments and exposition which will follow them.

RULES OF NOMINATION IN COLUMBIA COUNTY:— ADOPTED DEC. 26, 1870.

"I. The annual county convention shall be held at the Court House in Bloomsburg on the second Tuesday of August, at one o'clock, P. M., and the delegate elections shall be held on the Saturday before at the places of holding the general elections in the several election districts, between the hours of three and seven o'clock in the afternoon.

"II. The representation of districts in county convention shall be in proportion to the party vote of each, as cast at the most recent election for Governor, but the whole number of delegates shall not exceed seventy nor be less than fifty-four, and no district shall be allowed less than two or more than four delegates.

"III. Until the next election for Governor, delegates shall be allowed to districts upon a ratio of sixty voters for a delegate, allowance being made for the largest fractions of a ratio.

" IV. The Standing Committee shall, whenever necessary, make an apportionment of delegates to the several districts under these rules, and publish it, together with the rules, in the party newspapers of the County, at least two weeks before each annual convention.

" V. Voters at delegate elections may give their votes to a smaller number of candidates than the whole number to be elected in the manner provided in the fourth section of the Bloomsburg act of 4th of March, 1870.

" VI. The delegate elections shall be by ballot, and shall be held and conducted by a judge and clerk, . . . and the said officers shall keep a list of voters, and tally of votes counted, to be sent by them to the Convention with their certificate of the result of the election.

" VII. All cases of disputed seats in Convention shall be disposed of openly by vote after hearing the respective claimants and their evidence.

" VIII. All delegates must reside in the districts they represent. In case of an absent delegate he may depute another to serve in his stead. . . .

" IX. The voting in Convention shall be open, and any two members may require the yeas and nays on any question pending."

Rule 10 authorizes special Conventions to be called by the Standing Committee. Rule 11 provides that all County nominations and appointments of district conferees and delegates to State conventions shall be made in County Convention.

" XII. The Standing Committee shall consist of one member from each election district, who shall be elected by the people at the delegate elections, who shall choose their own Chairman, and any five of them shall be a quorum when called together by the Chairman.

"XIII. No member of the Legislature shall be chosen by this county as a delegate to a State Convention during his term of office.

"XIV. In Convention a majority of all the votes given shall be necessary to a nomination, and no person named shall be peremptorily struck from the list of candidates until after the fourth vote, when the lowest name shall be struck off, and so on at each successive vote until a nomination shall be effected.

"XV. Delegates instructed *by the voters who select them* shall obey their instructions in Convention, and votes given by them in violation of their instructions shall be disallowed by the Convention. All instructions shall be reported by the election officers.

"XVI. Conventions shall be called to order by the Chairman of the Standing Committee, or in his absence by some other member thereof, who shall entertain and put to vote motions for the election of a President and two Secretaries for purposes of temporary organization."

Rule 17. No person shall be eligible to a nomination who has opposed the ticket of his party at the next preceding election. Rule 18. Any voter may be challenged who has voted against his party at a Federal or State election within two years, or opposed his party ticket at the last preceding election, or has taken or agreed to take money or any valuable consideration for his vote at the delegate election, or has corrupted or attempted to corrupt any voter of the district at such election. Rule 19. If it shall be made to appear that any candidate for nomination has paid or promised any consideration to any delegate to influence his vote, or that the same has been done by another with his approbation, the name of such candidate shall be struck from the list of candidates, or if already nominated his name shall be struck from the ticket and another nomination be made, and he shall be ineligible as a candidate or delegate for two years.   Rule 20. Any delegate who shall receive, or accept the promise of, any consideration for himself or for another for his vote or influence in Convention, shall on proof of the fact be forthwith expelled from the Convention (by a majority vote), and shall be ineligible for any nomination or to serve as a delegate for two years.   Rule 21. A two-thirds vote in a regular annual Convention is required to alter or amend any of the Rules.

In Convention, August 8, 1871, the following additional Rule was unanimously adopted :—

" XXII. Candidates for nomination may be voted for directly at the Delegate Elections, and shall receive delegate or district votes in Convention in proportion to their popular vote in the several districts, upon the same principle on which delegates are electable under the 5th rule."

OBSERVATIONS ON THE COLUMBIA COUNTY RULES OF NOMINATION.

REPRESENTATION OF DISTRICTS.—The maximum of four and minimum of two delegates to each district, are judiciously fixed for several reasons. First, The number of districts to be represented being twenty-seven, the result is a representative body of convenient size: Second, The numbers two, three and four are convenient ones for the application of

the new plan of voting in the selection of delegates:
Third, Liberal representation of the smallest districts, and a limitation upon the representation of
the largest ones, gives play to the principle of territorial representation, (as distinguished from that of
mere numbers,) without carrying it to excess, and
in the particular case in hand avoided the dissatisfaction which would have been produced in the
smaller districts by a reduction of their representation in Convention. (Before the new rules were
adopted in 1870, each district, without regard to the
magnitude of its vote, was entitled to two delegates.)
But in the case of a county much larger or much
smaller than Columbia, good reasons may exist for
adopting a different scale of representative numbers.
Where the districts to be represented are but few in
number, as many as six or eight delegates might be
allowed to some of the largest ones; while in the
case of a great county, with numerous electoral divisions, the smallest districts might be limited to one
delegate each. It is true that in such case proportional representation could not be secured for such
small districts along with separate representation,
but the evil of over-representation in convention—
of an unwieldy representative body—may be
greater than that of partial disfranchisement of district electors by the majority vote. Besides, it is
evident that in the case of single districts, (i. e. districts with but one delegate,) the evils of the majority vote are at their minimum; the disfranchisement is always likely to be much less in such than
in plural districts where the total number of voters
must be greater. And, practically, in any ordinary

case, it will be found that delegates in convention
from single districts will constitute but a small percentage of the whole Convention membership, and
will not constitute a great disturbing force opposed
to the reformatory action of the new plan.

That proportional representation of districts in
nominating conventions is a great improvement
over' equal district representation therein, will not
be questioned by any one when the objection of
minority disfranchisement in large districts has been
removed.   For if the representation of large districts is broken up, or divided between parties or
candidates by the free vote, the vote of those districts will not ordinarily overwhelm or swamp the
smaller ones in Convention and give to the former
absolute control of the nominations to be made.

THE FREE VOTE FOR DELEGATES.—The 5th Rule
given above is the first application ever made of the
free vote to primary elections connected with nominations for public office, and it has been found to be
most satisfactory upon trial.   The scale of representation under it is not difficult of ascertainment or
remembrance.   In a district entitled to two delegates, any number of voters exceeding one-third of
the whole can elect one delegate, and, exceeding two-
thirds, both.   In a district of three delegates, any
number of voters exceeding one-fourth can elect one
delegate, exceeding two-fourths (or one-half) two,
and exceeding three-fourths, all three.   In a district of four delegates, any number of voters exceeding one-fifth can elect one, exceeding two-fifths,
two, exceeding three-fifths, three, and exceeding
four-fifths, all four.   In each case the denominator

of the fraction is one number above the total delegate number. For the plan upon which votes may be actually cast to realize these results, reference may be had to the 4th section of the Bloomsburg act to be found at a prior page of this volume.

It is to be remembered constantly that the new plan of voting is not *compulsory.* It is permissive merely, and need not be resorted to in all cases. Whenever there is an understanding between candidates, or among the voters of a district, as to the persons who shall be elected delegates, a common ticket may be used by all the voters, and cumulation of votes be dispensed with. The right to cumulate must however exist with the voter in order to his certain obtainment in any case of just representation by the concession or agreement of his co-electors of the district.

INSTRUCTION OF DELEGATES.—The 15th rule is superseded in part by the new or 22d rule, but yet invites examination because it presents a clear case of unwisdom in stopping short of the ultimate point to which a sound principle of reform would lead us. The 5th rule having provided a just plan for the selection of delegates, it was seen that the old practice of voting district instructions by a majority would no longer work. It would not do, for instance, to allow a minority in a district to elect a delegate and then permit the majority to instruct him. Thereupon, the attempt was made to harmonize the old practice of instruction with the new voting rule by a modification of the former, expressed by the words *italicized* by us in the 15th Rule. " Delegates instructed *by the voters who select them* shall obey their instructions in Convention," &c. By this clause it was intended that election officers should report separately instructions voted by majority and minority voters to the delegates elected by them respectively and not combine them in the return. But by this device simplicity was sacrificed to some extent, while questions of difficulty connected with the old plan of voting instructions remained uncorrected.

THE POPULAR VOTE FOR CANDIDATES.—By the new or 22d rule, authorizing a direct vote by the people for candidates, all the advantages of the old plan of voting instructions are retained, while its inconveniences are wholly avoided. It is perhaps the most perfect rule ever devised for taking the sense of the people upon nominations for office; for it is convenient, effectual, popular and just, and stands free from all the objections which condemn other plans of popular-vote nomination, and especially the plan known as the "Crawford County System."

But here a brief explanation of its practical working—or of the manner in which it is applied—is necessary to its full comprehension; and such explanation can be best made by tracing the proceeding of nomination under the rules in its successive stages from its commencement at the election of delegates to its consummation in county Convention.

1. The officers who hold a delegate election in any district are provided with election blanks or papers on which they keep a list of the persons who vote, and score tallies or counts at the close of the

election of all votes polled, whether for delegates or candidates for nomination, and these papers, with returns certified, are transmitted by the election officers to the county Convention.

2. The voters at such election vote sheet or slip tickets (ordinarily printed or partly printed) for delegates, and for candidates for nomination to the several offices to be filled; but as the free vote applies to the choice of delegates by virtue of Rule 5, any voter may cumulate his delegate votes on one or more delegate candidates in the manner provided in the 4th section of the Bloomsburg act.

3. Returns of the votes cast in each district for candidates for nomination being produced before the county Convention when it meets, it can be readily ascertained how many district or delegate votes in Convention each candidate is entitled to, and in fact the record can be made up from the returns by a Secretary or Clerk and announced by the presiding officer. But if the districts be called over the vote of each must be reported correctly by the Delegates and recorded by the Convention officers, for the former are bound by the 15th rule to obey the virtual instructions of the home-voting, and the 22nd rule is imperative as to the principle on which district or delegate votes shall be assigned to candidates by the convention.

What is material to observe here, is, that the popular vote polled in any district is not reported in order to be itself counted upon the result in Convention; it is simply reported to direct and control the casting of the Convention votes to which the district is entitled. There is, therefore, no motive to swell the popular vote in a district in order to increase its power or influence in nominations, and hence a fertile cause of fraud inherent in other plans of popular-vote nomination is entirely excluded.

4. If upon a report of the district voting throughout the county it shall appear that any candidate is entitled to a majority of Convention votes, his nomination will of course be forthwith recorded and announced.

5. If no candidate shall be entitled to a Convention majority by virtue of the district voting reported, the Convention will proceed to make or perfect a nomination. This is most conveniently done by calling over the districts in alphabetical order and receiving the vote of each from its delegates; in other words, the vote is taken by districts, as it is taken in national conventions by States. But still the delegates from any district must report or give their votes according to the home-vote in their district; they must still obey their home instructions and execute the twenty-second rule. But from this obligation as to some of the candidates, they will be at once or presently discharged by the declination or withdrawal of candidates, or by the striking off of names lowest on the list of candidates, under the fourteenth rule. By one or the other, or both of these means, delegates from districts will have some of their votes freed, and can bestow them according to their best judgment, thus securing a nomination within a reasonable time. The idea is, that a candidate shall be entitled to all the Convention votes which the people have ordered to be given to him,

so long as he remains before the Convention; but when he is no longer before it, the vote pledged to him may be cast freely for others.

6. Necessarily the delegates from a district must cast the freed vote or votes of their district according to the decision of a majority of their number, except in one case, to wit: when all the votes of the district become free, when each delegate may cast a single or separate vote. The only alternative to this would be the allowance of fractional votes to be cast by delegates or reported, which would require a special or additional rule. But mostly nominations will be made before this question can arise.

Having now traced out the successive stages in the proceeding of nomination, it only remains to remark, under this head, that upon the popular-vote plan, contained in the rules, *the principle of the free vote is substantially applied in the nomination for each office to be filled;* for the same popular vote which would carry a delegate for a candidate, if used for that purpose, will carry for him a Convention vote when given to him directly. In a district of two delegates a popular vote exceeding one-third of the vote polled will entitle him to one Convention vote; in a district of three delegates a popular vote exceeding one-fourth of the vote polled will entitle him to one Convention vote, and a like result will follow in a district of four delegates when he obtains over one-fifth of the total vote. In other words, the same number of popular votes is required to secure a Convention vote that is required for the election of a delegate, under the fifth rule.

THE CONVENTION.—This body, when assembled,

represents truly the whole mass of voters in the county who have taken part in the primary elections, and is well constituted for the transaction of business, for the selection of district conferees and delegates to State Conventions, etc., as well as for perfecting nominations which have not been determined by the people; and in practice it has been found that conventional action under the new rules (and particularly since the adoption of the twenty-second one) has been fair and satisfactory.

THE PLAN IN AMENDED FORM.

For general adoption and use the Columbia County plan might be expressed in a series of Rules somewhat as follows:

RULES.

A.—Voters at the primary elections may cast their delegate votes for any less number of candidates than the whole number of delegates to be chosen from their respective districts, in the manner authorized by the fourth section of the Bloomsburg act of 4th of March, 1870, and delegate candidates highest in vote shall be declared elected.

B.—Each voter at a primary election may vote directly for one candidate for each of the offices for which nominations are to be declared or made in Convention, and all votes so given shall be duly counted and returned by the election officers, to the Convention.

C.—Any candidate for nomination who shall receive popular votes cast as aforesaid at a primary election in any district shall be entitled to at least one Convention vote of such district, for his nomination, whenever his popular vote therein shall equal or exceed the number of voters required to elect one delegate therefrom under Rule A; and the number of such Convention votes to which he shall be entitled, when more than one, shall be a number equal to the number of delegates who could be elected under said rule by the voters who voted for him at said primary election.

D.—The Convention votes to which a candidate shall become entitled under Rule C shall remain to him so long as he continues a candidate before the Convention, but in case no candidate shall have a majority of Convention votes reported from the districts, the Convention shall proceed to perfect a nomination under the following regulations :

1. The districts shall be called over, and the delegates from each shall report to the Convention the Convention votes of their district; first the vote or votes pledged by the popular home-voting to candidates who remain before the Convention, and next any vote or votes unpledged to candidates or freed by the withdrawal of candidates.

2. Convention votes shall become freed by the voluntary declination of candidates and by striking off the name of the candidate lowest on the list at each vote after the first.

3. Unpledged and freed Convention votes from a district, when less in number than the whole Convention vote of the district, shall be cast by the delegation therefrom or by a majority of them acting jointly; but when all the Convention votes from a district shall be unpledged, or shall become freed, each delegate therefrom may cast one vote separately, or have his vote separately reported.

APPENDIX.

PROCEEDINGS AND DEBATE IN PARLIAMENT UPON LIMITED VOTING IN THREE-MEMBERED DISTRICTS.

In the House of Lords, July 30, 1867.

The reform bill being under consideration—

Lord CAIRNS moved an amendment, to come in after clause eight of the bill, as follows:

"At any contested election for any county or borough represented by three members no person shall vote for more than two candidates."

In supporting this amendment he explained that there would be at least eleven constituencies to which the plan proposed by it would be at once applicable, and he foresaw that if there should be a further alteration in the distribution of electoral power the great probability was that such alteration would go in the direction of increasing those three-cornered constituencies. This consideration made him more anxious that some proposition of this kind should be adopted. He then proceeded at length to present the reasons which had occurred to him in favor of his amendment, and to answer and repel certain objections which might be urged against it.

A debate followed, in which the amendment was supported by Earl Russell, Earl Spencer, Earl Stanhope, Earl Cowper, the Earl of Carnarvon, Lord Houghton, the Earl of Shrewsbury, and Viscount Stratford de Redcliffe; and was opposed on behalf of the administration by the Earl of Malmesbury and the Duke of Marlborough. Lord Denman suggested that the proposition should be made the subject of a separate bill.

Upon a division the vote stood:

For the amendment,.. 142
Against it,.. 51

Majority,... 91

Lord CAIRNS then proposed the following additional clause:

"At a contested election for the city of London no person shall vote for more than three candidates."

The clause was agreed to.

The London *Times* the day following contained an elaborate and powerful editorial in support of the proposition and in commendation of the action taken by the House of Lords. It declared that that House had "by a single vote covered many errors and justified the opinions of its warmest admirers. Such a triumph of reason and truth," it continued, "may well startle us, accustomed as we have been during this session to the rapid growth of convictions." "The idea of modifying our electoral machinery so as to secure in three-membered constituencies the proportionate representation of both the great divisions of party has made its way by its inherent justice. The verdict of the lords has been decisive, but we do not believe that it in any degree outstrips the independent opinion of the House of Commons, still less that it is at variance with the deliberate judgment of the country. It has been everywhere confessed that the adoption in one form or another of the principle of cumulative voting was essential to maintain the character of our institutions, and that through it, and through it alone, could the redistribution of electoral power (which all prescient statesmen regard as inevitable) be reconciled with the preservation of our representative government."

"The arguments on behalf of the proposal advanced by Lord Cairns were overwhelming. He himself treated the question in the succinct dialectic style, of which he is a master, and the chain of his reasoning was perfect. But he did not stand alone. In fact every one who took part in the discussion, with the exception of the ministers who represented the Government, was on his side. It mattered not whether, like Lord Russell, they spoke from the front bench of the Opposition, or like Lord Stanhope and Lord Shrewsbury, they avowed themselves faithful supporters of the administration and resolute to do nothing which should interfere with the success of the bill; whether, like Lord Spencer and Lord Cowper, they expressed the views of independent Liberals; like Lord Carnarvon, they argued from the position of a thoughtful Conservative; like Lord Stratford, they uttered the sentiments of a man above party; or, like Lord Houghton, confessed their sympathy with pure democracy, the result was the same. One and all saw in the proposed representation of minorities a suggestion consonant with the strictest principles of justice and equity, and therefore to be depended upon as stable when artificial securities must prove worthless."

"It is only necessary to remember that the House of Commons consults and deliberates as well as votes to see how necessary it is to the due performance of its functions that it should contain members representing all sections of the community. The power of decision can never be endangered by the proportionate representation of minorities, but the deliberate formation of opinion is exposed to great hazard if the moderating influences of dissenting minorities be excluded. Parliament itself must be improved by the addition of such men as will be chosen by the wealthy and intelligent merchants and manufacturers who are now unrepresented in the largest towns, and of the members who will be returned by the Liberal minorities of counties. The effect of Lord Cairns's amendment on the members for three-membered constituencies must be equally beneficial, and its consequences on the constituencies themselves will prove of transcendent importance. The voters who are now hopelessly outvoted and whose political energies become feeble by disuse will start into fresh vitality. Enfranchised in deed, and not merely in name, they will be animated by the consciousness of power. They will be brought into direct relation with the Legislature." "The Lords have shown their independence and their foresight. At a point of the highest importance in the history of the representative institutions of the country they have been faithful to themselves and to their duties. On minor questions they have shown themselves too ready to defer to the decision of the ministers of the Crown, but when the character of the future government of the nation was at stake they asserted their own judgment against all attempts to betray them to a false position."

In the House of Commons, August 8, 1867.

On the order of the day for the consideration of the amendments made by the House of Lords to the reform bill, the

Chancellor of the Exchequer, Mr. DISRAELI, said that the Cairns amendment "had been opposed on the part of her Majesty's Government in the House of Lords with all the authority that a Government can fairly exercise over a deliberative assembly; but he was bound to say that it was carried by an overwhelming majority; indeed, he must confess that it was almost unanimously carried by the House of Lords, because, when the minority was told, he observed that it consisted almost entirely of the members of the administration." He therefore, in deference to this strong expression of opinion by the House of Lords, advised a concurrence in the amendment.

Subsequently, the same evening, when the amendment came up for distinct consideration, Mr. BRIGHT moved to disagree with the amendment of the Lords. He expressed surprise at the speech of the Chancellor of the Exchequer, in view of his former speech when the same matter had been previously before the House. He wished he could find a suitable word to express his contempt for the proposition without expressing in the slightest degree anything that might be offensive to honorable members on his side of the House. But the member from Westminster (Mr. Mill) and his friends thought that the plan was in some degree an approach to the principle of the plan under which everybody should be represented and under which such things as majorities and minorities in election contests should hereafter be unknown. [Hear, hear, from Mr. Mill.]

Now, he thought those gentlemen who were in favor of Mr. Hare's plan were not in the slightest degree bound to support this plan. There was no intention in the country at present to establish Mr. Hare's plan, and the carrying of this proposition would be an unmixed injustice to the boroughs affected by it. The proposition was not likely to lead to the plan of Mr. Hare, but probably to have a contrary effect by reason of the ill will it would create in these large boroughs and in the country. The change proposed to be made was a fundamental change. There was no precedent for it in parliamentary history. It affected fundamentally the power of not only the constituency but of every individual in it. The alteration proposed had not been asked for. During six hundred years the principle of election by the majority had prevailed in the selection of members of the House. He suggested that the House at least suspend its decision in favor of the proposition until it had been a longer time before the country and a fuller opportunity afforded the constituencies of making up their minds upon it. He cited the cases of Liverpool, Manchester, Birmingham, and Leeds. They had been entitled to two members each, making eight altogether. By the bill they were each to have one additional member, and under the plan proposed there would be eight on one side and four on the other upon important public questions, and of course the four on one side would neutralize four of those on the other. Assuming that party ties were adhered to these four great constituencies would be so emasculated and crippled that they would have but four votes to bestow which would affect any of those great questions to which he had referred. The assigning of additional members to those boroughs upon this plan would not increase but would actually diminish their power in the House. He could speak, he was sure, for Manchester and for Birmingham, that the great majority of the constituency and population of those towns would be opposed to the proposition that additional members should be given them, if given under this crippling and injudicious clause.

Mr. BERESFORD HOPE declared himself unable to rise to the heights of democratic Toryism which had characterized the speech of the honorable member for Birmingham, [Mr. Bright.] Was the case of Birmingham miserable above that of all other boroughs? Birmingham was the seat of one of our great staples; Stoke was another. He himself was the majority member for Stoke, and his honorable colleague was the minority member for that borough. The Conservatives were entitled to one member, but he was of opinion that from their wealth, position, intellect, and numbers the Liberals of Stoke were likewise entitled to send a member to Parliament. Well, one Conservative and one Liberal were returned by the borough. Would the honorable member from Birmingham say it was humbled in consequence of that circumstance? So far was he from taking such a view that he had refused to be concerned in bringing down a second Conservative member because he believed it would be tyranny to do so. There were, say fifty-five thousand Conservatives and forty-five thousand Liberals in Stoke.

Now, would it be fair that either of those parties should be unrepresented? By the existing arrangement the whole population of Stoke was better served in that House. So much for the case of the two-handed boroughs; and if they took the case of the three-handed boroughs it was a juggling with words and a misrepresentation of fact to say that a representation of minorities would deprive the majorities in those boroughs of a fair share of representation in that House. If the minority in Birmingham should secure a member who could equal the honorable member (Mr. Bright) in eloquence it would give them a very great advantage indeed; but he denied that giving the third member for that borough to the minority would be a political injustice to the borough. If honorable members came to the House of Commons merely to count noses at the table there would be something in the honorable member's argument; but in no other sense would the influence of the two Liberal members for Birmingham be counterbalanced. The honorable member, whom he was happy to see on the first Opposition bench—(Mr. Bright was in conversation with Mr. Gladstone)—for no man had a better right to that position, and he would be there hereafter, [a laugh,] had drawn a touching picture of four towns who had at present eight members and would have twelve, but who, if this amendment of the Lords were adopted, would only have four; but if he might ask the honorable gentleman to descend from the regions of eloquence to those of plain fact, he would invite him to examine how matters really stood on these four boroughs. Manchester had two Liberal members; Liverpool had two Conservative members; so that these two boroughs wrote each other off. Leeds had one Liberal member, and one Conservative; thus its two members wrote each other off. Birmingham, however, had the good fortune to be represented by two Liberals; so that according to the doctrine of the honorable member the whole four boroughs were represented by his colleague and himself. [A laugh, and "hear, hear."]

Sir J. JERVOISE advocated the proposition for giving representation to the minority. He observed that if any argument were needed in support of such a proposal it would be found in the fact that the Government, though in the minority, had brought in this reform bill. [A laugh, and "hear, hear."]

Mr. SCOURFIELD had voted for the proposal before and would support it again. He cordially agreed with what had been said by the honorable member for Westminster a few evenings since—that he would not desire to see oppression practiced, even by the side to which he was most attached. When the honorable member for Birmingham said that the liberties of England would suffer detriment if there were no election contests, he could not help thinking that the honorable member spoke as if the life-blood of all the election agents and lawyers in the kingdom were flowing in his veins. [Laughter.] The fact was, that election contests were frequently unmitigated curses, and many places had been seriously injured by their means. ["Hear, hear."] He was not aware, for instance, that Lancaster, Totness, Reigate, and Great Yarmouth were any better off because they had been the scenes of contested elections. ["Hear, hear."]

Mr. BUXTON wished to touch upon a single argument which had not, he thought, received the attention it deserved. It seemed to him that valuable as the other results would be of the adoption of the proposed arrangement, no one of them would be of greater importance than this: that it would call forth so much political vigor and life in the constituencies to which it was applied. It was curious that those who had not given this subject much consideration often objected to this proposal, because they said that by extinguishing contests this arrangement would destroy political vitality. He was confident that its effect would be exactly the reverse; that it would be of singular use in preventing political stagnation. That would be clear if, instead of dealing with the question in the abstract, they took a concrete example. Take, for example, the town of Birmingham, in which it was proposed to adopt this plan. Could there be a doubt that if no such arrangement were made Birmingham would henceforth return three gentlemen of the same political hue?

The Liberal committee would select three candidates, and the majority of householders in the borough would be certain to support them. If there were ever a contest it would be a contest between the Liberals bidding against each other; but in all human probability there would be no contest at all; and those electors, perhaps a very large and important body of men, but who might not go so far in their political views as the mass of small householders, would be politically extinct. They would feel it totally hopeless to attempt to carry a candidate, and they would resign themselves with more or less bitterness to political death. They would feel that they were altogether excluded from any influence whatever over the destinies of their country; not merely that they could not hope to rule, but that they could not even be represented in the council of the nation. They would accordingly sink into hopeless apathy, while the majority having everything their own way, not enjoying the advantage of being opposed and forced to struggle and strive, would themselves also be likely to grow at once apathetic and arrogant. He was not devising this state of things out of his own imagination; they knew that exactly this had happened in many instances both across the water and in certain constituencies at home, where one party, be it Conservative or be it Liberal, had held irresistible sway. It would be invidious to do so; otherwise he could easily remind the House of many boroughs and many counties in which utter apathy and stagnation had actually resulted from the feeling of the minority that any exertion of theirs must be vain.

But now suppose, on the other hand, that instead of all the three seats being at the disposal of one committee the arrangement now proposed were adopted; immediately every elector in the constituency would be stirred into life. Those who belonged to the minority instead of giving up the whole affair as a bad job, shrugging their shoulders, and feeling that although they were Englishmen they were as destitute of political influence as if they were so many Indians, would immediately begin to organize themselves as a party to form a committee to look out for a candidate and combine to carry him. He admitted that very possibly no contest would ensue; but there would be as much demand for strenuous exertions and for individual self-sacrifice on the part of the minority as if a contest were certain. Political deadness would be exchanged for political animation. But to the majority this change would bring no less cause of excitement and vigor. Instead of gleefully accepting their three candidates and carrying them without an effort the party would be driven to keep its machinery in high order, to choose the best candidates that could be found, and, in short, to strain every nerve to hold their own. And yet, though each party would thus be compelled to be on the alert and to maintain its vigor, actual contests would probably be rare. The beauty of this arrangement would be that it would give all the political activity that contests are supposed to engender, but without that grievous moral injury that contests almost inevitably inflict. Now, it has been shown that these eleven constituencies affected by this proposition would contain 2,300,000 persons. If, then, the minority should not be able to carry its candidate no harm could ensue; but if they carried them all they must represent a body of some 600,000 or 700,000 persons. It could only be for the advantage not only of the minority itself but of the majority as well, and of Parliament, and of the nation, that such a body of men, comprising a large proportion of the wealth and intelligence of our largest cities, should enjoy some share of influence over the destinies of their country.

Sir C. Russell, as a representative of one of the three-cornered constituencies, opposed the Lords' amendment, but his remarks were not important nor prolonged.

Mr. Knatchbull-Hugessen, in supporting the amendment, differed from many to whose judgment he was accustomed to defer. But he was about to give his vote with the sanction of high authority, for the proposition had previously received the support of a large minority of that House taken in about equal proportions from both political parties, and had now received the support of a large majority of the other House, embracing names identified with the growth of liberal principles in the country. The honorable member from Birmingham (Mr. Bright) had said that Birmingham ought to have a larger representation than Arundel; but if a third member were given to Birmingham on the plan proposed he would pair against one of the majority members, and the representation would be reduced virtually to a level with that of Arundel, which had one member. The fallacy of that argument was this: what the honorable gentleman and his colleague represented was not really the whole community of Birmingham, but some 6000 or 8000 electors as opposed to some 4000 or 5000 who differed from him and were totally unrepresented. But to go one step further. It was true that upon questions in which party interests alone were involved, under the proposed system the three members from Birmingham would go into the lobby, two on one side and one on the other. Yet with regard to all questions affecting local interests as well as those great commercial and manufacturing questions on which Birmingham was peculiarly entitled to be heard, the three members would be found voting together and throwing their whole weight into the scale in the interest of that great constituency.

The honorable member said Birmingham would not have its full weight in the representative body. Did he mean to say that the wealth, the importance of a constituency was derived only from the majority? Had the conservative minority in London nothing to do with the weight and importance of the constituency? It was plain that they ought to give representation to all the elements that constituted the importance of a constituency.

He insisted that two great advantages would be secured by adopting the proposed system of representation. In the first place, in times of popular excitement it would insure the return to Parliament of eminent men who would otherwise be excluded. Did the honorable member from Birmingham recollect the result of the China vote and his exclusion from Parliament? [Hear.] Similar cases might occur in time to come, and honest and able men might be excluded from Parliament when their services would be most necessary for the welfare of the country, and when thousands of their fellow-countrymen would be willing to combine to secure their return.

The second great advantage from the adoption of this system was the inducement it would offer to large numbers of persons to take part in the political affairs of the country, who might otherwise be indisposed to give their votes. This was neither a party nor a class question, because there were large Liberal minorities in counties, as there were large Conservative minorities in towns, which were now unrepresented, and had no inducement to vote. He desired to see the greatest amount of intelligence and the largest number of persons possible engaged in taking part in our political affairs. Such participation was one of the most essential elements of democracy—that every man in the community should feel himself to be a component part of the State—should assist in framing the laws which he had to obey, and should throw his whole individual strength and vigor into the constitution. Now, if this principle of representation was a right one, why should they shrink from adopting it because it was said that, for the last six hundred years, the precedents had been the other way? [Hear, hear.] England was the foremost in the van of civilization, and why should she not, in reforming her whole representative institutions, introduce a plan of this sort, if it were shown to be a good one, and thus render her constitution a model for the world? [Hear.] But the honorable member from Birmingham had asked why the proposal, if adopted, was to be limited to a few large boroughs, and not be applied to every constituency throughout the country? He would reply, that if it were shown to be good, why should they reject it because its application was limited? If it turned out that it worked well, nothing could be easier than to extend its operation hereafter. The vote which he was about to give he believed to be a wise and patriotic one, and he knew it to be an honest one, as it was founded upon sincere convictions.

Mr. NEWDEGATE supported the amendment. He believed that if it were adopted it would be possible hereafter further to redistribute the representation of the country so as to secure justice both in boroughs and counties. He should vote for it because he hoped the result of it would be to give the people, as they advanced in intelligence, fuller opportunities than had been hitherto accorded them of making their opinions known in that House.

Mr. GOSCHEN spoke against the amendment, insisting that it had not been duly considered; that it was an innovation and not conservative in character. The remainder of his remarks was composed principally of criticisms upon the various positions occupied by members who supported the proposition.

Mr. HUBBARD said the bill was full of innovations, that the objection that this proposition was an innovation applied to the whole bill. Was not household suffrage itself an innovation?

Mr. GLADSTONE spoke at length and against the amendment.

A prominent point in his speech was that if the proposition were agreed to it would have to be extended hereafter to the constituencies generally; and he distinctly indicated that such extension would be made. He insisted upon further time for considering so important a proposition, and repeated the argument that the addition of one member to Birmingham and each of the other boroughs mentioned in the bill would not be advantageous to them upon the new plan of voting; for the power of majorities therein, instead of being in point of fact increased, would be diminished. His most important observation, however, should be given in his exact language. It was as follows:

"If adopted at all, this proposition must be adopted with perhaps the knowledge, and at least with the certainty, that whether we admit it ourselves or not it must unfold and expand itself over the whole country and completely reconstruct the system of distribution of seats." [Hear, hear.]

Mr. LOWE concluded the debate with an animated and able speech in favor of the amendment. He remarked that his right honorable friend (Mr. Gladstone) had said that he considered the constituency and the majority of the constituency the same thing; in those few words summing up the whole fallacy which had pervaded the debate. The honorable member from Birmingham's speech rested on the groundless assumption that when anything was true of the majority of Birmingham it was true of the whole of Birmingham. Taking their own arguments, he wondered that gentlemen who refused to give representation to minorities were willing to even admit their existence. He should like to know on what principle they acted in forcing on the Government a third member in the boroughs except as an homage to numbers. [Cheers.] It was said that in introducing personal representation you were doing away with local representation. This is again the same fallacy. Gentlemen have accustomed themselves so much to overlook the existence of minorities that they will not allow them to live even in the places where they actually reside. [Laughter.] He could not in the least understand what there was in a minority that should make it less local because it was less numerous.

Mr. LOWE concluded as follows: There is a sort of worship

of the majority which, after all, is a mere political superstition. True representation, the idea of true representatiqn, is to leave no portion of the constituencies unrepresented. [Hear.] We have a specimen of the old and rugged way of doing things in the case of juries. We require them to be unanimous, and as that is not in the nature of human things, we shut them up in "durance vile" until they come to an agreement. That system not having been found practicable under all circumstances, mankind hit upon the plan of representation by majorities as a better mode of settling their differences. Well, there is no absolute reason for stopping there. The art of representation, like other arts, is progressive; and if means can be found for increasing the number of members, and then adapting your system to that increase by the cumulative vote, so as not to disfranchise minorities and to give some representation to the whole of the constituency, so far from regarding that as an innovation upon the constitution, I think we ought to hail it as an advance in the science of government. [Cheers.]

The great difference between ancient and modern societies lies in the invention of the principle of representation. It was from the want of that power of representation that the Roman empire was reduced to place itself under the tyranny of a Cæsar. It is only by the existence of that power that large free governments have become possible. This is just an instance of the changes which may be produced by the use of the most simple expedients. Instead of regarding this principle with hatred and jealousy, I think we shall act more wisely if we investigate and accept it as a just and necessary improvement of that system of representative government which has obtained among us, upon which, in a great measure, the perpetuity and glory of our country depend.

The House then divided, when there appeared:

Ayes...204
Noes...253
Majority... 49

So the motion to disagree to the Lords' amendment was lost, and the clause stood a part of the bill. The announcement of the numbers was received with cheers.

The next amendment, that at a contested election for the city

of London no person should vote for more than three candidates, was then, after a brief debate, agreed to by a majority
of sixty-four.

When the reform bill was first considered by the House of
Commons the cumulative vote was proposed by way of amendment, but rejected. The motion for it was made by Mr. LOWE
on the 4th of July, in the following words :   '

"That at any contested election for a county or borough represented
by more than two members, and having more than one seat vacant, every
voter shall be entitled to a number of votes equal to the number of
vacant seats, and may give all such votes to one candidate or may distribute them among the candidates as he thinks fit."

This amendment was debated on the day of its introduction
and again on the next day, and received the support of the
mover and of Mr. Liddell, Mr. Thomas Hughes, Mr. Gorst,
Mr. Morrison, Mr. Beach, Mr. Fawcett, Mr. Newdegate, Viscount Cranborne, Mr. J. Stuart Mill, and Mr. Buxton, while
it was opposed by Mr. Shaw Lefevre, Sir Robert Collier, Mr.
Adderley, Mr. Bright, Mr. Henley, and the Chancellor of the
Exchequer.

It was lost by a vote of, yeas 173, nays 314. The large
number of votes it received upon its first consideration was
evidence of its strength whenever it should be subjected to
examination and debate, and inspirited its friends to further
exertion.   In fact, it appeared evident that the opposition of
the administration, through the Chancellor of the Exchequer,
alone prevented its adoption at that time, and such explanation
of the result was distinctly stated by the *Times* of August 9
in editorial comments upon the adoption of the Cairns' amendment.   It is to be remembered constantly in following the
debates in the House of Commons that the prominent men
who spoke against the cumulative vote and the Cairns' amendment represented districts which were to elect three members
under the provisions of the bill.   Consequently they were
deeply interested as political men in securing in their home
districts the election of the third member by the majority.
Buckinghamshire, represented by Mr. Disraeli, Birmingham,
represented by Mr. Bright, and other districts that contributed
speakers to the debate in opposition to the proposed reform,

are all three-member districts, in which the local political majority could not, under the new plan, elect the third member.

It remains to be observed in this review of the proceedings in Parliament that the Cairns' amendment secures substantially the same result as the cumulative vote would in the districts, the counties, and boroughs, to which it is applied. In the triangular districts it will ordinarily secure the third member· to the minority, and in London (which elects four members) the fourth member. But it is very evident that it is a proposition which is incapable of extended application, and therefore inferior to the plan of the cumulative vote. The latter will adapt itself conveniently and effectually to all districts elect-·ing more than one member, while the Cairns' amendment can hardly be extended beyond the triangular districts to which it has a convenient application.

MINORITY REPRESENTATION.*

It must be admitted that Government is, with us, in an un-satisfactory condition. Many evils exist, notwithstanding pop-ular control and the efforts of just men in public life to prevent or repress abuses. It is, therefore, timely and proper to in-quire wherein our plan of Government is defective, and to adopt some amendment of it, which will improve its practical action.

With us, the people are to govern, instead of one man or a few. They are to govern themselves, constituting ours, a sys-tem of self-government. But this is not to be taken absolutely and without qualification. Sovereignty resides with the State electors, who constitute but one-fifth of the population. But the powers of sovereignty, as exhibited in the laws, extend over the whole.

The fact is thus, because it has been so agreed upon and settled. For political powers are conventional, being founded in compact or assent. Ours is a Government of the most

* Printed for private circulation, February, 1862. *"Republican"* print, Bloomsburg, Pa.

worthy—of those best qualified, most fit, most capable. Those members of the social body who are incapable, or least capable, are excluded from political power,—as, minors, females, paupers, and unnaturalized foreigners.

In the electors, then—a select body or part of the population—resides the power to rule or govern, and this power is exercised through agents, who represent them. Government, then, in its restricted sense of an organism for legislation and administration, is an Agency, and possesses only such powers as are imparted to it by the electors. And those powers are held in trust, and subject at all times to change or revocation.

In what manner the electors shall be represented—the rules by which such representation shall be secured and regulated—and what shall be the laws of representative action, are questions for agreement among those who constitute the sovereignty, and their solution is shown by the Constitution, the fundamental law established by the electors. A practical difficulty arises in representing a numerous body of electors, from the diversity of interests and opinions which will always prevail amongst them. Identity of interest and unanimity of opinion will scarcely ever be found to exist. To secure action, therefore, in an electoral body so constituted, or in a numerous body representing them in the Government, it is necessary to adopt the doctrine that a part only may act for the whole. And hence arise practical rules by which the power of the whole electoral or representative body is wielded by three-fourths, two-thirds, a majority, or even a smaller number. A plurality rule is ordinarily provided for popular elections, and a majority rule for legislative action, except in reviewing a measure vetoed by the Executive, when a two-thirds rule is substituted. And the judicial department decide by the majority rule the cases that fall within its jurisdiction.

But these several arrangements, or rules, are founded upon considerations of convenience and expediency, and involve no fundamental principle of right. It is perfectly competent for the sovereign power to substitute one rule for another, in any of the cases just mentioned, or to introduce one altogether new. The great principle to be regarded is that of the government of the people by themselves, and the practical rules by which it is attempted to apply this principle, should be adapted to their object, and should be changed whenever shown to be insufficient or injurious, or should be limited or supplemented by other constitutional provisions.

That arrangement would be most perfect in theory, which would secure to every member of the political body a voice in the government. But this result, or any near approach to it, cannot be attained by a majority or plurality rule for popular elections. And a rule requiring unanimity, or a three-fourths or two-thirds vote, at such elections, would be intolerably inconvenient if not wholly impracticable.

If, then, no practicable rule among all those named, will secure complete popular representation, or any near approach to it; and if, on the other hand, the virtual disfranchisement of a large part of the electors be objectionable and injurious, (as it certainly is,) it is plain that something further must be proposed.

And such further proposition for the more perfect representation of the people, must be based upon some division of the electoral body into parts, and must deal with those parts separately and distinctly. Now, the most marked, extensive and permanent division of men in a Republic, is into political parties, usually two in number, and whenever greater in number tending to consolidate into two. For all practical purposes we may assume that there will be, always, a division of electors into a major and a minor party—a greater and a less—each representing opinions and interests different and distinct from those represented by the other, and sometimes, though not always, in conflict with them. But, it is certain (as already shown,) that a majority or plurality rule for popular elections, especially under a system of nominations by party conventions, will cause the disfranchisement of the minority party, and subject it to the will and pleasure of the greater. Any rule, or device, therefore, which will secure to the minority the power of defending itself against the aggression of the majority, will secure one of the main objects of the constitution, to wit: the protection of individual rights, and of all the leading interests of society, against government abuses. Without such power of self-defence, lodged somewhere in the system, a majority rule will change the Government into a despotism of numbers, and prepare the way for anarchy or revolution. For the

19

despotism of many is just as intolerable to the individuals and interests oppressed, as that of one or a few, and just as certainly tends to produce resistance and convulsion.

To secure the community against the despotism of a majority, and against government abuses mainly consequent thereon, our Constitution provides many peculiar arrangements of power, usually described as "checks and balances," as well as prohibitions against the exercise of particular powers. Of all the checks so provided, that of the Veto is most important and useful, and it deserves a particular examination.

It is secured in the Legislative branch of the Government by dividing that branch into two Houses, and requiring the assent of both to the enactment of laws. Thus each possesses the power to veto any measure originating with the other.

An Executive Veto is also provided, extending to all acts of the Legislative branch in the nature of laws. But this veto is not absolute, as it may be overruled by a two-thirds vote of both Legislative Houses.

There is also a Judicial Veto, less extensive but more absolute than that of the Executive. It is confined to unconstitutional acts of the Legislature, but as to such it has complete effect in any given case, and cannot be overruled.

But these checks, although useful and proper, are manifestly insufficient to secure wise and just government. In point of fact, they do not secure it, and in consequence wide-spread dissatisfaction exists in the community. The Legislative Houses will not check each other upon partisan measures when they agree politically, nor upon many others when strong corrupting influences assail both. Nor will the Executive Veto be applied when the Legislative majority and the Governor are of the same party—the very case where a check is most needed. And we have seen that the Judicial Veto is of limited application. The judges cannot annul an act although shown to be unjust, inexpedient, and profligate, unless it be also unconstitutional.

An additional check is therefore necessary and ought to be provided at once, by an amendment of the Constitution. Let the minority be represented directly, in the Government, and be armed with a power of self-defence against majority aggression. Let ampler representation of the people correct the evils in government, exhibited by experience—by time and trial—and furnish additional evidence of the wisdom of our fundamental principle of government by the people.

A proposition with these objects, may be stated in the following form :

The candidate second highest in vote at Gubernatorial elections, to become President of the Senate, and possess the power of vetoing bills.

By this provision the minority, for the time being, would be represented by its chosen chief for purposes of defence against a hostile interest, and the existing vetoes of the Constitution would be supplemented by one which will apply, in proper cases, where they will not. And thus the assent of both political parties will be given to new laws, and neither one can impose upon the other a measure grossly obnoxious or injurious. From which will result greater contentment among the people, an abatement of party violence, and a great decrease of injustice and corruption in the Government itself.

Substantially, the proposition is, that the minority shall have power to protect itself. Through its representative, the President of the Senate, it may require a two-thirds legislative vote for the enactment of laws. It is not a power to initiate laws—to establish an affirmative policy—to wield patronage—to interfere with executive or judicial duties; but to object to new projects—to defeat, or delay legislation, except against a decided public opinion represented by a two-thirds vote. And, as a Constitutional check, it operates where the judicial veto cannot reach, and when the executive veto will not be used.

As a curb upon legislation, this Protective, or Minority Veto, (as it may be called,) would be efficient, appropriate, and salutary, in a high degree; as will appear from considering the following results to be attained by it:

1. (As already stated,) an increased amount of popular assent to the enactment of laws, thus carrying more fully into effect our fundamental principle of government by the people. Laws will not go upon the statute book branded by party hostility; they will be more heartily accepted by the community, and be better obeyed and enforced.

2. Conciliation of the minority, inducing an increase of attachment to the Government and a decrease of hostility to its

administration. Participating in the powers of the Government, and thereby secured against aggression, the minority would be less passionate and violent, and the peril of insurrection or revolution would be removed.

3. Increased stability of the laws, and preservation of a consistent policy in their enactment.

4. But the principal utility of the Protective Veto, would be found in its prevention of bad laws. Most of these may be classed as corrupt, partisan, or unconstitutional; as, the re-charter of the United States Bank, in 1838; the Main Line Sale Bill, of 1857; the bill transferring the State Canals to the Sunbury and Erie Railroad Company, in 1858, and its supplements; and the Tonnage Tax repeal, of 1861. To which may be added an extensive list of corporation acts, and local laws. Nor are we to omit from mention those offensive and flagrant examples of injustice, called Apportionment laws, which would, standing alone, demand the establishment of a Minority veto. The septennial Apportionments, in 1850 and 1857, of Senators and Representatives throughout the State, were in many of their provisions unjust, and in some unconstitutional. And the most recent Apportionment—that of 1861, for Members of Congress—was an extreme outrage. By a just bill, proportioned to the relative strength of parties as shown by the Gubernatorial election of 1860, twelve members of Congress would have been assigned to one party, and eleven to the other. By the bill actually passed, the numbers stand nineteen to four, the minority being disfranchised to the extent of seven members for ten years, and the representation of the people of Pennsylvania, in Congress, being to that extent perverted.

Were the Protective Veto a provision of the Constitution, it would prevent the passage of laws like those just mentioned, and thus, to a great extent, preserve the purity of the Government and the integrity of the Constitution, as well as the rights and interests of the minority. Its benefits would not be confined to the minority. The whole body of the people would enjoy the advantages of improved action in the Government, which it would produce.

By our State Constitution of 1776, a Council of Censors was established, whose duty it was to review the action of the several departments of Government, and to declare to the people all departures from the Constitution by either. It was intended that this body should hold the Government, in all its branches, responsible to public opinion; that thereby the system of republican rule then established should be preserved from abuse, and, especially, that all minority and individual rights under the Constitution, should be preserved from invasion. But that body had no power to enforce its decisions, and from this cause, and from its breaking into factions on account of the number of its members, it fell into disrepute, and was not continued in existence by the Constitution of 1790.

But, the objects in view in constituting the Council of Censors, were laudable and proper, and can be attained, to a great extent, by the Protective Veto now proposed. Thereby an officer, of the first rank of ability, would be placed in a suitable position to check and limit the action of the Legislature; to defend the principles of the fundamental law against invasion; to baffle the agents of corruption in their attempts to prostitute the Government to their purposes; and to protect those interests of society which would, otherwise, be sacrificed or injured by partisan injustice. Whenever objectionable measures were proposed by the dominant party, it would be the interest and desire of the minority represented by the President of the Senate, to have them sent to the people for examination and discussion, which could be effected by this veto, operating as it would in the nature of an appeal to them from the legislative majority; while, at the same time, there would be no motive for interposing this power of appeal upon measures of real merit, the discussion of which, before the people, would strengthen, instead of weakening the party proposing them. And if a proper measure were vetoed, its discussion would secure a two-thirds vote for it in the Legislature, or an abandonment of objection to it by the President of the Senate. It would only be delayed, and it would, eventually, go into effect with an increased weight of public sentiment in its favor.

That "the world is governed too much," and that "that government is best which governs least," are maxims of common acceptation. And with us, in view of our experience, there is good cause for holding, that laws are supplied to the community beyond its wants and to its injury; that the influences in favor of legislation are unduly strong in the absence of effective checks; and that constitutional limitations and declarations of rights, will not be duly observed in the absence of power distinctly and suitably provided for their enforcement. A majority will be apt to construe the principles and provisions of a constitution according to their interests and passions, and there must be, therefore, powerful checks upon them, to prevent over-action, or wrong action of the government they control.

Our Election Boards in Pennsylvania represent both political parties, and exemplify some of the advantages of minority representation. A single Inspector is voted for by each elector, but the two candidates highest in vote are chosen; thus securing in all ordinary cases the representation of both parties in the board. This arrangement has proved most useful in practice, and is justly esteemed to be a valuable guard against partisan injustice, as well as fraud. It has, no doubt, contributed greatly to preserve our popular elections from degeneracy.

By the division of the State into districts for the election of Senators and Representatives, minority representation is obtained, to some extent, in the Legislature. For the majority party in the State will not have a majority in all the districts into which it is divided; and a plurality rule for elections somewhat disturbs the regularity of results. Upon the whole, however, it is nearly certain that the party in a majority in the State will control the Legislature and act its pleasure in the enactment of laws. And it will so district the State by Apportionment laws that the opposing party will be deprived of its due share of representation. And it is certain that in most cases of conflict between parties in the Legislature, the representation of the minority, resulting from district apportionment, is quite illusory; except where the two Houses happen to differ politically, the power of the majority will be as complete as its exercise will be unscrupulous.

Representation of the minority by a negative power or veto, then, stands vindicated by all the considerations detailed in the present paper. And it does not depart from principles already in the Constitution, but only gives to them a new and necessary application. The principle of the veto, and the principle of minority representation, we already possess.

What is proposed is that these be combined in a new provision, simple in character, but effective in action, which shall stand as a bulwark of defence against great and notorious evils. Political parties, considered as embodiments of all the main interests and opinions of society, are to be regarded in the distribution of power, and one of them be made to check another. And as such parties are inevitable, and as they thoroughly and permanently divide the mass of the people, what objection can there be to a recognition of their existence in the Constitution? In fact, is it not necessary that these, the most powerful forces which act upon the government, shall be dealt with and regulated, or at least put under a measure of control, by the fundamental law? If this be not done, we hazard nothing in saying that they will pervert the action of the government, and eventually destroy it. There being no actual balance of political powers, but on the contrary unchecked party domination, violence, injustice, and corruption will come in as a flood, until discord and passion reign supreme, and a divided and exasperated people be prepared to abandon free government and accept the rule of a master.

NOTE.—The election of a Lieutenant Governor would complete the proposition discussed in this paper. But being a subordinate question it is omitted.

[EDITOR's NOTE.—The *date* of the foregoing Essay shows the early inclination of the author's mind in matters of electoral reform. The proposition of a *minority veto*, contained in it, is quite novel, but may deserve consideration and development hereafter. It is believed that the writer intended it to be accompanied by provisions looking to the choice of *alternates* for both the Governor and President of the Senate, so that their offices would always be fitly filled and controlled by the proper political interest.]

INDEX.
